MW01120723

Between Families and
Frankenstein

Between Families and Frankenstein

The Politics of Egg Donation in the United States

Erin Heidt-Forsythe

UNIVERSITY OF CALIFORNIA PRESS

University of California Press, one of the most distinguished university presses in the United States, enriches lives around the world by advancing scholarship in the humanities, social sciences, and natural sciences. Its activities are supported by the UC Press Foundation and by philanthropic contributions from individuals and institutions. For more information, visit www.ucpress.edu.

University of California Press
Oakland, California

Cataloging-in-Publication Data is on file with the Library of Congress.

ISBN 978-0-520-29818-7 (cloth)
ISBN 978-0-520-29819-4 (paperback)
ISBN 978-0-520-97043-4 (e-edition)

27 26 25 24 23 22 21 20 19 18
10 9 8 7 6 5 4 3 2 1

For Mark

CONTENTS

Conclusion

191

ILLUSTRATIONS

FIGURES

TABLES

ACKNOWLEDGMENTS

Works about reproduction often begin with the adage that writing a book is often like the joyous, long, and sometimes painful process of having children. While I resist this particular simile to describe my decadelong process of writing about the politics of egg donation, I borrow from another metaphor: it truly took a village of colleagues, friends, and family to cultivate what has become my first book. I am a lucky beneficiary of the generosity, kindness, creativity, and intellect of so many people, inside and outside of academia, and am grateful to thank them.

I am immensely thankful for Jocelyn Crowley, without whom this book would not be a reality. Through hurricanes, heartbreak, and Hillary, Jocelyn has generously given me her time and support over the years. I hope to one day repay my great debt of gratitude for her support. My advisor and dissertation chair, Cynthia Daniels, guided my early zeal about reproductive policy toward new and innovative questions about the intersections of reproduction and technology. Cyndi offered me important opportunities to ask interesting questions, work across disciplines, and expand my thinking about the boundaries of political science and gender.

As a first-generation PhD, I would have never completed this book without the support of women and men who have taught and mentored me over the years. At Occidental College, I was inspired to pursue this profession because of the brilliance of Roger Boesche. He is deeply missed. Jane Jaquette's class Women, Politics, and Power illuminated the exciting field of gender and politics to a drifting undergraduate. Heartfelt thanks to Michelle McGowan, one of the people who most significantly shaped my scholarship, from challenging my thinking across feminist studies and bioethics, to providing crucial comments and feedback on the arguments that underpin this project. Thank you for your friendship. And thank you to Lee Ann Banazsak and Carolyn Sachs at Penn State for their warm mentorship, support, and professional guidance.

Faculty, staff, and students at Rutgers University, Case Western Reserve University, and Pennsylvania State University were instrumental at multiple stages of this project. Many thanks to Beth Leech for her early feedback and comments on this manuscript as it developed. Thank you to the Rutgers Political Science Department and Rick Lau for providing funding and Grace Howard for research assistance at the earliest stages of this project. From 2012 to 2013, I was in residence in the Bioethics Department at Case Western Reserve University, which shaped my thinking about feminist bioethics. Thank you to the Center for Genetic Research Ethics and Law at Case Western Reserve University for providing funding and resources for this project, as well as an opportunity to share early portions of this book with an interdisciplinary audience. I finished this book as a faculty member at Penn State, which has provided me the resources, funding, and leave I needed. Thank you to my wonderful undergraduate research assistants, Julia Gurule and Jennifer Heckman. I am especially grateful for the Penn State Women's, Gender, and Sexuality Department, where an amazing group of intersectional and interdisciplinary scholars has created a welcome community for my work. I am truly lucky to be part of this community.

Many thanks to the individuals, groups, and organizations that helped me develop the ideas and methods in this book. The Women and Politics Reading Group and the Center for American Political Responsiveness at Penn State provided important opportunities for feedback on early chapters. I also have immense gratitude for the Gender and Political Psychology Writing Group. This group epitomizes shine theory: I don't shine if you don't shine. Members of the group provided enthusiastic feedback, advice, and support. Additionally, I thank Karen Baird, Rebecca Kreitzer, Kimala Price, and Rebecca Traister for their scholarship, writing, observations, and feedback, which have significantly influenced the arguments, methods, and orientations of this book.

I offer thanks to my editor at University of California Press, Naomi Schneider, for her enthusiasm and support of this project. She has cultivated groundbreaking books on reproduction and the social sciences for UC Press, and I feel deeply privileged to join this list of authors. I am grateful for the editorial assistance of Benjy Malings, as well as the anonymous reviewers, whose keen eyes and critical comments immensely improved this manuscript.

Friendship has sustained me throughout this process. In particular, a group of women have consistently reminded me to stay sharp, keep fighting, and bloom despite the conditions: Krista Chambers, Colleen McKeever, Laura Palotie, and Aubry

Parks-Fried, thank you for your sustaining friendship. Thank you to The Gang, particularly Sarah Cohn Hickey and Aaron Bawol. Doctors Hayley Baines and Nimish Parekh were incredible sources of strength and hilarity throughout the long years I have worked on this project. Among those at Rutgers and beyond, I am lucky to know and count on over a decade of friendship with Kelly Dittmar, Tessa Ditonto, Wendy Wright, Anna Mahoney, Sara Angevine, and Dave Andersen. And thank you to my friends Allison Harris, Zach Baumann, Amir Fairdosi, and Michael Nelson at Penn State. The future of the profession is bright with folks like you.

My family instilled in me a deep curiosity about the natural and social worlds. My mother and father, Susan and Stephen Forsythe, deserve more thanks and credit than an acknowledgments section can provide. From supporting my decision to study gender and politics for a living (with only one question, "Can you get a job in that?") to literally providing a sanctuary so I could finish my book, they have been a source of strength and inspiration every single step of the way. Ryan Forsythe and Kelly O'Hara, thank you for being a source of feminist love and support. Eamon O'Hara-Forsythe, I never anticipated how much joy you would bring into my life, and I can't wait to watch you take on the world. Thank you to the extended Major family for their long-standing support.

This book is dedicated to Mark Major, my husband. My deepest love and gratitude is for Mark, whom I met at the same time I began this project. Over the course of a decade—in which we fell in love, got married, and each wrote a book—we have continued a long and lovely conversation, one that I hope will never cease. From long walks in the woods to crisscrossing the country with Sloan and Gilmore in the back of the car, he listens my ideas, challenges my thinking, comforts me when things get tough (as they always do), and shares in my joy. Mark read every word of this manuscript, many times over, which is a testament to his unflagging patience and support. I am privileged to be your partner, and I benefit from your sharp intellect, loyalty, love, and humor more than I can express here. I am better, and this book is better, because of you.

Introduction

Fifty years before donor eggs would be used to conceive a child in the US, journalists breathlessly speculated about the strange new world of human egg research. Experimentation could "lead to a new stock of fatherless human being, given birth by women not actually their mothers" (Lawrence 1939). Aldus Huxley's fictional process of exogenesis could ultimately be achieved through the insemination of eggs outside of the body, and unfettered scientific research might prove that "the Frankenstein myth is real" (Lasagna 1962). Mixing donor eggs and donor sperm outside of the body could "constitute a vision of long-distance adultery ... between total strangers" in a context that could be a "dream" or a "nightmare" (Lasagna 1962). Women involved in egg donation would come into "sociologically perilous conflict" over who was the rightful mother of the donor-conceived child (Rorvik 1974). More insidiously, consumers and states could use reproductive technologies to create "perfect" citizens: "Some voices fear that the procedures, once perfected, will, almost inevitably, give rise to undesirable and ever-escalating expectations that parents and governments, respectively, might find irresistible. Many recoil at the thought of an embryo 'prefabricated' to exhibit at birth a set number of physical and mental characteristics, whether ordered by the parents or some other, possibly less benign, 'authority'" (Rorvik 1974).

These overwhelming anxieties have subsided over the late twentieth and early twenty-first centuries in the US, having been replaced by a culture that regards egg donation as yet another normal option by which to create a family. University newspapers regularly advertise the immense earning possibilities of egg donation, enticing young, college-aged women with rewards of ten thousand dollars or more for a single cycle of egg donation. Egg donors have their own Facebook support groups and tell-all documentaries on public television, and some have even brought a suit against the American Society for Reproductive Medicine (the largest advocacy group for fertility medical professionals) for price-fixing. Consumers seeking donated eggs have a huge array of choices and can view highly detailed, intimate profiles of potential donors online and order eggs with a credit card number and a click of a mouse.

However, antiquated anxieties about reproduction and science using human eggs have never gone away, mixing with contemporary practices to shape the politics of egg donation in the United States. Egg donation has breathtakingly diverse uses: donated eggs can be used for third-party reproduction to create and enlarge families; individuals may use egg donation procedures to procure and cryopreserve eggs for their future as mothers and fathers; donated eggs are also used in stem cell research, where donated eggs can be fertilized and developed into blastocysts, from which human embryonic stem cell lines are derived.[1] Rarely is this diverse array of egg donation issues discussed within the context of politics and policy, and seldom does our thinking about egg donation connect the interactions between medical, economic, social, and political institutions to regulation of egg donation in the US. While many decry the strange, highly commercialized system of egg donation in the US that lacks serious politics and policymaking, I aim, in this book, to dismantle this notion, shining light on the unexplored political spaces between idyllic visions of the family and the abject horror of Doctor Frankenstein's monster.

Science fiction–fueled fears about egg donation seem to have been replaced by a contemporary, laissez-faire system of regulation of egg donation in the US today. "The United States is the Wild West of the fertility industry," declared Marcy Darnovsky of the Center for Genetics and Society (Ollove 2015).[2] This sentiment—that reproductive technologies like egg donation have been left to the unrestrained forces of multibillion-dollar fertility and stem cell research industries—prevails across popular media and scholarship.[3] In a *Los Angeles Times* article about egg donation, a lawyer who specializes in reproductive medicine calls the egg market "the wild, wild West of reproductive medicine" (Li 2012). In an interview with PBS's *Frontline,* Harvard bioethicist George Annas concludes that "the whole world of assisted reproduction has been described aptly as a kind of Wild West. But I'd go further than that.... [I]t's the Wild West [if] it mated with American commerce" (PBS 1999). Debora Spar, former president of Barnard College and a scholar of the economics of reproductive technology in the US, wrote in the *New York Times* that in contrast to the heavy regulation of egg donation in western Europe, Canada, and Israel, the US is a "free market for assisted reproduction, a Wild West of procreative possibilities" (Spar 2011). Bioethicists, legal scholars, philosophers, gender studies, and policy scholars use the term *Wild West* to describe the seeming lack of political attention to egg donation (e.g., Sauer 2001, Dresser 2000, Hecht 2001, Mamo 2013, Chang and DeCherney 2009). Beyond this rhetoric, scholarship across disciplines, from women's and gender studies to sociology, from political science to anthropology, observes and analyzes the hugely profitable, privatized, and loosely regulated commercial systems of egg donation in the US context (e.g., Thompson 2005, 2007, Dickenson 2007, Ikemoto 2009, Almeling 2011, Clarke et al. 2010, Bonnicksen 1989, Daniels and Heidt-Forsythe 2012, Jasanoff 2005, 2011, Franklin and Ragoné 1998).

Although the US has regulated contraception, abortion, childbirth, and other issues related to reproduction, conventional belief holds that the nation simply does not regulate egg donation, that the latter is market-based and free of politics, as evidenced by the fact that only one federal egg donation law exists, one aimed to protect consumers rather than donors. In the US, donor compensation, medical practices, and commerce are not centrally regulated by a bureaucratic agency or a set of federal laws. In contrast to this unique system, countries across the globe have established complex and restrictive policies regarding egg donation (Jasanoff 2005, 2011, Ouellette et al. 2005). Germany bans egg donation outright; Canada allows uncompensated egg donation; the United Kingdom has established a complex bureaucratic agency that regulates compensation for lost wages and medical care, the distribution of eggs, and the ways that consumers can choose donor eggs for reproduction. There is no parallel, centralized system of regulating egg donation in the US, which seems strange in light of the fact that most forms of reproduction are regularly controlled, systematized, and organized. From abortion to childbirth, the US political system has never been reticent to engage with reproductive politics; moreover, there have been colorful and passionate moral debates about controversial scientific research in the political sphere throughout the twentieth century and the beginning of the twenty-first century.

This creates a puzzle: If egg donation is publicly recognizable and provokes such social interest, then why does the US political fail to regulate it? In this book I challenge conventional thinking while answering this question: I explore answers to *how* egg donation is defined, debated, and regulated in the US, and I explain the logic of *why* the US political system is organized the way it is in response to egg donation. Using three major areas of inquiry—framing, body and morality politics, and representation by gender and party—I answer long-standing questions about egg donation and politics in the fields of women's and gender studies, political science and policy studies, and bioethics. Using case studies, narrative analysis, and comprehensive public policy analyses, I highlight the ways that state legislative institutions and actors make sense of (and act on) egg donation as a political issue. Rejecting the conventional thinking that there simply is a lack of regulation in the US, I demonstrate that a vibrant and important politics of egg donation exists.

Moreover, the politics of egg donation can be explained through the ways the US political system makes sense of egg donation for reproduction *and* research. Despite the fact that a single medical act of egg donation provides the building blocks for life in the reproductive and research sectors, we can trace strikingly different political responses and policy solutions to egg donation over time. Throughout the histories of egg donation for reproduction and research, political actors and public stakeholders (such as religious organizations, bioethicists, advocacy groups, and infertility patients) have used different rhetorical concepts to discuss and deliberate over egg donation. While at some points in the history of egg donation in the US the reproductive technology has elicited moral outrage from elites and the public, at other historical moments this reproductive technology has been normalized as a conventional way to treat infertility and involuntary childlessness for the socioeconomically and racially privileged. Stakeholders have relied on moral and ethical rhetoric while, at the same time, embracing logics of reproduction and state intervention to "frame" egg donation, using these ideas to define, deliberate, and create diverse policy responses to egg donation. As discussed later in this introduction, these diverse "frames" have gained and lost traction during the history of egg donation, creating and maintaining this country's unique politics of egg donation.

THE EMERGING POLITICS OF EGG DONATION

Egg donation was used in about 10 percent of all fertility treatment cycles in 2013, resulting in over nine thousand births of egg-donor-conceived children in that year (SART 2013). Between 2005 and 2014, the use of donor eggs increased 27 percent (CDC 2014). Cryopreservation, or egg freezing, has created greater availability of donor eggs; moreover, individual egg procurement and banking (where a woman freezes her own eggs for the future) has skyrocketed since 2011, when cryopreservation became accessible to a wide swath of consumers (CDC 2014). While not as prevalent as other reproductive technologies, egg donation is crucial for a significant segment of infertility patients, who rely on egg donation owing to "diminished ovarian reserve," in which the number and quality of a person's eggs declines with age

(Resolve 2016, ASRM 2014). The explosion in the demand for and supply of women's eggs, particularly in the twenty-first century, has drawn the attention of US scholars and policymakers. In light of the concurrent explosion of egg donation for third-party reproduction and fertility preservation, many characterize the nation as having an incomplete and incoherent regulatory system; as previously noted, only one federal law governs egg donation in a broader context of reproductive technologies and infertility care. Missing in this research is the important consideration of federalism, and few scholars have investigated the diversity, nuance, and richness within the patchwork of state policies that regulate egg donation (e.g., Von Hagel 2014, Kirkpatrick 2012).

Although the US system has been identified as a strange and unique regulatory system, no scholarly consensus explains why it exists in its current form. Many contemporary scholars simply avoid the question of politics (which is conventionally seen as a settled question) and focus on professional and other nongovernmental oversight. Analyses of commercial markets, networks of kinship and families, medical practices, and the very meanings of reproductive technology are often considered separately from political deliberation and policymaking in the US (Almeling 2011, Thompson 2005, Franklin 2013).[4] Among contemporary scholars in the areas of politics and reproductive technologies, one dominant explanation is that the concept of privacy, an individual-centered concept of protection from regulation by the state, has molded the democratic culture of egg donation (Thompson 2005, Holland 2007). Using donor eggs for reproduction has been defined as a private choice for family formation, which enables individuals to make reproductive decisions away from the prying eyes of the state. Commercial egg banks, infertility medical professionals, and consumers can, without the political influence of state intervention, efficiently coordinate their activities to maximize access to donor eggs and treatment for involuntary childlessness (Thompson 2005).

A second prevailing explanation of the US system is that abortion is so central to US politics that political elites have avoided engaging with the topic of egg donation (Bonnicksen 1989, Jasanoff 2005, Goggin and Orth 2004). The connection between abortion and egg donation is not always clear, but conventional wisdom holds that both involve the nature of personhood and the moral status of the embryo, and that the broader social meanings of human eggs for kinship and family are political landmines. The third explanation for the status quo in the US is that, in general, there is a lack of *any* substantive public discussions of bioethics in political discourse (Jasanoff 2005). As evidenced by highly polarized discussions of cloning, stem cell research, and chimeric research, there is no common language (or infrastructure) for coherent democratic debates about egg donation. Moreover, such debates, when they are attempted, get mired in discussions of fundamental moral principles and religious traditions, which are not universal across the US. Like many bioethical issues, discourse about egg donation falls by the wayside because there is no coherent, structured way to talk about moral and ethical debates inherent in the reproductive technology.

These arguments are useful in explaining the absence of a federal politics of egg donation, but they are incomplete in accounting for two important observations about egg donation governance: first, the existence of egg donation laws at the state level, and second, the different purposes that donated eggs serve in reproduction and research. Federalism is a deeply understudied component of reproductive technology in the US; while many decry the lack of a centralized organization to regulate egg donation in the US, the importance of federalism in reproductive and scientific policy is lacking in this area. The majority of policy in the US—particularly policy that regulates "controversial" issues like reproduction—is crafted and executed at the state level, given the state powers of regulation under the Tenth Amendment to the Constitution. States act as laboratories of democracy, where innovative and new policies can be created, carried out, and observed for their effectiveness before making their debut in other states or on the national stage. While comparative policy scholars note the relative lack of centralized policy on egg donation in the US, the states are a more natural place to find the politics and policymaking we would expect in relation to reproductive technologies (e.g., Goggin and Orth 2004). Rather than being a strange, fragmented system, the US system of regulation reflects a strong reliance on states to function as central actors in policymaking. Even major federal health and medical laws (such as the Affordable Care Act, which extended accessible health insurance nationally) were customized and implemented at the state level (Sonfield and Pollack 2011). This book is the first to comprehensively examine the multiple streams of state politics and policymaking in relation to egg donation in a system of federalism. Importantly, other work on reproductive technologies has highlighted the centrality of states as policy makers (and often policy entrepreneurs) in the US system (Von Hagel 2014, Kirkpatrick 2012).

That egg donation can be used for different outcomes is not only an important component of the fertility industry but also a part of stem-cell and cloning research (Benjamin 2013). Even though some believe that the federal government simply stays out of these issues, state legislative commissions released research reports on the implications of reproductive technologies for public policy as early as the mid-1980s (New York State Task Force on Life and the Law 1989). In the first decade of the twenty-first century, states like Massachusetts, New Jersey, California, and New York each established taxpayer-funded, state-directed stem cell research centers, which rely on procured eggs for material. States are in fact politically engaging with the topic of egg donation—and there is a gap in the explanation of why and how these politics are unfolding. To understand the practical why and how of politics and policy, we must first step back and examine the underlying social, economic, and medical assumptions made about egg donation in the first place—traditions, expectations, and norms about femininity that shape the politics of egg donation in the US.

GENDER NORMS AND FEMININITY IN THE POLITICS OF EGG DONATION

Egg donation is defined socially, economically, and politically through dominant imagery and narratives, religious and ethical beliefs, and cultural ideologies of gender, sexuality, and reproduction. Norms of femininity drive the framing of egg donation in politics, defining egg donation practices as "natural" or "unnatural." Normative femininity shapes body and morality politics frames, and how these frames gain salience or lose traction over time. Reflecting the inherently unstable nature of femininity, norms regarding the proper and improper use of women's bodies are complex, overlapping, and sometimes contradictory, and they change over time in different contexts (Hawkesworth 1997, Thompson 2005, Almeling 2011). While at some points in history, norms have been used to make the act of egg donation for reproduction and research seem conventional, at other times these norms have shifted and portrayed egg donation as an unnatural and strange practice—thereby shaping how egg donation is ultimately framed by stakeholders in egg donation markets and politics.

Gender norms and normativity are understood, in gender studies scholarship, as two aspects of the "process by which people claim that a given way of being is good ... or to be endorsed," through which definitions of what it means to be female are established, managed, and monitored (Shotwell 2012, 991–992). For many, gender norms and normativity can be limiting, as they may restrict gender expression and fail to acknowledge the subjective experience of the sex/gender system.[5] Rather than reflecting objective realities of sex and gender, norms create the conditions of female bodies; like Simone de Beauvoir's contention that gender is constructed from social ideas, beliefs, and values, norms create ideals about the appearance and function of female bodies, as "bodies are not born; they are made" (Mamo and Fosket 2009). Bodies defined as female are assigned characteristics (even if these bodies do not fit these characteristics) that reflect dominant definitions of femininity, or gender norms. These norms are seen as naturally occurring, rather than as constructed by society, and are used to describe and understand the biology, anatomy, and genetic characteristics of bodies. For example, the X chromosome and the egg have been historically described in science texts as passive, unpredictable, and dependent, despite the biomedical research that contradicts these narratives (Hawkesworth 1997, Richardson 2012, Martin 1991, Mamo and Fosket 2009). Closely linked to prevailing norms of "natural" femininity is the function of the body in reproduction: according to an "ideology of procreation," female bodies are intended primarily for reproductive purposes (Barrett 1980, Hawkesworth 1997, Connell 1987). If individuals resist this ideology of procreation, they are treated as if they are aberrant and disabled, in need of highly technological medical interventions (Garland-Thomson 2002, Mamo and Fosket 2009).

Normative femininity determines many aspects of how we understand gender in relation to egg donation: norms define gendered social relations, characterize sexed embodiedness, and explain the gendered division of labor of egg donors and consumers alike (Hawkesworth 1997). In terms of social relations, normative femininity works to define women in accordance with their relationships with men and children: women are defined as mothers and wives, reflecting their function as sex objects and/or caregivers in families according to the ideology of procreation. Norms about wives and mothers, reflecting racial, class, and sexual hierarchies, shape how we understand the relationships between women and their partners and families. The literal bodies of women are also determined by normative femininity: as female bodies are considered strange, unpredictable, incomplete, unstable, and innately threatening, normative female bodies must be controlled and regulated to achieve norms of purity, passivity, cleanliness, fitness, and sexiness. In the last category of normative femininity, there are socially constructed standards of women's work that are considered hallmarks of the feminine: in a gendered division of labor inside and outside of the home, women are expected to be mothers and caregivers and to play a maternal role. Even though women may not be mothers or wish to become mothers, normative femininity mandates that women do extensive care work, both inside their relationships and in their communities.

NORMATIVE FEMININITY AND EGG
DONATION FOR REPRODUCTION

Normative femininity in the contemporary egg donation market reflects two major characteristics: one emphasizing an ideology of care, and another enforcing beauty and obedience. In the first set of emphasized gender norms, egg donors and consumers are largely required—both formally and informally—to adhere to a framework of altruism and care. Despite the fact that donated eggs are not in fact a gift (as thousands of dollars are exchanged), the language of altruism pervades these commercial relationships. Potential egg donors are screened according to their expressed motivations regarding donation. If they express reasoning that does not reflect altruism, care, and selflessness, women are often excluded from donation (Almeling 2011, Daniels and Heidt-Forsythe 2012). Women who seek to donate eggs for compensation are often paid more for already being biological mothers (Almeling 2011, Thompson 2005). Advertisements to attract potential egg donors emphasize the norms of passivity and selfless emotional labor—asking potential donors if they want to be an "angel" for potential parents of a donor-conceived child (Daniels and Heidt-Forsythe 2012). Although women are paid significant amounts of money to donate their eggs for third-party reproduction, potential egg donors are encouraged to "give the gift of life" to someone suffering from involuntary childlessness (Daniels and Heidt-Forsythe 2012, Markens 2007).[6] Gift language is also part of the donor experience: intended parents are encouraged to buy extra items for their donor as a gift for her donation, such as flowers, a phone, and jewelry (Daniels and Heidt-Forsythe 2012).

Gender norms about egg donation also work within what Rosemarie Garland-Thomson (2002) calls the "disability/ability system," where "natural" facts about a body's deviation from the norm interact with beliefs about female beauty and submissiveness (Daniels and Heidt-Forsythe 2012, Almeling 2011, Garland-Thomson 2002). These norms emphasize the hyperfertility of egg donors in contrast with the infertile bodies of intended parents. On one hand, you have the unconventional bodies of consumers, which break with reproductive norms; on the other hand, you have egg donors, who are full of youth, sexuality, and beauty (Mamo and Fosket 2009, Almeling 2011, Daniels and Heidt-Forsythe 2012). While the egg donation market highlights egg donors' feminine eroticism and reproductive vitality, there is also an emphasis on obedience to the procedural requirements of egg donation (Daniels and Heidt-Forsythe 2012). For example, egg donors are regularly advertised on egg bank and fertility clinic websites. Each donor has a page where conventionally attractive, even sexy, photos of the egg donor are available for public viewing. Women in these profiles are highly stylized, posed in ways that emphasize their youth, small body size, and whiteness. Commercial egg banks emphasize the idea of beauty to their potential egg donors, whom they entice to donate by offering them extra benefits such as professional photo shoots to create images for their online profiles (Daniels and Heidt-Forsythe 2012). However, there is distrust of unfettered norms of beauty and eroticism: commercial egg banks also seek to regulate the unpredictable and threatening bodies of potential egg donors. Women are warned that drug use, alcohol use, sexual promiscuity, and relationships with nonheterosexual men will prevent their selection as donors (Egg Donation Center of Dallas 2017). Potential egg donors are also warned of the behavioral and medical requirements of egg donation: donors are told to be polite and well behaved and to adhere to their schedules of pharmaceutical drug injections and surgeries (Daniels and Heidt-Forsythe 2012).

Normative femininity in relation to altruism, beauty, and passivity is an important component of framing egg donation for reproduction as a natural and established practice. Moreover, egg donation is considered conventional in a context of "stratified reproduction," a system whereby some individuals and couples are encouraged to reproduce—through dominant images of motherhood, fatherhood, and families, through public policies and law, and through cultural beliefs about reproduction— while others are discouraged or prevented from doing so (Colen 1986, Roberts 1998). The US system allows access only to those who have the economic resources to pay the high cost of egg donation, placing impossible barriers for those who cannot pay out of pocket or do not enjoy private insurance coverage of infertility treatment. Such a system, where the wealthy are privileged and individuals bear risk for reproduction, fits snugly with the inequalities related to parenthood and stratified reproduction: as egg donation is a pronatal practice, the narrative of egg donation for reproduction is one that is increasingly conventional and natural, particularly for those who have historically been considered "good" mothers. In many ways, the US system is rewarding an ideology of the "natural" in reproduction: egg donation is simply an assisted reproductive procedure that emphasizes the body's natural biological processes, done by bodies that *should* be reproducing, according to state ideologies—those who should be providing biological material (and receiving biological material) for reproduction according to norms of maternal altruism, beauty, and submissiveness to authority. Although egg donation challenges notions of traditional families, given that it is available to single individuals and same-sex couples, arguably the socioeconomic and pronatalist definitions of egg donation for reproduction serve state ideologies about the "natural" feminine body and what it is intended to do: reproduce.

NORMATIVE FEMININITY AND EGG DONATION FOR RESEARCH

Egg donation for research intrinsically violates some of these norms of femininity, owing entirely to the fact that it cannot serve the ideology of procreation. Eggs donated for genetic research—via a process identical to that of donation for reproduction—are instead part of a procedure in which no reproduction of humans will take place. This alternative path for donating eggs has long been the source of fiction, speculation, and horror at the use of women's finite reproductive material (Bonnicksen 2002, Thompson 2013, Benjamin 2013, Franklin 2013). Egg donation for research violates norms of femininity which determine that a body is meant for reproduction of the family, because egg procurement for research (and the inevitable destruction of egg cells in the process) creates a new potential for women's bodies that is delinked from traditional and naturalized expectations of reproduction. Willing participants can donate eggs without regard for family, kinship, and state pressures regarding reproduction.

Instead of helping build families, women who donate eggs for research are more akin to patients and participants in scientific research: their activities are often stripped of the gendered characteristics that so often accompany egg donation for reproduction. In research settings, eggs are yet another important human material for research. While biological material may be reproduced in research settings—such as the reproduction of stem cells—the creation of organisms in research is for far different purposes, for developing treatments and cures for the already living. The labor of donation for research is subject to institutional protocols of clinical research, rather than policies that enforce normative femininity like altruism, beauty, and obedience (Waldby and Cooper 2010). This labor has historically provoked horror, distrust, and even protectionism as women's bodily processes and materials are moved away from the sphere of reproduction (Thompson 2005).

FRAMING EGG DONATION IN US POLITICS

The premise of this book is that norms of femininity provide the basis of the politics of egg donation. Often, slippery definitions of and ideas about femininity, in relation to gender, sexuality, reproduction, and labor, shape the rhetoric and logic that political actors and stakeholders use to define and solve the problems of egg donation. Broadly, egg donation is like other perceived social and political problems: it has been identified as important for deliberation and regulation on the basis of claims-making activities by elites and publics alike, and a concerted effort has been made to construct a definition of the issue for debate and regulation. Scholars who study the emergence of social and political problems have increasingly demonstrated that these problems don't necessarily arise out of objective conditions of conflict or uncertainty about an issue—social problems can be constructed for many reasons that have little to do with political urgency. However, in the case of egg donation, a combination of increasing use by consumers and scientists, of public recognition in popular media and culture, and of extreme uses of egg donation has precipitated regulation. There have been significant delays in recognizing egg donation as a social and political issue, and these delays have contributed to the idea that it goes unregulated in the US system.

To explain the ideological constructions of egg donation for reproduction and research, I engage with, and contribute to, the research paradigm around framing of social and political issues. Framing is a way of describing the power of communicating discourse and texts, of giving an issue like egg donation meaning. This meaning is derived from verbal discourse and rhetoric (often by political elites and others who are trying to lay claim to an issue), as well as from written texts produced by those interested in the issue and by the media (Entman 1993, 51, Feree et al. 2002). Analyses in this book engage with both written texts (bills, press releases, media coverage of policy debates, and media interviews with political elites) and discourse (verbal communication by political elites in and out of state legislatures) to explain the power of framing of egg donation. The act of framing an issue has important implications for normative democratic theory, particularly when elites control the framing of an issue; it demonstrates the exertion of political power and identifies the ways that certain political actors and interests intersect in an issue (Zaller 1992, Entman 1993). It is through framing processes that political debates and strategies unfold (Markens 2007, Jesudason and Weitz 2015).

How an issue is framed has tremendous impact on how policy is formulated, who the policy targets, how the policy is debated, and whether it gets adopted. Controlling issue definition means that one can control the public policy process: by being the "winner" among competing interests in defining an issue, one has control over how the government regulates (or does not regulate) a given issue (Baumgartner et al. 2009). The norms of femininity in policy are especially important, as assumptions about gender, sexuality, and reproduction shape policymaking. Public policy scholars have demonstrated that the gendered definition of *target populations* (those who will be directly affected by the proposed policy) has a powerful influence on public officials, and that it shapes both the policy agenda and the actual design of the policy (Schneider and Ingram 1993). Moreover, how women's issues (such as abortion) are framed can determine who puts issues on the legislative agenda, as there is significant evidence of descriptive representation by women of particular categories of issues, such as reproductive health (e.g., Swers 2016). How a policy is framed has a lasting impact on gendered policymaking regarding private behavior (see for example Petchesky's [(1984) 1990] discussion of antiabortion advocacy), as well as on economic issues that disproportionately affect women (see for example Theda Skocpol's [1992] discussion of motherhood as a central construct of welfare policy).

BODY POLITICS, MORALITY POLITICS, AND FRAMING EGG DONATION IN THE US

In this book I forward the idea that rhetoric and logic of body politics (a broad area of inquiry from women's and gender studies) *and* morality politics (a common framework used in political science and policy studies) best explain the politics of egg donation in the US. These frameworks operate simultaneously over time: while at some points a body-politics definition of egg donation has gained traction (particularly in reference to reproduction), at other points actors and stakeholders have used morality politics to explain the issue and create policy to address it. Both frameworks explain the unusual American politics of egg donation. Despite the common convention that the US is apolitical on the topic of egg donation, or that egg donation for reproduction is treated as a phenomenon separate from donation for research, I argue that body and morality politics contour egg donation in important ways.

In the case of egg donation in the US, framing has been unstable over time; as norms of femininity change, so does the salience of certain frames regarding reproductive technologies. As discussed at length in chapter 1, the two explanatory frameworks of body and morality politics have been deployed in framing egg donation in the US, sometimes simultaneously and often separately. These frameworks have been deployed at different moments in time in the politics of egg donation: for example, during the emergence of egg donation as a reproductive technology in the early to mid-1980s, consumers, critics, and scholars relied on moralistic frames (emphasizing moral debates over fundamental principles) to define and regulate egg donation. These moral debates predominated in the context of a small but growing egg donation market. During the 1980s and early 1990s, legislatures sought to understand the technical and ethical complexities of reproductive technology, learning about egg donation with an intent to structure regulation of it (Bonnicksen 1989, New York State Task Force on Life and the Law 1989). Medical institutions, guided by hospital ethics boards, were entrepreneurs in creating policies to address moral and ethical issues. Critics and scholars responded in kind, analyzing how the rush of technological innovation was being trailed by moral and ethical inquiry into egg donation. Moralistic frames during this early period defined egg donation through a set of moral lenses, identified fundamental ethical problems of reproductive technologies (such as compensation and inducement for egg donation), and debated egg donation through a discussion of first principles, often rooted in religious belief. However, these morality frames lost traction by the mid-1990s as egg donation normalized and became both increasingly used by consumers and publicly visible.

By the first decade of the twenty-first century, increasingly nuanced views of egg donation began to predominate, and moral frames gave way to an increased scholarly and public interest in body politics and the role of the state in private decisions about reproduction (Thompson 2005). Rather than defining egg donation as a clash of fundamental principles, political, medical, and social institutions normalized the reproductive technology as a way to make families (Franklin 1995, Thompson 2005). Use of this frame was further advocated by policy entrepreneurs, such as Resolve (an infertility support group) and the American Society for Reproductive Medicine. For example, state legislatures, as well as Congress, passed consumer protection laws for fertility clinic patients rather than addressing fundamental moral debates. Political actors defined egg donation as an important issue, identified problems with egg donation practices, and found policy solutions to these problems by protecting consumers of donated eggs (among other reproductive technologies; Bonnicksen 1989, Heidt-Forsythe 2012, Almeling 2011).

During the late 1990s and early in the twenty-first century, technological innovation in stem cell and cloning research produced not only Dolly the sheep but also the first stem cells created from a human blastocyst—a blastocyst formed by joining donor eggs with donor sperm. Suddenly, egg donation was not just for reproduction but also supplied important materials for stem cell research—a controversial, and morally framed, issue in US politics (Bonnicksen 2002, Thompson 2013). During the early years of the twenty-first century, egg donation for research elicited strong moral condemnation from political actors—who were silent on the moral and ethical issues surrounding egg donation in reproductive contexts. While morality frames lost traction to define egg donation for infertility and involuntary childlessness, morality frames arguably dominated the ways that politicians and the public defined, debated, and made policy regarding stem cell research (Ryan 2014, Bonnicksen 2002).

What accounts for this contingent framing? In this book I explore how body and morality frames are always present, and how policy entrepreneurs in the form of political actors, advocates, and other stakeholders make certain frames more salient than others in the diverse politics of egg donation. Different interests have spurred this framing process. Increasing consumer demand for and access to egg donation is one important influence on the framing processes regarding egg donation for reproduction (Franklin 1995). Similarly, increasing public awareness of and technological sophistication in regenerative medicine, with leadership from the biotechnology and pharmaceutical industries as well as professional and patient advocacy groups, has pushed forward alternative ways of defining, debating, and regulating egg donation for research (Thompson 2013, Benjamin 2013, Jesudason and Weitz 2015, Heidt-Forsythe 2016). Advocates and stakeholders—such as interest groups and professional societies—also have a vested interest in framing processes, and the growth of these groups (in size and power) has also guided how egg donation is framed. These diverse interests come up against each other in struggles over how to frame egg donation in US politics. To understand how policy entrepreneurs create dominant frames for the diverse issues related to egg donation for reproduction and research, I explore—in both micro and macro processes—how frames are utilized by stakeholders to define and create a politics of egg donation in the US.

GENDER AND POLITICS IN EGG DONATION

Who is driving the politics of egg donation in the US? In the last third of the book, I examine the role of gendered, partisan political actors in the politics and policies of egg donation at the state level. In the field of gender and politics, scholars have long debated how women legislators are different from their male colleagues, and how the inclusion of women in political spaces makes a difference for policymaking, particularly regarding reproductive and family issues. Scholarship has long been interested in the links between descriptive representation of women and substantive representation of "women's interests" in federal and state legislatures (Bratton 2002, Carey, Niemi, and Powell 1998, Carroll 1992, Darcy, Welch, and Clark 1994, Swers 2002, Osborn 2012). In the long-standing question of whether women in government "act for" women in general, there are theoretical and empirical disagreements in the field over the definition of women's interests, the benefits and drawbacks of thinking about women as a cohesive identity group, and the precise causal relationships between descriptive and substantive representation with respect to gender. Considering the presence of women in state legislatures and the topic of egg donation in these debates, I explore the boundaries and relationships of descriptive and substantive representation of reproductive technologies and how they shape the politics of egg donation.

Gender has an important impact on what issues are introduced, how they are debated, and how policy solutions are created (e.g., Tolbert and Steuernagel 2001). One would expect women in political spheres to have an important role in framing processes about egg donation, particularly because women in legislatures have historically been crucial in illuminating how the "personal is political," how seemingly private issues (such as egg donation) are in fact subject to political forces. Women legislators in the state and federal legislatures are more likely to be policy leaders on issues that are particularly relevant to women and families, such as health care, social welfare, and reproductive issues. Women introduce and sponsor more women's-issue bills than their male counterparts, particularly in the area of health care; their voting records reflect the fact that women's issues are often a legislative priority for women legislators (Tolbert and Steuernagel 2001, Caiazza 2004, Cowell-Meyers and Langbein 2009). Constituents expect women legislators to be experts in the women's issues, and some women work strategically to represent women's issue legislation to appeal to their voting base (Swers 2002). While the area of reproductive technologies is understudied in these debates, reproductive health care, such as abortion, contraception, breast and ovarian cancer care, and infertility care are more likely to be on the legislative agenda when more women legislators occupy political spaces at the federal and state levels (Tolbert and Steuernagel 2001, Caiazza 2004, Cowell-Meyers and Langbein 2009).

Gender does not operate in political isolation, however: partisanship of the individual legislator, as well as partisan context, matters in policy leadership of women's issues. In fact, diverse behavior and leadership is created when we consider the interactions between gender and partisanship. Partisanship modifies and shapes how gender operates in political spaces: individual ideology, party agendas, and polarized partisan contexts all change how women represent issues (Dodson 2006, Swers 2002,

Frederick 2009). Democratic women are the most likely among all partisans to introduce women's issue bills, particularly about women's health (Osborn 2012). While less likely to be policy leaders on "culture war" reproductive issues like abortion and contraception, Republican women have been observed to be policy leaders on women's health issues where there is no strict party line on the issue, such as maternal health care (Osborn 2012). Partisanship *and* gender work in concert to shape policy solutions, particularly in observations about women's health (Osborn 2012, Deckman 2016, Schreiber 2008). Other studies have noted that partisan women, despite strict party lines on reproductive health, have diverse opinions and approaches to issues like motherhood, technology, and family roles—for example, Tea Party women have expressed more flexible expectations about gender roles, reproduction, and working outside of the home than previously expected (Deckman 2016, Schreiber 2008).

While the political behavior and policy preferences of women legislators are indeed distinct from those of their male counterparts, women represent diverse issues, sometimes representing feminist concerns (like abortion), and sometimes representing issues that disproportionately affect women and children but which are not explicitly feminist (such as social welfare programs; e.g., Swers 2002, Thomas and Welch 1991, Cowell-Meyers and Langbein 2009). Women's issues and interests are often broadly defined in gender and politics research. One of the primary questions in this research is whether women can be understood as a cohesive group with similar interests, issues, and preferences. Critics, sensitive to the diversity of women's experience in intersecting structures of social, economic, and political oppression and privilege, argue that some women have interests in common owing to the effects of social structures like race, class, gender, and sexuality (among other social categories) that delineate a single social category for women (e.g., Smooth 2011, Beckwith 2011, Young 1994, 2002). As gender and politics scholars have come to agree that women are a diverse and heterogeneous social group, they have acknowledged that women may have similar patterns of experience with respect to traditional gender roles, particularly those in the family. Women's issues often reference concepts relating to the family, such as reproduction, children's welfare, health, and education. Feminist policies come out of these interests, issues, and preferences, as advocacy groups and legislators draw ideological lines around women's issues. Amy Mazur (2002, 3) defines feminist policies according to three core ideas of Western feminism: the idea of defining women as a group within contexts of heterogeneous identities and social structures; the goal of advancing women's rights, status, and condition within the public and private spheres; and the reduction or elimination of gender-based inequalities in the public and private spheres. Others measure feminist legislation similarly, arguing that it must promote women's equality or women's rights in the public and private spheres (MacDonald and O'Brien 2011, Saint-Germain 1989, Swers 2002, 2013).[7] Issues that may be included in a category of feminist policies that adhere to these core goals are equal pay policies and laws against gender-based employment discrimination; sexual harassment and domestic violence policies; and increasing access to abortion and contraception. As noted above, gender and politics research has consistently shown a large gender gap on feminist issues: the difference between which issues women and men represent in legislatures is greatest among feminist issues, with far more Democratic women taking the lead on feminist policies than their counterparts (MacDonald and O'Brien 2011, Swers

2002/2013, Wolbrecht 2000, Dodson and Carroll 1991, Carroll 1992, Osborn 2012).

How egg donation fits into feminist policy is complex and not as neatly defined as other reproductive issues that are more widely studied, such as abortion and contraception.[8] Feminist approaches to egg donation have been heterogeneous, with different feminist viewpoints articulating diverse concerns, debates, and policy solutions to problems associated with egg donation (Jesudason and Weitz 2015, Thompson 2005). The dominant feminist approaches to egg donation—liberal and radical feminisms—promote very different ideas about how egg donation should be regulated. While liberal feminists identify egg donation as disproportionately affecting women, they believe that bodily autonomy and decision making are paramount, and that the state should stay out of regulating the reproductive technology. While radical feminists also identify egg donation as an issue that disproportionately affects women as a group, they see the threats to women's liberty and freedom differently. They believe that—owing to stratified reproduction and the inequalities that women experience in response to the structures of race, class, sexuality, and others—regulation by the state can protect women from threats of eugenics, patriarchal oppression, and medical harms (Jesudason and Weitz 2015, Daniels and Heidt-Forsythe 2012). While there has been little research into how these diverse feminist claims are expressed in explicitly feminist policymaking regarding egg donation, examples from other research are helpful in guiding this inquiry into the politics of egg donation.

Swiveling to antifeminist policy addressing abortion and assisted reproductive technologies (ART) is key in understanding how gender and politics research may play a role in egg donation politics and policy. In the case of abortion policy, conservative advocates and policy makers witnessed the success (and failure) of a certain type of rhetoric to create policy and change public opinion. In one study of state female legislators between 1997 and 2012, Reingold and colleagues (2015) found that conservative Republican women were more likely to introduce explicitly antifeminist, antiabortion legislation.[9] This came after decades of little success in changing public opinion about abortion by using rhetoric about the rights of the fetus (Jesudason and Weitz 2015). After the mid-1990s, antiabortion legislation was increasingly introduced as a matter of "women-centered" health and well-being, where the policies to restrict abortion would ultimately protect women from physical and psychological harm (Reingold et al. 2015). In a case study of California state legislation regarding abortion and egg donation, Jesudason and Weitz (2015) came to a parallel conclusion, although they do not label the legislation as specifically antifeminist: pro-choice and anti-choice stakeholders used similar "woman-protective" rhetoric to justify two bills, one that restricted abortion access, and one that enabled legal, paid egg donation. Women-centered and women-protective rhetoric has a long history in feminist scholarship and advocacy, as the feminist women's health movement has utilized the rhetoric since the 1960s (Solinger 2005, Luker 1984). Feminist women's health movement activists argued that policies that disproportionately affect women should identify women as the central subjects of the legislation; moreover, women should be protected from biased, discriminatory, and unfair medical institutions. In the women's health movement, this meant empowering women to be active subjects in their health and medical care, which would be tailored to enable autonomous decision making about health and medicine. This rhetoric of placing women and women's health and well-being at the center of policymaking has been co-opted by women's conservative groups, as well as by conservative legislators (Schreiber 2008, Deckman 2016, Reingold et al. 2015). This co-optation is unsurprising, given the ways that conservative women's organizations (such as Concerned Women for America) have increasingly focused on women's economic independence, reproduction and motherhood, and political engagement as important goals. Clearly, the use of feminist rhetoric by conservative women's organizations and conservative women does not mean their aims are feminist; the use of women-centered, feminist rhetoric is to achieve goals that reinforce, rather than reject, the inequality of women's rights, status, and condition, as well as patriarchal structures concerning gender, sexuality, and the family (Jesudason and Weitz 2015, Mazur 2002, Reingold et al. 2015). How feminist rhetoric is co-opted—used by social and political conservatives to weaken women's equality and status in regard to reproduction and research—is an important question in the egg donation regulation system; it also has broader impacts on politics and policy around reproduction in the US.

This is where several strands of gender, partisanship, and feminist policy-making research intersect: if there are no party agendas present in an issue, and partisan women create diverse policy solutions, then there is a story to tell about the ways that gender, partisanship, and legislation on egg donation interact in the US, shaping the overall politics of egg donation. For example, while Republican and Democratic women may agree that egg donation is a pressing issue, they likely have different policy solutions (shaped by their own ideology, by which party controls their chamber, and by the polarization between political parties in their state) for problems that arise from egg donation for reproduction and research. As women legislators have been crucial in influencing the politics of reproduction more broadly—and there is case-by-case evidence of the importance of women in advocating genetic research at the state level—the story of the politics of egg donation is incomplete without an examination of the diverse ways that gender, partisanship, feminist policy, and issue leadership shape the US system.

CHAPTER OVERVIEW

The conventional thinking that the US system of egg donation is the Wild West is incomplete, failing to take into account the state politics of egg donation and the diverse policy outcomes related to egg donation for reproduction versus research. Moreover, current explanations for the US system fail to account for these characteristics of egg donation. What are the politics of egg donation at the state level, and how do gendered norms of femininity in egg donation shape these politics? To answer these questions, I engage in this book with three major areas, analyzing how *framing* of egg donation plays a key role in the politics and policymaking, particularly through the frameworks of *body politics* and *morality politics,* and how *gender and partisanship* create diverse roles for women legislators in the politics of egg donation. This analysis is the first of its kind to look at egg donation politics over time, and at how women in politics play nuanced and complicated roles in the politics of this "women's issue" of reproduction, technology, and medicine.

In order to clarify the development of the politics of egg donation in the US, chapter 1 examines the history and politics of egg donation through the lenses of body politics and morality politics, two major frameworks in political science, policy studies, and gender studies. I argue that these frameworks, considered together, better explain the development and regulation of egg donation in the US than current understanding—particularly that which looks through the lens of historical change in response to the deployment of body and morality politics by stakeholders in egg donation. Since the mid-1990s, egg donation for reproduction has been considered a private, conventional choice to expand one's family, whereas egg donation for research is couched in fiery debates about fundamental moral principles—discourse that defines stem cell, cloning, and egg donation research as akin to Dr. Frankenstein's experiments. However, these conventional logics of egg donation have not always been accepted; at different points in history, morality and body politics have gained and lost traction in the US system. To demonstrate the explanatory power of body and morality politics frameworks, I explore the history of scientific research on the human egg, which culminated in the rise of commercial markets in eggs for fertility and research. This chapter builds upon current explanations of the politics of egg donation as the result of privatization (of reproduction, science, and business), abortion politics, or a lack of bioethical discourse, by arguing that body and morality politics shape the US system. Moreover, the history and contemporary oversight of egg donation are more fully explained by the concept that body politics and morality politics create divergent beliefs, attitudes, and ideas about reproductive technologies and research.

The politics of egg donation are created through framing—the process by which issues are defined, debates drawn, and policy solutions created. Chapter 1 introduces how my argument tests the theory that norms of femininity—processed through body and morality politics—shape the process of framing egg donation. Chapter 2 introduces policy narrative analysis, an interpretive technique of finding "policy stories" in discourse and texts, and explains how and why this method is an effective way of analyzing processes of framing egg donation. This chapter also provides an overview of the cases that I analyze in chapter 3. These case studies—California, New York, Arizona, and Louisiana—provide important insight into the fact that bills about egg donation for reproduction and for research are subjected to different framing strategies related to body and morality politics and, thus, political outcomes. Focusing on the topic of bans on compensation for egg donation, these four cases provide the first comprehensive, comparative analysis of the diverse framing processes, and thus politics and policymaking, about egg donation in the US.

Drawing on policy narrative analysis of egg donation bills, chapter 3 describes and analyzes how stakeholders frame the issues of egg donation for reproduction and research across California, New York, Arizona, and Louisiana. Observing and analyzing bill text, hearings, meetings, press releases, and other legislative materials created by egg donation stakeholders, I lay out the strategies in advocating bans on compensation for egg donation for research (California and New York) and, in all contexts, reproduction and research (Arizona and Louisiana). The subsequent cases rely on gender and norms of femininity that shape body and morality politics frames. Moreover, each of the cases relies on certain narratives of egg donors' vulnerability to justify policy solutions. Finally, each case demonstrates the moral responsibility of the state and defines the role of the state in regulating some aspect of egg donation. These themes—gender and agency, vulnerability, and the moral responsibility of the state—reflect prevailing attitudes, beliefs, and values in body and morality politics and demonstrate the ways that diverse political stakeholders use, and co-opt, feminist policy rhetoric.

To further test the theories forwarded in this book, in chapter 4 I examine a third major area of inquiry: gender and partisanship in politics. This chapter demonstrates that states are in fact active on the social issue of egg donation and its implications for medical practices, parentage and kinship, and research. Using an original data set of bills about egg donation across state legislatures in forty-nine states between 1995 and 2010, this chapter identifies the role of body and morality politics in shaping policymaking about egg donation. I also use event history analysis (also known as hazard analysis), which can determine how time-dependent and time-independent variables are implicated in policy change over time, to determine how the introduction and passage of egg donation policy is associated with body politics, morality politics, and state demographics. I argue that, against some conventional thinking found in bioethics and feminist studies, egg donation legislation is predicted by *both* morality and variables in body politics, lending support to the theory that these frameworks have dual and central influence over the politics and policymaking regarding egg donation in the US. Importantly, this analysis also uncovers the prominence of gendered representation in the politics of egg donation in the US, uncovering surprising and counterintuitive findings about the roles of gender and party identification in agenda-setting on the subject of egg donation and related issues such as parentage, compensation, disposition, and research, among others. Combining theorizing about motherhood and pronatalism in conservative women's representational behavior, this chapter presents new findings about the role of partisan women in representing reproductive and scientific issues, in contrast to current analysis and theorizing about reproductive issues such as abortion and contraception. Not only has there been a vibrant politics of egg donation across the states in the late twentieth and early twenty-first centuries, but also these politics uncover new truths about the roles of diverse women in politics.

In the conclusion, I return to some of the conventional thinking about the politics of egg donation in the US. Despite more than thirty years of visibility of egg donation regulation in public life—a visibility that has only intensified with the development of new procedures, such as the use of egg donation in stem cell research and cryopreservation—the US is often characterized as having incompletely regulated egg donation in a highly commercialized environment. While egg donation is increasingly part of a constellation of conventional reproductive options, it has emerged as an important political issue connected to questions of morality and first principles. Egg donation for reproduction in recent years has come under scrutiny because fertility clinics may be illegally fixing the price of human eggs, preventing donors from receiving increased sums of money for their donations (Lewin 2015). Websites now connect egg donors to one another and disseminate information about the procedure, particularly in light of the potential health risks of egg donation.[10] Long-standing ethical questions, such as exploitation of egg donors in the US system, remain in the public sphere (Daniels and Heidt-Forsythe 2012). Since the late 1990s, egg donation for genetic research has stimulated a sense of moral panic, causing governors to exclaim that "not everything in life is for sale nor should it be," and state senators to warn against "endangering our young women's lives ... for a massive egg harvesting industry" (Brown 2013, Hamilton 2010). While egg donation for reproduction seems unfettered and unregulated, scientific research using human eggs has been a source of vivid political controversy. Although current explanations for the politics of egg donation do draw attention to the ways that we conceptualize privacy, the influence of polarized politics, and the intersection of deliberation and bioethics, the previous chapters observe and analyze egg donation politics in motion, particularly at the state level.

To best confront these future debates, we must examine our own gendered assumptions about the body, sexuality, and reproduction in relation to donors and consumers in the world of egg donation. For donors, definitions of reproductive labor must be confronted. New conceptualizations of this labor must be formulated to keep up with the lucrative, growing industries of egg donation for reproduction and research. Moreover, given that egg donors are in fact the targets of so much policy—and yet are largely silent in this analysis—we must take seriously their role as policy stakeholders in the policymaking process. Little is known about women who donate eggs, and who are often targeted by legislators, but who so rarely speak for themselves in the political sphere. Women face a politics of egg donation in the US that is largely driven by gendered norms of femininity, a politics that does little to help increase their say in the policy that regulates the experiences and transactions. Similarly, consumers of egg donation face a similar scenario: while policies have been developed to represent their interests, many women (particularly disadvantaged women at the intersections of race and class) experience a politics in which policy solutions increase, rather than alleviate, structural inequalities in the experience and financing of infertility treatments, including egg donation. Through this analysis of reproduction, research, and gender, I argue that political stakeholders must challenge gender norms of femininity, resist the urgings of politics to reinforce inequalities, and create new visions of equality, justice, and representation in the politics of egg donation.

CHAPTER ONE

Dream or Nightmare?

*Theories and Histories of Egg Donation in the
United States*

Traveling through New Brunswick, New Jersey, drivers find
that tedious stretches of highway are dotted with billboards;
not terribly unusual, except that these billboards advertise egg
donation. Festooned with brightly colored chicken eggs, warmly
smiling doctors, and chubby babies accompanied by storks, these
advertisements reveal the large, lucrative fertility industry in
New Jersey. Young women at nearby Rutgers and Princeton
Universities can earn eight thousand to ten thousand dollars for
signing up, passing a battery of tests, and having their eggs procured through outpatient surgery. However, New Brunswick is
also home to the Stem Cell Institute of New Jersey. In contrast
to the fertility industry, which put up those cheerful billboards
soliciting egg donation for reproduction, the institute has faced
major political attention and turmoil. In 2008, only eight months
after breaking ground for the Christopher Reeves Pavilion in
the future eighteen-story research tower in the center of the
city, voters rejected a ballot measure allocating almost half a bil-
lion dollars in funding for the institute (Jackson 2008). While

young women can easily apply to become egg donors at the seventeen clinics across New Jersey, moral and ethical debates about using state money for research—some of which involves human eggs—plague stem cell science in the state. The dream and potential of egg donation to create life on one hand, and to create cures on the other, can easily slide into a political nightmare.

THE POLITICS OF EGG DONATION: REPRODUCTION VERSUS RESEARCH

One of the key questions I explain is why, given the robust regulation of egg donation in comparative industrialized countries, the US is so different in its approach to the politics of egg donation. In a system of federalism like that of the US, states have an important role in crafting and implementing policy, even when the policy has been created at the national level. States have been vested in issues surrounding egg donation since the 1980s, and interest in human eggs for research has burgeoned since the development of stem cell research in the late 1990s (Bonnicksen 1989, Bonnicksen 2002, Markens 2007, Thompson 2013). Egg donation also developed and changed in the public imagination: while early depictions of egg donation for reproduction portrayed the technology as morally suspect, it has transitioned into a highly conventional practice for those privileged to access infertility care in the US. However, the belief that egg donation is a conventional choice for family formation has not always prevailed; moral and body politics have informed the histories and policies of egg donation. I argue that existing explanations for the US regulatory system—that privacy, the controversial nature of abortion, and the lack of bioethical discourse explain regulation of egg donation in the US—are incomplete. These arguments fail to account for two important patterns in the politics of egg donation in the US: first, why egg donation for reproduction has summoned diverse framing and policy responses; and second, why state political actors have engaged with issues related to egg donation. In this chapter I argue that two explanatory frameworks work together to illuminate the unique regulatory approach of the US to egg donation, as described in table 1.

As discussed in the introduction, the US is viewed in the public imagination (as well as in scholarly observation) as the Wild West of reproductive technology, where egg donation practices and regulations are determined and policed by multibillion-dollar commercial markets. On one hand, the US has been perceived as too passive on bioethical issues, refusing to regulate private reproductive decisions, scientific research, and commercial markets; on the other hand, the US has been described as being mired in debates over abortion, precluding any reasonable discussion of egg donation (Jasanoff 2005). This characterization is rooted in comparison: while other nations have centralized regulatory regimes restricting egg donation practices, a cursory examination of the US shows no such regulatory framework. For example, some nations (such as Germany, Austria, Italy, and Norway) have banned egg donation outright. Other nations (such as the UK and Canada) allow egg donation, but donation cannot be compensated. Some nations (Israel and Switzerland) restrict the use of donor eggs to those who are legally married, a privilege often reserved for heterosexual couples. The US stands out among these examples of centralized regulation, with its seemingly unfettered system attracting domestic and international consumers looking to purchase third-party eggs for reproduction.

TABLE I

The Politics of Egg Donation
Body Politics and Morality Politics

Egg Donation Type	Theoretical Framework	Framing Strategy	Political Outcome
Reproduction: 1990s–Present	Body politics / stratified reproduction	Natural, conventional	Individual choice and reproductive privilege
Reproduction: Early 1980s–Mid-1990s; Some Issues from 1990s–Present	Morality politics	Unnatural, strange	Matter of moral values, moral responsibility of individual/government
Research: Late 1990s–Present			

In order to solve this puzzle, in this chapter I examine two major frameworks—body politics and morality politics—that explain the diverse politics of egg donation. At different moments in the history and regulation of egg donation, these frameworks have gained and lost traction in defining egg donation in the US context. Body politics, as an area of inquiry in gender, women's, and sexuality studies, has traditionally examined gender, sexuality, and reproductive issues in the context of state power. Overarching questions about how the state intervenes in reproduction have long underpinned body politics; since the 1990s, feminist scholars have used the lens of body politics to consider the relationships between state power and reproductive technologies (Franklin 1995). Egg donation fits into body politics: the state uses its powers of regulation to advance political ideologies about gender and the family, particularly as they interact with other social structures like race, class, and sexuality (e.g., Roberts 2009, Daniels and Heidt-Forsythe 2012, Thompson 2005). However, missing from these conversations within body politics is how this framework informs egg donation politics and policies.

Egg donation in the US is not only shaped by considerations of body politics and interventions by the state into reproduction; it is also structured by discussions of ethical and moral values. Morality politics—a field of study within political science and policy studies—considers how certain issues are defined in the public sphere through the lens of fundamental moral principles. This lens shapes how political actors define an issue, what the terms of debate are, and how distinct partisan, contentious politics are provoked by the issue. For example, those who study abortion politics and policy have noted the ways that the issue is defined through the lens of morality related to life and bodily autonomy, how discourse occurs between opposing actors who represent different fundamental principles, and how distinct politics and policy are created in relation to abortion (e.g., Mooney and Lee 1995, Norrander and Wilcox 1999). In the scholarship on morality politics, there is increasing attention to the ways that the politics of stem cell research and cloning are defined through morality politics (e.g., Ryan 2014, Bonnicksen 2002). However, this research lacks attention to the intersection of reproduction and controversial research—the place where egg donation exists. In egg donation for reproduction and egg donation for research, morality politics potentially has important explanatory power in conjunction with body politics.

Part of the overarching premise of this book—that norms of gender create divisions between the "natural" and abject and shape the politics of egg donation—is that body politics and morality politics have played roles in this process in the past and still do so today, and in this chapter I break down these roles. Discussing the broader existing debates in body and morality politics, this chapter traces how body and morality politics have shaped the US system of egg donation and how they have gained and lost relevance in this system. After laying out the ways that these frameworks help explain egg donation for reproduction and research, this chapter connects body and morality politics to the practical, scholarly, and political histories of this reproductive technology in the US context. I argue that rather than being a strange, Wild West system of regulation that makes little sense in light of nearly universal regulation of egg donation in Europe, North America, and Oceania, egg donation reflects the simultaneous logics of body politics and morality politics. Contemporary politics surrounding egg donation in the US have taken two different trajectories, where egg donation for reproduction is defined according to body politics, and egg donation for stem cell and cloning research is defined through morality politics as an abject, strange, and unnatural use of women's bodies. However, these patterns have not always existed—and the histories of egg donation illustrate how stakeholders employ body politics and morality politics to frame the reproductive technology in the US.

BODY POLITICS OF EGG DONATION: THINKING CRITICALLY ABOUT STRATIFIED REPRODUCTION

While conflicts over egg donation for reproduction and research seem new and discomfiting, they are an echo of much older debates about inequality, reproduction, and the state. For nearly fifty years, scholars have carefully observed and analyzed how the combination of reproduction and technology provides "a terrain for imagining ... contested claims of powerful religious and political ideologies" (Ginsburg and Rapp 1995). State power is exercised over the body and its processes—particularly practices that literally reproduce the population of the nation—and this power communicates and enforces hierarchies of identity (among these are gender, race, and class), citizenship, and representation in political spaces (Roberts 1998, 2012, Ginsburg and Rapp 1995, Franklin and Ragoné 1998, Luker 1984, Dickenson 2007, Browner and Sargent 2011, Ehrenreich and English 1978, Gordon 2004). Reproduction and motherhood are sites of contestation in political institutions and policymaking, particularly at the state level (Skocpol 1992, Petchesky [1984] 1990, Daniels 1993, Roberts 1998, Jelen and Wilcox 2003, Kreitzer 2015). As is the case in other reproductive issues, egg donation is a site of debates and confrontations about the role of the state in commodification and exploitation, procreation, kinship and the biological family, and bodily autonomy (Mamo 2008, Farquhar 1996, Franklin 2013). More broadly, politics surrounding egg donation (and indeed, the body in general) serve the aims of the state to not only define civil society and citizenship but also define the meanings of the state's economic and political powers (Waylen et al. 2013). Egg donation's role in stem cell and cloning research has also opened up broader debates on inequalities within scientific research and innovation, particularly on issues of access to the benefits of such research (Thompson 2005, 2013, Benjamin 2013).

Stratified reproduction is a process by which "physical and social reproductive tasks are accomplished according to inequalities that are based on hierarchies [of social categories], of class, race, ethnicity, gender" (Colen 1995, 78, Rapp 1999). Reproductive stratification is based in—and further aggravates—inequalities in lived experiences inside and outside of reproduction. In experiences ranging from sexual activity to access to contraceptive technologies, from access to abortion to access to pregnancy care, from childbirth to socializing children, individuals encounter the work of forming families in different and often unequal ways. This "reproductive labor" of physically reproducing and sustaining children, families, and domestic tasks is not only strongly associated with femininity and the lived experience of women but is also often devalued and discredited as valid and important paid or unpaid work (Colen 1995, Rapp 1999). Reproductive labor is not, however, equally disregarded or rewarded across the population; according to hierarchies of class, race, gender, sexuality, and ability, some individuals are highly incentivized and rewarded for reproductive labor, while others are shamed, punished, and prevented from reproducing and raising families (e.g., Roberts 1998). State authority and control over technologies in reproduction and research are used to promote hierarchies of gender, race, class, and sexuality within and across national borders, and inequalities are anchored in complex webs of laws and policies that enforce ideologies of reproductive value (Farquhar 1996, Petchesky [1984] 1990, Mamo 2007, Markens 2007, Thompson 2005, Colen 1995, Rapp 1999, Roberts 2009, 1998).

Although the use of egg donation has skyrocketed over the past twenty years, not all people have experienced increased access to infertility treatment or sophisticated reproductive technologies (Roberts 1998). Stratification has arguably become more intense with egg donation (among other reproductive technologies): in the US context, the high costs of procedures and pharmaceutical drugs come out of patients' pockets for those without comprehensive health insurance. Intense reproductive stratification in reproductive technologies is not simply a product of economic resources: as Roberts (1998, 2009) notes, historically the entire fertility market in the US has been built upon white, middle- and upper-class consumers, while women of color face high levels of scrutiny, surveillance, and legal restrictions regarding fertility and childbirth (see also Smith 2007). Historically, infertility clinics aimed their services at white, economically privileged, urban couples, as evidenced by commercial practices that heavily advertised to and served these populations (Roberts 1998, Markens 2007, Thompson 2005, Almeling 2011).[1] With the increasing sophistication and application of genetic testing, pharmaceutical drugs, and obstetric technologies, there has been a shift to individual responsibility in reproduction across the entire population, where individuals are increasingly being asked not only to accept personal risk during reproduction but also to access all possible technologies in order to have a "successful" reproductive experience (Roberts 2009, Thompson 2005, 2013, Harwood 2007).[2] From the Centers for Disease Control advising "pre-pregnant" women against alcohol consumption to seemingly mandatory amniocentesis, from genetic testing during the first trimester of pregnancy to increasingly sophisticated technologies for visualizing fetuses in the womb, women face intense pressure in a stratified system of technology access: one's ability to access the best medical care, reproductive technologies, and pharmaceuticals determines one's fitness as a mother (Roberts 2009). Despite the prevalence of these technologies, not all people have equal access to even a minimum level of health care, much less sophisticated reproductive technologies like donated eggs. Additionally, the benefits of research using donor eggs—such as regenerative medicine—have not been spread equally across the population, particularly failing to reach socioeconomically disadvantaged groups (Benjamin 2013). The values, beliefs, and assumptions about inequality, reproduction, and research shape the politics and policy outcomes related to egg donation—while the state must intervene in some cases to alleviate inequality in access to reproductive technologies, in other cases the inequality may be reinforced by state inaction (Roberts 2009).

MOTHERHOOD AND EGG DONATION IN STRATIFIED REPRODUCTION

Although stratified reproduction and access to technologies have changed through biomedicalization and the use of egg donation, these patterns are rooted in the US's history of using race, gender, class, and other identities to determine what makes a good mother versus a bad one. Popular culture, media representations, legal cases, and public policy demonstrate prevailing ideologies about who is a good or a bad mother: for example, President Theodore Roosevelt warned of "race suicide" during the Progressive Era, a historical moment when increasing numbers of single women agitated for increased liberties in sexuality and reproduction, the workplace, and education, while delaying marriage, pregnancy, and childbirth (Traister 2016). During this same era, other women were deemed innately unfit to be mothers owing to their sexuality, race, ethnicity, immigration status, gender identity, or disability. Whereas the state made an explicit call for white, single women to settle down and form families, it enforced punitive and oppressive reproductive policies (such as state-mandated sterilization) on marginalized women (Solinger 2005, Roberts 1998). However, there is no "good" mother without a corresponding "bad" mother in popular culture and political life, and this binary has hinged on race, class, and sexuality. African American, Latina, Asian American, and Native American women, particularly economically disadvantaged women, have been historically defined as unfit mothers in a stratified system of reproduction. Among these groups, nonwhite, young, and unmarried women have been subject to a litany of negative sociopolitical representations that define their motherhood as criminal and damaging. Reflecting these representations, punitive policies and social practices prevented women from fulfilling their goals of motherhood (Solinger 2005, Roberts 1998, 2009).

This division between good and bad mothers is reinforced through commercial and political practices related to egg donation in the US—particularly the ways that *certain* women's bodies are deemed appropriate and natural for reproduction and motherhood, while other women's bodies are defined as deviant or unfit, disqualifying them for reproduction and motherhood. Importantly, there are multiple roles women's bodies can play in egg donation markets and politics: the bodies that provide the raw materials for reproduction are not always the intended or legal mothers of donor-conceived children, and intended mothers do not always provide biological material or a bodily environment to carry a pregnancy and give birth to a child. In the US market system, who is deemed a "good" parent is determined in part by whether one can navigate the immense financial barriers, bias and discrimination, and social stigmas to access medical care. "Good" mothers and fathers not only identify their infertility and/or involuntary childlessness but also seek out medical advice and treatment for these conditions—a process that varies widely by race, class, gender, and educational attainment level (Bell 2009, 2010, 2014, Ceballo 1999, Ceballo et al. 2010, Ceballo et al. 2015, Greil et al. 2011). Despite the social stigma of infertility, the dominant belief in the US is that individuals who want to become parents should extend themselves emotionally and financially to achieve parenthood, despite the immense physical, psychological, and economic costs of using reproductive technologies to treat infertility (Zelizer 2010, Harwood 2007, Thompson 2005, Greil et al. 2016).

On the other hand, "unfit" mothers are economically prohibited from using reproductive technologies, or they find themselves excluded (through commercial or legal policies) from the possibility of accessing "good" motherhood. Because infertility is covered only by private insurance, those who are poor and working class (and rely on public insurance like Medicaid) cannot benefit from reproductive technologies to treat infertility and involuntary childlessness.[3] Medical professionals' preconceived notions about immigrants, religious affiliations, and familial norms shape how they treat women's infertility, particularly that of women from Latinx and Muslim communities in the US (Greil et al. 2016, Ceballo 1999, Inhorn and Fakih 2009). Clinical practices often rely on biased and discriminatory beliefs about the hyperfertility of women of color, rather than relying on a patient's personal testimony or empirical evidence about infertility (Roberts 1998, 2009, Bell 2009, Ceballo 1999). Even among those with the economic resources and community support to finance medical treatment and access to reproductive technologies, many are excluded from dominant white, middle- and upper-class, heterosexual, and female-centered models of infertility (Bell 2009, 2014, Ceballo 1999).

Marital status, sexuality, and perceptions of disability have also historically delineated "good" and "bad" motherhood. Throughout the first two decades of reproductive technology use in the US, those with nonnormative sexuality and relationship statuses—particularly same-sex and queer couples, and single individuals—were prevented from using infertility medicine and technology to address involuntary childlessness. Biased commercial practices, bans on same-sex and single adoption, and state bans on in vitro fertilization (IVF) treatment for unmarried individuals prevented many from accessing infertility care and reproductive technologies. Historically, disabled or diseased bodies were the subjects of legal debate, with arguments addressing the question of whether they were "unfit" to be the parent of a child conceived through assisted reproductive technologies (ART): in one Michigan case in 2009, a surrogate sued to keep the donor-conceived twins she was carrying, owing to the intended mother's history of treatment for mental illness (Saul 2009). While the pressures may shift and change, and the role of the state may become more obscured in its promotion of ideologies of gender, race, class, and ability, stratified reproduction and access to technologies is the context in which politics occurs and policy is made (Roberts 2009). The systems of inequality surrounding access to and benefits from scientific research and technology define egg donation and set the parameters of political debate. Stakeholders—legislators, advocacy groups, and political actors—hold beliefs about reproductive technologies and genetic research, foregrounded by values about good and bad motherhood. These beliefs and values shape the current US system of egg donation politics and policy in a framework of body politics.

The relationship of body politics to egg donation is one where policy and practice create conditions in which some individuals, identified by race, gender, sexuality, and class identities, are privileged over others in reproductive practices and policy. These social structures of identity shape access to participation in, and benefits of, genetic research involving human eggs (Benjamin 2013, Thompson 2013). State ideology is exercised through the power of regulation, whereby policies are constructed to allow some to access egg donation for reproduction and/or research, while creating insurmountable barriers for other populations. Moreover, the exercise of state power over egg donation is always shifting, as evidenced by the introduction of new and innovative technologies such as egg freezing for future fertility. Thinking about egg donation for reproduction as a conventional, personal choice for family formation reinforces reproductive stratification, the valuing of some individuals' reproduction over that of others. Moreover, commercial and political practices related to egg donation markets also reinforce inequalities in how eggs are valued: while some women donate eggs prized for their phenotypical characteristics, others are shut out of this commercial market (Daniels and Heidt-Forsythe 2012). This ostensibly creates different markets (one for reproduction, and one for research) according to state and commercial ideologies of reproductive value (Waldby and Cooper 2008, 2010). Although body politics provides an important lens for understanding the logic of egg donation, it is an incomplete framework—while body politics has been used to frame egg donation at some points in history, morality politics has taken precedence at other points to define the reproductive technology.

MORALITY POLITICS AND EGG DONATION FOR RESEARCH

Soon after the first egg-donor-conceived child was born, the press speculated about the moral and ethical implications of the practice for women, their partners, future children, and the meaning of life itself (Brozan 1988). Later, when egg donation was a crucial source of biological material for research, it elicited dramatic and conflict-oriented media coverage, morally based discourse between medical and religious communities, and the morality-based debates around stem cell research (Nisbet et al. 2003, Bonnicksen 1989, 2002). In the last decade, states (such as California and New York) have established state-funded stem cell research, and debates over egg donation as part of this research have been framed as a matter of the ethical orientation and value-driven interests of stakeholders (Thompson 2013, Benjamin 2013, Heidt-Forsythe 2016). In contrast to the dominance of body politics in contemporary framing of egg donation for reproduction, these examples demonstrate the salience and traction of morality politics in contemporary research using donated eggs. The simultaneous power of body politics and morality politics better explains the unique system of egg donation in the US.

MORALITY POLITICS AS CONCEPT AND CATEGORY

Egg donation is but one of many issues that elicit debates over morals, ethics, and values. Morality politics as a theoretical concept addresses the distinct politics of issues that regulate morality in social life. Theodore Lowi's (1972) seminal work on organizing policy into discrete categories is considered to be the starting point of this research, where he aimed to create a "proper, analyzable, relationship [between public policy] … and those dimensions of political science that are already well developed" (1972, 299). Lowi argues that there are four types of public policy in American politics: "constituent policies" that target governmental institutions and procedures; "distributive policies," which determine how benefits are allocated across society; "regulatory policies," which impose restrictions on individuals and resources; and "redistributive" policies, where material goods and services are reallocated among groups in society (Lowi 1964, 1972). However, rising controversies during the twentieth century—particularly regarding gender, sexuality, and reproduction—challenged these clear policy boundaries. The changes brought about by *Griswold*[4] and *Roe*[5] that eased legal access to contraception and abortion, the movement of middle-class and mostly white women from the private to the public sphere, climbing divorce rates, the increase in LGBTQ rights, and the diversification of family structures all challenged conventional ways of thinking about policy issues and how they could be categorized (Sharp 2005). Specifically, issues concerning the body, reproduction, and science invoked new kinds of debates and political deliberation: not about constitutive, representative, distributive, or redistributive policies, but about those issues that seemed to deeply divide the public and politicians on the basis of fundamental, moral values.[6] New issues were debated in ways that emphasized arguments over first principles (like the meanings of *personhood* and *life,* in the case of abortion debates) and provoked a new kind of politics. To respond to these new kinds of deliberations and politics focused on moral and ethical debates, scholarship in the 1980s and 1990s emerged that defined a new policy category: morality politics and policy (Haider-Markel and Meier 1996, Lowi 1998).

Issues can be labeled *morality politics* when political actors seek to regulate social norms, the issues conjure a strong moral response from the public, and deliberation reflects a clash over fundamental, moral principles (Tatalovich and Daynes 1998, Mooney and Lee 1995). In morality politics, how an issue is defined determines whether it is a matter of morality or not: rather than reflecting an inherent morality, some issues are defined as a competition between fundamental moral principles and claims, and there is a privileging of moral reasoning over instrumental reasoning in political debates and deliberation (Mucciaroni 2011). Morality issues are easy to digest for the public and politicians alike: generally, morality politics issues are technically simple and highly salient to the public, allowing everyone to be an expert (Haider-Markel and Meier 1996, Gormley 1986, Carmines and Stimson 1980).[7] Often divisive, these politics create situations where political compromise is nearly impossible, as moral values cannot be negotiated (Mucciaroni 2011). Abortion (Mooney and Lee 1995, Norrander and Wilcox 1999), the death penalty (Mooney 2000), gay rights (Haider-Markel and Meier 1996, Mucciaroni 2011), drugs and alcohol (Meier 1994), gambling and lotteries (Pierce and Miller 2004, Berry and Berry 1990), the sex work industry (Sharp 2005), and stem cell research (Ryan 2014) are among the diverse issues that fit the definition of morality politics and policy in the US context.

While morality politics scholarship has observed the ways that stem cell research and cloning are subject to being defined, debated, and solved through morality politics frames, I argue that morality politics has historically and contemporarily shaped the politics of egg donation. At different points in time, morality politics has gained traction in defining egg donation: in the media and political arena, egg donation for reproduction has been debated in terms of fundamental, often religiously based, principles (Nisbet et al. 2003, Ryan 2014, Bonnicksen 2002). In the contemporary period (since the mid-1990s) morality politics has increasingly been used to define and debate egg donation for research purposes. From the birth of the first child conceived by means of a donated egg in 1984 to the birth of Dolly the sheep in 1996, debates on egg research and reproduction have stirred up contentious, morally couched politics and public clashes over fundamental principles (Bonnicksen 2002). The 1998 development of somatic cell nuclear transfer, or "reproductive cloning," in human eggs, as well as President George W. Bush's 2001 ban on new stem cell lines for federal research, illustrate how egg-donation-related research has attracted not only public interest but also political outcry. In studies of public opinion, federally funded stem cell research ranks among the most controversial of ethical issues surveyed, evoking strong feelings about morality (Ryan 2014). Since the mid-1990s, egg donation for research has been closely connected to scientific research on cloning, chimeras, and stem cells, and many characteristics of public deliberation and policymaking in response to egg donation for stem cell research also fit into a morality politics framework.

Contemporary debate and policymaking reveal the salience of morality politics frames for egg donation for reproduction and research. In California's venture to become a policy leader in 2007 via Proposition 71, stakeholders consistently debated stem cell research in terms of morality, claiming the state was morally compelled to find cures for disease and disability as a matter of life and death for Californians (Benjamin 2013, Thompson 2013). In opposition, others argued their position in moral terms, stating that stem cell research dehumanized, exploited, and commodified bodies and life (Benjamin 2013, Heidt-Forsythe 2016). Outside of California, state legislators have characterized egg donation in moralistic terms, portraying egg donation as "endangering young women's lives" (Hamilton 2010). Others have argued that egg donation creates a "commodity" and is therefore akin to "prostitution … the buying, selling, and trading of women's bodies" (Hamilton 2010, Concerned Women for America 2010).

As is the case of egg donation, there can be a lot of variation in how issues are defined as morality politics. This variation depends on how stakeholders define an issue (as rooted in moral debates, or not), what actors are involved in the issues (such as religious organizations, medical professionals, or feminist groups), and how debates about an issue are constructed (whether they refer to moral principles or are more relevant to other societal factors). As Sharp (2005), Mucciaroni (2011), and Kreitzer (2015) convincingly argue, just because an overarching issue has been categorized as a morality policy in the past does not mean that every subissue qualifies as a morality policy. For example, laws against abortion access were subject to morality politics, while laws in favor of abortion access were more responsive to the ways that gender and the partisanship of legislators influenced pro-abortion access issues (Kreitzer 2015). The dynamics of morality politics can also vary widely within a single issue category: for instance, different subissues within abortion—such as targeted regulation of abortion provider laws (which impose building code restrictions on abortion clinics), parental notification (laws that require a parent to be notified when a minor seeks an abortion), and bans on public insurance coverage of abortion—vary in how they adhere to the morality politics paradigm (Kreitzer 2015).[8] Not only can politics vary quite a bit within broad issues, but also issues can be "demoralized": if an issue is framed as something besides a debate over fundamental values, then that issue can slide into other policy and politics categories. For example, debates over abortion can shift into debates over judicial oversight and administration rather than debates over moral values (Kreitzer 2015). Elites will "bracket" moral concerns, putting aside debates over values to place greater emphasis on "instrumental" concerns such as the proper role of government in regulating a policy issue (Mucciaroni 2011). This slippage speaks directly to the issue of egg donation in the contexts of body and morality politics: depending on the purposes of donated eggs and their historical and political contexts, politics and policy can reflect questions about state intervention in reproduction, or represent a clash over fundamental ethical principles. The politics of egg donation in the US reflects morality and body politics—and the historical development of these technologies and practices reflect these multiple frameworks.

THE BLURRING OF THE ANIMAL AND
THE HUMAN: THE HISTORY OF
EGG DONATION

Body and morality politics provide important lenses for understanding the complex and sometimes contradictory histories and regulations of egg donation. As body and morality politics work simultaneously to define, set the terms of the debate about, and shape the politics of egg donation, we may begin to understand the multiplicity of egg donation, as egg donation is considered conventional in some contexts, while it is akin to Dr. Frankenstein's experiments in others. In line with the changeable norms of femininity and the waxing and waning influences of body and morality politics, the history of egg donation is one of blurred boundaries. It is a history where constructions of the "natural" and "unnatural" shift with technological development, consumer use, public attention, and political regulation. For an expanded discussion of the medical and psychological processes (as well as risks) associated with egg donation, please see appendix 1.

As far back as the eighteenth century, reproductive science related to gametes, assisted reproduction, and reproduction management was first used to improve the reproductive lines of livestock. Starting in the mid-1700s, humans began to determine whether human sperm procurement and insemination would work in ways similar to insemination in livestock; historians argue that the first sperm-donor-conceived children were probably born in the eighteenth century (Almeling 2011). However, it took far longer for experimentation with animal (or human) eggs to occur: not until the beginning of the twentieth century was the manipulation of animal ova used in livestock reproduction.

This manipulation opened the door for experiments on human eggs for reproduction outside of the body.

Despite the early promise of sperm donation and artificial insemination of cattle, it would take much of the early twentieth century for egg donation to develop as a reproductive technology. Doctors Gregory Pincus and John Rock (who would later become the fathers of the birth control pill) began researching how manipulation of rabbit ova might yield parallel insights into human reproduction (Eig 2014). In 1934, Dr. Pincus created a "near-riot among medical men" when he became the first to successfully fertilize a rabbit egg in vitro and presented his findings to the medical community (Kaempffert 1934). Ten years later, Dr. Rock and Dr. Miriam Menkin achieved the same goal, but this time with three human eggs (Lawrence 1944). After this groundbreaking discovery, Rock attempted to fertilize nearly 140 human eggs, but none of the eggs successfully divided into a blastocyst, the cluster of cells that develops after an egg has been fertilized and before the cells form an embryo (Cohen et al. 2005). In 1959, Dr. M.C. Chang—a collaborator with Rock and Pincus on the birth control pill—connected the dots: after fertilizing a rabbit egg and growing it into a blastocyst, Dr. Chang implanted the embryo in a rabbit, who successfully gave birth. For the first time, eggs fertilized outside of a mammal's body resulted in a live birth, demonstrating that at least in rabbits, IVF was a medical possibility for assisted reproduction (Cohen et al. 2005).

The race to figure out a way to join these experimental threads began in earnest in the 1960s. Researchers at Cambridge and Johns Hopkins Universities used women's eggs—procured largely through surgeries to treat polycystic ovarian syndrome—for experiments in fertilization inside of animals (Almeling 2011, Cohen 2005). In 1965, the researchers at Johns Hopkins com-

pleted the first gamete intrafallopian transfer of egg cells in the
fallopian tubes of cynomolgus monkeys—although at the time,
it was deemed unsuccessful in its clinical application to humans.
Increased scientific collaboration throughout Australia, the
United Kingdom, Sweden, and the US finally produced the first
IVF birth. Gynecologist John Edwards teamed up with Cambridge embryologist Patrick Steptoe to successfully complete
the first IVF birth after a decade of experimentation on in vitro
fertilization. Louise Joy Brown was the first baby born via IVF:
her mother's eggs and father's sperm were procured and mixed
outside of their bodies in a "test tube", and the resulting embryo
grew into a healthy baby girl born in the fall of 1978.

This history demonstrates how the boundaries between experiments and medical procedures, fertility and infertility, animals
and humans, and the "natural" and "unnatural" are porous—and
how developments related to egg donation further complicated
questions of gender, sexuality, reproduction, and research. As
many patients and their doctors realized, the breakthrough of
IVF was not the answer for all fertility problems. For many
women, early IVF procedures required a healthy couple's eggs
and sperm. What could be done if a woman's eggs were damaged
or she could not ovulate? While there was some experimentation
with embryos procured from the wombs of donors and implanted
in women who sought to become pregnant, this procedure was
largely abandoned owing to the immense risks of disease and
pregnancy complications. Instead, fertility doctors turned back to
the nearly two-century history of assisted reproduction in livestock: this time, they would focus on procuring eggs from healthy,
ovulating women who would be a third party to the eventual
pregnancy. Monash University of Australia reported the first live
birth using a donor egg in 1983. In the US, the first child conceived

using a donor egg was born in the Harborview Medical Center at University of California, Los Angeles, in 1984.

Once the floodgates had opened for those who could not use their own gametes for reproduction, more couples came forward to access egg donation. There was so much demand that hospitals and medical centers began procuring third-party eggs in earnest. The first sources of "donated" eggs came from IVF and tubal ligation patients, who shared their eggs with clinical researchers without compensation, but demand for eggs soon outstripped this limited supply (Almeling 2011). Egg donation programs were always attached to fertility clinics in (often, university-run) hospitals, with infertility patients frequently obtaining potential egg donors from among their friends and families. Interestingly, even at this early stage of the egg donation market, potential donors were questioned about their altruism and motivations for donating, as well as given a battery of psychological and medical tests (Almeling 2011). In the earliest days of egg donation, women did not receive compensation. Later the demand for eggs created a new market system in which egg donation was paid (Almeling 2011).

Although this early period of egg donation brought about new innovations for infertile women, concerns about the morals and ethics of third-party reproduction dominated discussions of egg donation. In the 1980s, the press documented the rising moral concerns. The author of one 1988 *New York Times* article wondered if the reproductive technology was a "miracle" or "science gone haywire, severed from moral principles" (Brozan 1988). The Vatican denounced in vitro fertilization and, by extension, egg donation, during this period, arguing that reproductive technologies were not in line with "natural" procreation (Boffey 1987). In the US political sphere, members of Congress and state legislators alike raised the issues of ethics and morals concerning egg donation, in vitro fertilization, and surrogacy (New York State Task Force on Life and the Law 1989, Bonnicksen 1989). Four state bioethics commissions and committees, the Presidential Bioethics Commission, and the Congressional Bioethics Board were formed in the early-to-mid-1980s to study the moral and ethical implications of reproductive technologies (Heidt-Forsythe 2016).

Reflecting public and political concerns, feminists and bioethicists focused on the moral implications of the burgeoning practice of egg donation. Although early radical feminists like Shulamith Firestone foresaw the liberatory and oppressive nature of reproductive technologies long before the first successful use of egg donation, feminist and bioethical concerns grew louder and more noticeable with the skyrocketing use of donor eggs in IVF in the 1980s and 1990s. On one hand, reproductive technologies liberated women from their biological "destinies" of motherhood—giving women more autonomy over when and how (if at all) they would become mothers. On the other hand, reproductive technology was also foreseen as a tool of patriarchal control, by which male-centered power institutions (like the family, or medicine) would force women to become machines of reproduction. Firestone—as well as later bioethicist and feminist critics of egg donation—recognized the ways that women's oppression in a stratified reproductive system could be aggravated by reproductive technology. In the early 1980s, the United Kingdom, too, recognized these concerns, producing the 1984 Warnock Report and eventually instituting the Human Fertilisation and Embryology Authority, the regulatory body for reproductive technologies. In contrast, there was no parallel report in the US, although the Presidential Bioethics Commission during the Carter, Reagan, and Clinton administrations, as well as individual states, did take notice of the challenges of new reproductive technologies. Neither the Presidential Bioethics Commission nor state commissions pushed for federal legislation similar to what was developed in the UK during the mid-1980s to 1990s.

DEMAND GROWS: EGG DONATION IN THE 1990S AND BEYOND

Within this history of egg donation in the US, a few dynamics emerge as crucial to the development of the unique US system in the twenty-first century. Despite early attempts to control the egg donation market through patient recruitment of donors and/or egg sharing with fellow infertility patients, the growing demand throughout the 1980s and early 1990s required new systems of egg donation and distribution. Hospitals and medical professionals also began to compensate egg donation, unlike organ donation and blood donation, which are unpaid in the US—ostensibly to fulfill the immense demand by fertility patients.

By 1987, the Cleveland Clinic developed the first program to procure eggs from anonymous donors and compensate them for their labor in producing eggs. In this program, women could earn nine hundred to twelve hundred dollars per egg donation cycle (AP 1987, Almeling 2011). The small and often geographically variable market for eggs in the 1980s and early 1990s gave way to an explosion in demand for donor eggs and the emergence of modern, commercial egg banks by the late 1990s (Almeling 2011, CDC 2017). Competition for donors increased as demand by infertility patients grew, transforming commercial practices related to egg donation. Commercial egg banks in the late 1990s expanded their efforts considerably. Using collegiate newspapers and free weeklies, radio, and billboards, recruitment was aimed closely at college and university students. Later, recruitment would extend to websites and even subway-car advertising. Recruitment also expanded to disproportionately underrepresented racial, ethnic, and religious groups in the egg market (Roberts 2009). By the first decade of the twenty-first century, commercial egg banks advertised egg donors online with comprehensive donor profiles, extensive personal information, and publicly available photos (Daniels and Heidt-Forsythe 2012).

In parallel to the growth in clinics and advertising, the amount of compensation for egg donation also grew exponentially from the late 1990s on. Although the practice of payment for eggs dates back to the 1980s, competition among banks for the "best" donors (and thus the most expensive donors) increased the overall price of eggs. Donors with highly sought-after demographic characteristics were paid more for their eggs, and prices for procured eggs increased fivefold from the 1980s to the first decade of the twenty-first century. Compensation also increased according to location, as donors on the coasts often receive higher payments for their eggs. For example, one New York clinic's doubling of the average compensation for egg donors raised compensation for egg donors across the country (Almeling 2011, Kolata 1999). By 2007, egg donation compensation guidelines suggested that donors be paid a maximum of five thousand dollars, and that compensation over ten thousand dollars was not appropriate (ASRM 2007). Moreover, these guidelines suggested that the amount of compensation should not depend on egg sellers' medical, phenotypic, or familial characteristics (Klitzman and Sauer 2015, ASRM 2007).[9] "Competitive" donors with in-demand characteristics (such as educational attainment or musical talent) or rare racial/ethnic/religious identities, repeat donors, and donors whose eggs had already successfully helped create a healthy donor-conceived child may all expect increased compensation (Almeling 2011, Daniels and Heidt-Forsythe 2012). Beyond payment for the medical procedure of donation, egg donors may receive extra compensation for travel, freezing their eggs for future ART cycles, and donating eggs that result in a successful pregnancy. In most cases, donors remain anonymous and are protected by a significant informed-consent process and legal protections against maternity (Daniels and Heidt-Forsythe 2012, ASRM 2016a). Gendered norms of femininity also came into play in the early markets: even in the mid-1980s, there was an emphasis on women's altruism in the donation process—doctors and consumers expected women to act according to traditional, feminine norms of service, which entailed giving to others without compensation and complaint. While other kinds of donation are legally uncompensated, and altruism is considered to be an important element of market exchanges in blood and body organs, egg donation is unique: even though egg donation for infertility is highly compensated, there continues to be a strong discursive emphasis on women's altruism to other women in egg donation (Almeling 2011). Moreover, clinics enshrine this altruism in their practices, as many clinics require women to express feelings of giving, selflessness, and love of helping others, in order to be chosen as egg donors (Daniels and Heidt-Forsythe 2012).

After the mid-1990s, public and political responses to egg donation began to shift: as scholar Sarah Franklin presciently wrote in 1995, egg donation (and other reproductive technologies) had become normalized in the public imagination, as yet another consumer option for family formation (Franklin 1995). By the mid-1990s, media coverage of egg donation increasingly focused on the human stories—and consumer perspectives—of those seeking infertility treatment. Stories like those about the seemingly boundless promise of egg donation that allowed a sixty-three-year-old woman in California to become a mother, and about the desperation of the infertility "treadmill" of reproductive technologies, helped shift the public's perception of egg infertility. (Harwood 2007). Politically, the winds had changed as well: the only federal law regulating fertility clinics was passed in 1992, and state legislatures began to debate egg donation in the mid-1990s.

Faced with skyrocketing demand for egg donation and a proliferation of fertility clinics, US scholarship about egg donation became more nuanced and diverse after the mid-1990s (Thompson 2005). The new generation of scholarship focused on the multiplicity of experiences of egg donation, infertility and involuntary childlessness, kinship, and reproductive inequalities in the US system—and solutions to some of the problems inherent in the US system of egg donation (Thompson 2005). Interdisciplinary scholarship examining the cultural, economic, and political aspects of infertility and involuntary childlessness across the globe proliferated during this period, exposing the diversity of experiences of and perspectives on infertility and ART, mediated by nation, race, class, religion, and sexuality (e.g., Inhorn and Fakih 2009, Browner and Sargent 2011). Feminist science studies and poststructural feminist scholars emphasized the complicated ways that women and men are embedded in systems of power within egg donation markets, noting the ways that compliance and resistance to technology exist simultaneously (Thompson 2005, Markens 2007, Dickenson 2007). Reflecting a nuanced critique of a technology that could both enforce and rebel against traditional norms of the nuclear family, egg donation could both enable nonheterosexual individuals to form families and, at the same time, reinforce pressures on women and men to form biological families (Mamo 2008).

OVERSIGHT OF A GROWING MARKET
FOR HUMAN EGGS

The growing complexity of egg donation as a social and political issue gained attention as the markets in human eggs grew from the 1980s onward. Fundamental feminist and bioethical questions about the meanings of gender norms of femininity, reproduction, and kinship, and about the role of technology in social life, began to be asked in the 1980s and have not yet been answered: while there have been calls for oversight at the federal level, most medical and ethical guidelines have come from professional medical societies with few enforcement mechanisms. It was in this world that many of the characterizations of the US as the Wild West of egg donation emerged—as other nations, like the UK, established and strengthened regulation of egg donation, the US seemed only to grow its lucrative commercial markets in human eggs.

The market in egg donation, growing steadily throughout the 1980s and 1990s, was not free of critique or calls for oversight: as in other nations, such as the UK and Canada, feminist and bioethicist voices called for increasing attention to oversight of reproductive technologies.

The policy responses to this complex history of egg donation reflect two major political frameworks: body politics, where the state upholds particular ideologies through the regulation of the reproductive, bodily, and sexual lives of women and men; and morality politics, where issues are defined, debated, and solved through the lenses of morals and ethics. These frameworks have, at different times, shaped the political and regulatory approaches to egg donation. In contrast to strong regulations and outright bans on egg donation in other nations, the only federal law on reproductive technologies that exists in the US is the Fertility Clinic Success Rate and Certification Act (FCSRCA) of 1993. The bill, introduced by Senator Ron Wyden (D-OR), who wrote it in partnership with infertility patient groups and the American Society for Reproductive Medicine (ASRM), was a response to the growing commercial success (and ethical quandaries) of reproductive technologies. The law allows participating fertility clinics to register with a federal agency, adhere to clinical standards, and report their clinical activities, including successful birth rates. Although the FCSRCA was not initially funded and could not be implemented, by the mid-1990s parts of the act were put into effect by the Centers for Disease Control and Prevention (CDC). The parts of FCSRCA that were implemented allowed participating clinics to report their procedures, numbers of patients, and success rates (measured in live births). Since the bill was not funded, there is no mandate for all clinics to participate in reporting, although a majority of fertility clinics eventually did so. The CDC publishes these clinic reports annually and has done so since 1997. Even though there is only one federal law about reproductive technologies in the US, the House and Senate have interest in infertility and egg donation. For example, the Family Act (S881/HR1851) was introduced by Senator Kirsten Gillibrand (D-NY) and Representative John Lewis (D-GA) in 2013. This bill, like the 2015 Reproductive Treatment for Certain Disabled Veterans Act (HR 2247) or the Female Veterans and Families Health Services Act of 2015 (S469/HR3365), seeks to expand affordability and access to infertility care for women and their partners.

Outside of the FCSRCA and congressional attempts to regulate egg donation, nonbinding guidelines for clinics and commercial egg banks exist at the federal level. The National

Academies of Science (NAS), the National Institutes of Health (NIH), and the CDC have established best-practice guidelines for recruitment, informed consent, compensation, and clinical practices in egg donation. Additionally, federal funding of the NIH and National Institute for Communicable Diseases has served as a form of national regulation of egg donation practices in larger experimental contexts. For example, national debates over the moral status of the embryo have dominated the distribution of federal grants for ART research. Only a year after the first child was born using IVF, scientists applied for NIH grants to fund research. It is unsurprising—given the power of the president over federal funding, as well as the controversy over embryonic research—that presidents (and their cabinets) alternatively restricted and enabled federal funding for research involving egg donation. This arguably created a greater reliance on funding and regulation from other levels of governance, such as professional self-regulation by the ASRM and the Society for Assisted Reproductive Technology (Thompson 2005).

Lastly, the courts are an important source of regulatory guidelines in lieu of strong federal action on issues of gender, the family, and reproduction. Broadly, court cases about ART and the family extend back to the 1980s—such as the broadly publicized *Baby M* case, as well as cases regarding same-sex partnerships, child support, and legal kinship in cases such as *Elisa B. v. Superior Court, K.M. v. E.G., Kristine H. v. Lisa R.* (all decided in 2005), and the well-known case involving egg donation, IVF, and gestational surrogacy, *Johnson v. Calvert* (1993). This constellation of cases (many involving female same-sex couples) established important practical guidelines for family law in regard to children who were donor-conceived or carried to term by surrogates. Just as significantly, they established parental rights and responsibilities for same-sex couples before the national legalization of same-sex marriage (Smith 2009). In the last decade egg donors were at the forefront of legal battles over compensation. *Perez v. Commissioner* (2014) established that egg donor compensation could be taxed by the US government, while *Kamakahi v. ASRM* (2015) was a notable legal move by a former donor in protest of ASRM guidelines on compensation—suing the organization for price-fixing, although the case was settled out of court. In the US system, courts settled new contestations of gender, sexuality, and the family when federal and state law was seemingly absent or unclear.

PROFESSIONAL OVERSIGHT AND EGG DONATION

In response to the absence of national oversight, the American Society for Reproductive Medicine, in partnership with the National Academies of Science and the National Institutes of Health, led the ethical charge in the 1980s and 1990s, becoming the first medical organization to have an ethics body focused specifically on reproductive technologies. While these organizations are not lawmaking bodies, they provided crucial ethical recommendations for the burgeoning egg donation markets, which they continue to update. In lieu of federal regulations, ethicists and medical professionals in these organizations established voluntary guidelines for best practices regarding reproduction and research, guiding clinical and commercial practices related to egg donation. In parallel to other issues in reproduction and research, such as embryo research and in vitro fertilization, the ASRM, NIH, and NAS provided voluntary guidelines for practitioners. In lieu of federal guidelines for egg donation, the ASRM established ethical recommendations. These cover the subjects of the recruitment of donors; advanced maternal age; the interests, obligations, and rights of donors; financial compensation of donors; and disclosure of errors by medical professionals (ASRM 2016a). The ASRM also produced extensive guidelines for informed consent, conflict of interest, and conflict of commitment protocols related to egg donation (Blake et al. 2015). However, as many bioethicists have argued, while these guidelines are often followed, especially by clinics and banks that seek certification by the ASRM, they cannot be legally enforced on unscrupulous medical professionals and commercial egg banks (Blake et al. 2015, Daniels and Heidt-Forsythe 2012, Von Hagel 2014).

THE PUZZLE OF EGG DONATION:
RESPONSES TO THE US SYSTEM

The lack of federal regulation of egg donation has generated numerous critiques about the US system. A number of problems with the US system emerged during the 1980s and 1990s, such as rising compensation and questions of exploitation of egg donors, concerns over the long-term health of egg donors after exposure to hormones, and the inequalities in health-care access faced by women and men looking to expand their families using egg donation. Feminist bioethicists led scholarly and medical communities toward debates about the need for oversight of egg donation. They especially shed light on how unregulated compensation and transactions in eggs have negative implications for the autonomy of consumers and egg donors and their ability to make informed, independent decisions about ART. For example, egg donation advertising not only fails to represent the medical and psychological risks of donation but also falsely advertises the levels of compensation received by donors (Levine 2010). Egg donors may be induced by false advertising and high levels of compensation in a regulatory system that creates incentives for highly lucrative transactions, potentially resulting in exploitation of egg donors and desperate infertility patients (Kenney and McGowan 2010, Daniels and Heidt-Forsythe 2012, Holland 2007, Ikemoto 2009, Roberts 2009). Given the medical and psychological risks of egg donation, many have argued for increased attention to the ways that clinical ethics (such as informed consent and disposition policies) can support donor agency and autonomy over medical decisions in egg donation (Kenney and McGowan 2010, Kalfoglou and Gittelsohn 2000, Ellison and Meliker 2011). In response, others claim that while the US system is not perfect, egg donors and consumers are protected by the self-interest of the privatized market, which prompts it to ensure donor safety and compensation (Thompson 2005). Additionally, they assert, egg donors should be afforded the same autonomy over reproductive decisions—such as the decision to undergo medical procedures to procure eggs—as any other person making a medical decision about his or her body (Thompson 2005).

As described above, in general, the US has avoided implementing (or even debating) federal regulations surrounding egg donation (Jasanoff 2005). Yet, over time, as markets in donated eggs grew exponentially and practices related to egg donation, IVF, and surrogacy became increasingly normalized as a reproductive option, the state continued to regulate issues of gender, sexuality, and reproduction. For example, not only did major debates about abortion take place in Congress and in state legislatures, but also major legislation enforced policies that regulated, limited, and defined abortion. This interest in regulating questions of the body, pregnancy, and control seemingly did not extend to egg donation in the US between the 1980s and the present. This crucial difference is an important part of the argument of this book: egg donation is distinct from other reproductive issues—not only in the ways that it is regulated by the federal government and states, but also in how egg donation is shaped, simultaneously, by body politics and morality politics. Early studies of in vitro fertilization in the US, for example, noted that the politics of reproductive technologies overlapped with reproductive issues but were also held under different regulatory standards (e.g., Bonnicksen 1989). While explanations exist for why egg donation is different in the US compared to other reproductive issues—owing to privacy, the controversial nature of abortion, and the lack of bioethics debates—these current explanations incompletely capture why egg donation for reproduction is seen as a health choice for families, while egg donation for research is seen as akin to Dr. Frankenstein's experiments.

Despite the decades of rich debate and calls for oversight in multiple scholarly and practitioner communities, there has been a lack of sustained historical attention to *why* the US lacks the type of regulatory regime for egg donation found in comparable nations. Across legal, social science, and humanistic fields, scholars and practitioners point to three major reasons for this lack. First, some argue—particularly from a legal standpoint—that the US embraces a working concept of privacy in reproduction and science. Second, others, often from a politics and policy standpoint, contend that abortion is the third rail of politics. Considering the fact that bodily autonomy, personhood, and family formation are themes that connect abortion and egg donation, some believe that policy makers intentionally avoid the subject of egg donation to get around political controversies inherent in the practice. A third and connected argument points to the nation's lack of bioethical discourse and deliberation. Because of our polarized politics, culture wars, and lack of comprehensive bioethical infrastructure, the US dodges many crucial conversations about morals and ethics in reproductive technology, unlike comparable Western nations that have had extended debates on the bioethical implications of egg donation.

Speaking to the concept of reproductive privacy, John Robertson (1994) argues that the concept of "procreative liberty" characterizes the US regulatory approach to ART: in a liberal society, the government cannot impede individuals' access to ART, as that would be a restriction of fundamental autonomy over reproduction—a violation of individual rights. However, because procreative liberty is a negative right, the government cannot provide assistance for individuals to use ART (Robertson 1994). Throughout the twentieth century, the definition of reproductive privacy as a negative right (whereby reproductive decisions are protected from interference by the government) has been supported by political and legal institutions, such as Supreme Court decisions on family formation, contraception, abortion, same-sex intimacy, and marriage.[10] Scholars have argued that this sense of privacy understood as autonomy away from the prying eyes of the state has also governed the politics and economics of egg donation for reproduction and research (Thompson 2005). With the exception of one federal consumer protection law, the FCSRCA (1993), the private sector has relied on business compliance through self-regulation, primarily through the ASRM and the Society for Assisted Reproductive Technology. Research using eggs has relied on a combination of guidelines from the CDC, NIH, and NAS, although researchers have largely been moving toward increased autonomy throughout the twentieth and twenty-first centuries. In lieu of federal funding for stem cell and ART research, states (with their ability to fund research) have stepped in to make policy governing the science of ART and stem cell research (Levine 2006, Mintrom 2009). Privatization has allowed markets for human eggs for research to flourish, creating a greater number of available human eggs for reproduction *and* research. Although scientific research shifted toward increased autonomy in the post–World War II period, policy scholars have noted that this privacy has been mediated by federalism in parallel with institutional compliance with clinical and bioethical standards (Mintrom 2009).

While privacy has allowed markets in human eggs to flourish, providing increased material for reproduction and research purposes, the privatized system can have problematic effects on egg donors and consumers of egg donation. There is unequal access to egg donation for reproduction and to the medical benefits of research on human embryonic stem cell lines (Thompson 2005, 2013, Benjamin 2013). For consumers and donors, a privatized system may allow dangerous variation in compliance with professional and national guidelines, with negative consequences for the health and well-being of egg donors and intended parents (Blake et al. 2015). Rather than turning to the state for intervention, scholars call for improved self-regulation by medical professionals and researchers, as well as improved business practices to make expensive ART treatment more affordable to consumers (Thompson 2005, Blake et al. 2015). In response, others argue that only increased US regulatory authority over egg donation can mitigate health and psychological risks of egg donation, protect vulnerable populations from exploitation in a privatized market, and guard against violations of clinical ethics (Von Hagel 2014, Levine 2010, Keehn et al. 2012, Papadimos and Papadimos 2004, Daniels and Heidt-Forsythe 2012).

While debates over reproductive, research, and business privacy do clarify ideologies underpinning the political and economic characteristics of egg donation in the US, privacy does not fully explain this political context. In US political history, there has been significant oversight of seemingly private choices related to reproduction, from the availability and use of contraceptive and abortion technologies to the establishment of legal kinship outside of biological reproduction. Research privacy has also historically broken down in light of policy entrepreneurship at the state level regarding controversial science (Mintrom 2009). And, while the US system largely does protect business from interference by the state, this privacy relationship has, again, historically broken down in contexts of controversial reproductive services such as abortions (Rose 2006). State political institutions have shown compelling interest in the oversight of egg donation for research and reproduction within their regulatory purview under federalism, via actions ranging from establishing legal parentage of donor-conceived children to establishing state infrastructure to procure eggs for stem cell research (Bonnicksen 1989, Von Hagel 2014, Stapleton and Skinner 2015).

Besides privacy, the other alternative explanations for why the US regulatory system does not legislate egg donation are the controversial, combustible nature of political deliberation around abortion and the lack of a comprehensive discourse on bioethical issues in the US. In the setting of controversial, passionate, and sustained debates over morality and ethics in abortion, debates over bioethics largely focus on the moral status of the embryo. Unlike nations that have established long-standing infrastructure to implement bioethical recommendations in research and commercial markets in ART, the US relies on temporary iterations of the Presidential Bioethics Commission and guidelines from the

NIH and NAS, funded by the federal government. These commissions, institutes, and academies have an advisory role dependent on federal funding. Observing the debate over cloning after the birth of Dolly the sheep in 1996, Andrea Bonnicksen (2002) finds that while cloning incited divisive politics at the state and federal levels, ultimately no federal laws were passed condemning the practice. Sheila Jasanoff's (2005) comparative study of US deliberation in response to bioethics issues concludes that unlike the UK and Germany, the US has little "ethical biocapital" with which to deliberate the question of ART (Jasanoff 2005). Unlike the UK and Germany, the US has not successfully held public deliberations, despite media coverage and increased public awareness of ART (Jasanoff 2005). Moreover, egg donation for research has been the subject of divisive politics similar to debates over cloning: despite contentious debates over the morality of stem cell research, regulation has historically been enforced through funding (and the restriction of funding) of federal research in the NIH and NAS. The divisiveness and inability to come to policy compromises on controversial bioethical issues such as egg donation has been claimed to be one reason why the egg donation market goes nationally unregulated in the US.

However, the deliberation argument fails to account for the fact that issues of great moral controversy have a unique politics unlike other social and political issues. For example, research using embryos and fetal tissue has provoked the use of moral values in deliberation and policymaking. While a deliberation argument illustrates important qualities of US reproductive politics and the ways that abortion (and by extension, debates over the moral status of life) dominates questions of reproduction, medicine, and science, this explanation does not account for why egg donation is seemingly different than other controversial reproductive and scientific issues that come under sustained federal and state oversight. Egg donation is not a homogenous policy area, despite conventional thinking: egg donation for reproduction has prompted different politics and policy than egg donation for research; and issues within egg donation—such as kinship, medical insurance, embryonic research, and women's bodily autonomy—further complicate regulatory systems in the US.

EXPLAINING THE BIFURCATED POLITICS OF EGG DONATION: BODY POLITICS AND MORALITY POLITICS

Body and morality politics—built upon assumptions about the "natural" and "unnatural" in normative femininity—provide important contexts for the complex historical and regulatory developments in egg donation in the US. Despite the rhetoric that the US is the Wild West of egg donation, the overlapping histories of medical innovation, consumer markets, regulatory systems, and public perceptions of egg donation demonstrate a more complex picture. We can see how, over time, body and morality politics have gained and lost traction in defining egg donation, setting the terms of debate, and helping shape regulatory approaches. However, what is not as clear is how and why body and morality politics are more and less relevant over time.

States have emerged as the foci of politics and policymaking, in a context of lackluster federal policy, case law, and professional guidelines. In a framework of body politics, current systems of access to egg donation for reproduction are logical—it is not the case that the US ignores egg donation; in fact the state has an important role in promoting egg donation for some and preventing others from using this technology. In a system of stratified reproduction, certain individuals are encouraged and enabled to use egg donation according to hierarchies of gender, race, sexuality, and class, while others are prevented from doing so according to these same hierarchies. In the framework of body politics and stratified reproduction, egg donation for reproduction is framed as a conventional, natural choice for family formation—particularly for those who can afford it. It is transformed into a politics of reproductive "choice," where one has the "choice" (given one's privileges) to access egg donation in a system of stratified reproduction. At the same time, the history of egg donation for family formation reveals the strong role of morality politics. From historical concerns over the moral meanings of third-party egg donation, to concerns over family, romantic relationships, and sexuality, to contemporary concerns over embryonic research and embryo adoption, morality politics plays an important—if underemphasized—role in setting up the politics of egg donation for reproduction.

The use of human eggs in research has taken a far different trajectory. Since the late 1990s, egg donation for research has been subject to divisive, confrontational politics around values, akin to ethical debates about stem cell research, cloning, and chimeric research. Egg donation for research has been framed by media and political actors as a matter of fundamental values and moral debate. Like other morality politics issues, egg donation's connections to stem cell research, cloning, and chimeric research is often depicted as the Frankenstein story come alive, a highly salient and troubling exercise in scientific power. Although morality politics has dominated definitions of, debates on, and solutions to egg donation for research, the technology has also aroused concerns over the role of the state in reproduction. In the US, the egg donation market privileges some women over others in what some fear is a two-tiered system, where women with certain phenotypical traits are funneled into egg donation for reproduction, and women with less desirable traits can donate only for research purposes (Waldby and Cooper 2008, Daniels and Heidt-Forsythe 2012). This pattern has important implications for women, reproduction, and their eggs in public policy, as historically the US has pushed some women to reproduce and prevented others from forming families (Roberts 1998, 2009).

Illuminating the reasons why the US system of egg donation is unique, body politics and morality politics shed light on the ways that, in current political climates, egg donation for reproduction is seen as a natural, conventional choice, while egg donation for research is rendered unnatural, strange, and morally offensive. While these frameworks are the basis for understanding the unique politics of egg donation in the US, these explanations are not yet complete. The frameworks must also address how political actors deliberate on and make policy in response to these issues, particularly for women representing the ways that gender, sexuality, and reproduction enter into political debates about egg donation. To begin this exploration, the next chapter explores how political framing in state policymaking—the process by which issues are defined, problems are identified, debates are drawn, and policy solutions created—reflect body and morality politics at play in egg donation in the US.

CHAPTER TWO

Framing Egg Donation
at the State Level

In 2013, Governor Jerry Brown vetoed Assembly Bill 926, which, if signed, would have overturned California's ban on compensation for donated eggs used for stem cell research in the state-funded California Institute for Regenerative Medicine. California's ban on compensation for egg donation for stem cell research had been instituted in 2006, when Senators Deborah Ortiz and George Runner proposed Senate Bill 1260, which enjoyed broad bipartisan support and was signed into law by Governor Arnold Schwarzenegger. Reflecting on the moral implications of compensation for egg donation in the state's growing stem cell research sector, Governor Brown wrote in his veto letter that "not everything in life is for sale, nor should it be," arguing that "the long-term risks [of egg donation] are not adequately known. Putting thousands of dollars on the table only compounds the problem" of exploitation in research (Brown 2013). In stark contrast to these words of warning about egg donation for stem cell research, Brown failed to mention the sixty-two clinics in California that provide compensated egg donation services for intended parents suffering from infertility and involuntary childlessness (CDC 2014). Why does egg donation for research (particularly compensated egg donation for research) draw such condemnation, while egg donors in the fertility industry go seemingly unnoticed? In this chapter and the next, I examine these contradictions regarding egg donation for research and reproduction, because they speak to broader patterns in the politics of egg donation. If in fact beliefs about and norms of femininity and reproduction shape the politics of egg donation in the states—whereby egg donation for reproduction and research is framed by body and morality politics—then we will be able to explain why states like California produce such different politics in response to egg donation for research versus egg donation for reproduction.

Governor Brown's distinctions between paying those who donate eggs for stem cell research and those who donate eggs to fertility clinics echoes a conceptual difference found in the current politics of egg donation: while egg donation for research is subject to an array of ethical and moral debates inherent in stem cell research, egg donation for reproduction is described as a private choice for those privileged enough to participate in the fertility industry. Conventional wisdom points to this fractured system of regulation as typical of the US: because the nation lacks comprehensive federal regulation, states step in to create policies to guide egg donation for research and reproduction. While this fractured system does exist, what principles guide this two-tier system, and what is the logic of treating one procedure—egg donation—so differently in the contexts of reproduction and research? This chapter and the next answer this question by examining the processes of framing egg donation in case studies from four states: California, New York, Arizona, and Louisiana.

This chapter begins a response to the questions of what creates the unique system of egg donation regulations, by examining the ways that stakeholders—legislators, advocates, scientists, and invested citizens—frame the issue of egg donation for reproduction and research. Framing is a complex process done by political stakeholders to define an issue, construct explanations for problems, set out terms of debate, and ultimately, create policy solutions to these issue problems. In the case of egg donation, state-level stakeholders have immense power in politics, particularly owing to the lack of federal law regulating egg donation for research and reproduction. Advocates and opponents of egg-donation oversight define it as an important issue; debate the myriad ethical, moral, medical, scientific, and legal problems associated with egg donation; join together in political alliances; and create solutions for these diverse problems inherent in the US systems of egg donation for research and reproduction.

To begin this analysis, I explore one policy area of egg donation politics in the US: compensation. This emerges as a crucial topic in the politics of egg donation that engaged stakeholders across the political spectrum in California, New York, Arizona, and Louisiana during the first decade of the twenty-first century. This chapter explores and illuminates framing processes in relation to egg donation through the method of policy narrative analysis, an interpretive method of examining and analyzing the words, characters, and policy stories. Analyzing texts generated by stakeholders and the media, this chapter and the next investigate the ways that gender norms drive the definitions, problems, and solutions associated with egg donation policy at the state level. In the first study of its kind, this chapter explains the case selection in chapter 4, with particular attention to the diverse stakeholder perspectives in each case. To end this chapter, I survey the states' political contexts in which compensation bans emerge, and how these diverse histories inform analyses of framing in each state.[1]

COMPENSATION AND EGG DONATION

Although there is a wide array of policy categories that govern egg donation at the state level (as described in chapter 1 and the conclusion), the analyses in this chapter and chapter 3 focus on questions of egg donation and compensation for reproduction and research. Compensation for egg donation is an important topic that characterizes the politics of egg donation because of the multiple ways the issue is connected to stakeholders in reproduction and research. Egg donation for reproduction is done in a highly commercialized context, where donors can receive thousands of dollars per donation; there is no legal cap on the amount of money a woman can receive in egg procurement. Studies of commercialized systems in fertility clinics point to the ways that norms of femininity, race, and class are reproduced in this system, whereby certain eggs are not only coveted but also priced higher than eggs from women with lower-valued characteristics (Daniels and Heidt-Forsythe 2012, Waldby and Cooper 2008). Until 2016, the American Society for Reproductive Medicine recommended that compensation above five thousand dollars per egg-donation cycle required justification; compensation above ten thousand dollars per egg-donation cycle was described as "not appropriate" (ASRM 2007). While such compensation guidelines were discarded after the American Society for Reproductive Medicine's settlement in *Kamakahi v. ASRM* (2016), the organization still recommends that compensation not be scaled according to demographic characteristics, the number of eggs that have been produced by a donor, the number of previous donations made by the donor, or the outcomes for intended parents who receive a donation (ASRM 2016a). However, studies have demonstrated that clinics do, in fact, scale compensation—paying monetary amounts above fifty thousand dollars—according to demanded characteristics (such as race, ethnicity, gender, and religion), heritable *and* nonheritable traits, and a donor's medical and reproductive histories (Daniels and Heidt-Forsythe 2012, Levine 2010).

These financial costs deeply affect infertility patients and other consumers of egg donation. Without universal insurance coverage of infertility medicine, personal financial resources are necessary for individuals to access egg donation. To make matters worse, infertility is not always viewed as necessary and essential health care, and few policies address the financial hardship of infertility care and access to egg donation (King and Meyer 1997). There is a widespread belief that infertility and involuntary childlessness is a matter of personal, private concern that is best addressed not through public health provisions, but through personal "choices" and the assumption of individual risk. Compensation for egg donation reinforces existing structural inequalities in reproduction based on intersections of class, race, gender, and sexuality, and state intervention (such as infertility mandates) has done little to alleviate the inequalities (Roberts 2009, Daniels and Heidt-Forsythe 2012, Bitler and Schmidt 2006, 2012).

In contrast, stem cell research enterprises in the US historically have not paid egg donors for providing research material. This reflects the ways that bioethical principles guide research in the US, ostensibly protecting research subjects from financial and experimental exploitation. With the exception of plasma donation, altruism and a logic of "gift exchange" dominates organ and blood donation systems—it is considered unethical for researchers to entice subjects to participate in research using the lure of money (Titmuss 1997, Goodwin 2010). Stem cell and cloning research have historically provoked outcry, particularly in the media—the language of morals, bioethics, and fundamental principles accompanies discussions of paying research subjects to participate in research studies (Nisbet et al. 2003). This is particularly significant in the case of stem cell research, which is deemed morally suspect by conservative social critics. Stem cell research more broadly also prompts moral concern in public opinion surveys, where individuals not only have polarized opinions about the research but also feel a high level of emotion when considering stem cell research (Ryan 2014).

Discussions of egg donation for stem cell research have historically been highly salient to the public, simplified in public discourse and have prompted discussions over fundamental principles like personhood, the moral status of the embryo, and cloning—distinguishing characteristics of morality politics (Ryan 2014, Waldby and Cooper 2010, Heidt-Forsythe 2016, Thompson 2013).

Questions of compensation for research bring the body into sharp focus, highlighting debates about the appropriate and inappropriate uses of the human body (particularly the female body) in research. Historically, women, particularly pregnant women, have been excluded from clinical research. This practice of exclusion reflects the ideology that women should be protected against exploitation and any research that could possibly damage their reproductive health; such considerations have not been applied to men (Lyerly et al. 2012, Daniels 1993, 2006).

Underlying some debates about compensation for egg donation is the concern over the possible scarcity of eggs. Not having enough eggs for reproductive and research demands is a serious practical issue for consumers and intended parents, medical professionals, researchers, and donors themselves. Without compensation, the number of eggs donated for reproduction and research may decrease. While egg scarcity is not a major practical concern in fertility clinics in the US, it is of greater concern in research contexts, where donors are generally not paid. Interviewed by the *Washington Post* in 2006, the codirector of the Harvard Stem Cell Institute argued that bans on compensation are a barrier to research, as "the lack of compensation has meant it's been nearly impossible to get enough eggs" for research (Stein 2009). Concerns about scarcity have prompted more debates about the importance of compensation for egg donation for research, particularly in states like California, New York, and Massachusetts, where states have funded stem cell research (Benjamin 2013, Thompson 2013).

Compensation is not only a historically relevant issue across the states but also ties together major themes in this book: the debates and policies related to compensation can be explained by logics of body and morality politics, as well as by concerns over supply and demand. Questions about payment of egg donors have also been a common concern for state regulation: between 1992 and 2010, twenty-two states introduced at least one bill about compensation for egg donation for reproduction or research. First, compensation is a distinguishing characteristic of the unique US system of egg donation politics—no comparable countries have compensation systems for reproduction and research precisely like those of the US. Second, debates about compensation conjure concerns about buying and selling reproductive body parts, echoing similar debates about the appropriate and inappropriate commercial uses of women's bodies in sexuality and reproduction. Third, compensation highlights the moral and ethical boundaries of commercialized transactions: as Jerry Brown reflected in his veto of a compensation bill, some believe that not everything in life should be for sale—particularly in a context where the building blocks of life are used in controversial reproductive and research contexts.

FRAMING EGG DONATION IN FOUR STATES

Framing is a process by which actors "select some aspects of a perceived reality and make them more salient, in such a way as to promote a particular problem definition, causal interpretation, moral evaluation, and/or treatment recommendation" (Entman 1993, 52). The process is a series of steps toward defining a social and political issue. First, one identifies an agent precipitating social and political events. By isolating parts of reality out of an "unfolding strip of events"—which may be legal cases, medical events, scientific innovations, or debates over related reproductive issues—framing identifies them as the cause of certain shifts and changes in politics and society (Gamson and Modigliani 1987, 143). In the second phase of framing, actors diagnose the causes of social and political shifts. This second phase is not necessarily borne out of objective conditions; rather, a diagnosis may come from preconceived notions about the potential social and political problems that might arise from an issue. Third, actors make moral and ethical judgments about the perceived problem and the effects of it on other aspects of society and politics. For example, actors who identify egg donation as a social and political problem may make moral and ethical judgments about its impacts on traditional notions of heterosexual reproduction and the nuclear family (Markens 2007, Thompson 2005). After an actor makes a judgment about the effects of a social and political issue, the fourth and final step in framing is to suggest remedies for the problem by offering and debating solutions. In this book, I focus on this fourth step in the framing process by examining and analyzing the vastly different ways elite actors in state legislatures debate policy solutions when they are discussing egg donation for research versus egg donation for reproduction.[2]

The product of this complex framing process is the politics of egg donation in the US: first, meanings and definitions of egg donation have been established. These have arisen out of struggles over and debates on the issue—much in the same way that the meanings of abortion, contraception, and other reproductive technologies arose during decades of contention (Feree et al. 2002, Markens 2007, Almeling 2011). Although egg donation received disproportionately less attention in the public sphere than these earlier reproductive technologies, egg donation emerged from established political frameworks in the US. In particular, I examine how the framework for interpreting egg donation is rooted in stratified reproduction and body politics (particularly confrontations over gender and reproductive labor), as well as in debates over fundamental principles in controversial health and technology issues. Like other reproductive issues, egg donation has emerged as a form of symbolic politics, representing contentious debates about norms of femininity, appropriate and inappropriate forms of reproduction, and the role of technology in social life.

POLICY NARRATIVE ANALYSIS AND CASE SELECTION

Returning to a major theme in this book, framing, I discuss in this chapter the framing process (and policy outcomes) related to egg donation, particularly in response to social, ethical, economic, and political questions about compensation that have arisen. To show how egg donation is framed, I use four cases in this chapter and chapter 3—California, New York, Arizona, and Louisiana—to explain how egg donation is defined, in some cases, as conventional and, in other cases, as ominous and morally alarming. Understanding the ways that stakeholders create egg donation policy requires two steps. The first is to recognize that policies are not created out of thin air: even for "new" issues like egg donation, preceding political debates, policies, and external events play a role in policy creation. The second step is to grasp that the political contexts of policymaking are crucial to clarifying how stakeholders understand, debate, and argue for and against particular policy solutions to egg donation (Price 2011). By testing the idea that body politics and morality politics have both been deployed to frame policy solutions for egg donation in the contexts of reproduction *and* research, this process reflects the values, beliefs, and assumptions of stakeholders, shaping the ways that political issues are defined, conflicts are highlighted, and solutions are created. Examining the framing process can tell us if and how body and morality politics inform, shape, and alter the politics of egg donation at the state level.

In its simplest form, policy narrative analysis is a way of "making sense" of policy by uncovering stories, characters, and conflicts (Price 2011). In explaining how framing affects egg donation, narrative analysis helps the researcher clarify the stories, characters, and conflicts relevant to egg donation. Policy narrative analysis is a particularly strong method when the researcher is interested in the broader social context of political framing and in using diverse textual sources to explain the "entire scene—with expectations of actors and actions—that conform to a socially-constructed understanding which audiences often take as given and even immutable" (Jesudason and Weitz 2015, 262; see also Price 2011). Using political histories, legislative texts, advocacy discourse, and public debate, policy narrative analysis illuminates the ways that language (both written and verbal discourse) communicates sociopolitical meanings far beyond dictionary definitions, "objective" states of the world, and even the intent and aims of the speakers themselves. This also shines a light on how these "scenes" are connected more broadly to other social, political, and economic events. In one example of policy narrative analysis, the centrality of adolescent women's sexuality plays an important part in the history and politics of emergency contraception. Studying public narratives about and histories of teen girls and Plan B reveals that political context plays an important role in policy formation; that certain voices are amplified in policymaking, while others are silenced; and that "meanings, values, and beliefs" about sexuality, gender, age, and race played a fundamental role in passionate debates, political stalling, and partisan battles over emergency contraception in the US (Price 2011, 285).

Similarly, stakeholders are telling competing policy stories about egg donation, reproduction, and research in the policymaking process. Rather than simply accepting the definitions, problems, and solutions presented in the framing process as rational and objective, policy narrative analysis allows interpretations of the cultural narratives, the perceived antagonists and protagonists, and the preceding political debates that define the realities of egg donation. Narrations about egg donation allow stakeholders to tell a particular story and, thereby, control how the public interprets the uses of this reproductive technology in reproduction and research settings. In this study, multiple narrations exist: diverse interpretive communities offer different policy stories about egg donation. These communities tell different narratives about what egg donation is and why legislation is necessary, representing diverse political contexts to present their sides of the story (Price 2011, Stone [1998] 2002). Different backgrounds and stories lead to competing policy solutions for egg donation. For example, California legislators envisioned their role as ethical leaders in their proposed compensation ban, while the director of the California Institute for Regenerative Medicine argued that such a ban was overtly political, that it was redundant, and, further, that it interfered with the pursuit of scientific research. In contrast, Representative Bob Stump of Arizona claimed that a ban on compensation for egg donation would save women from exploitation and abuse. In response, Arizona governor Janet Napolitano viewed such a ban as a way to unfairly control women's reproductive choices and vetoed the bill (Napolitano 2007). Policy narratives are causal: structuring their narratives like arguments, stakeholders create policy stories with beginnings, middles, and ends (Stone [1998] 2002). In these stories, compensation for egg donation causes ethical, medical, and economic problems to emerge; it is then important to address these problems with particular policy solutions, such as a compensation ban. The policy narratives of different stakeholders not only have different beginnings and middles but also have different conclusions. To better understand the policy narratives constructed around egg donation—and to test the theory that gender norms determine different policy pathways for egg donation for reproduction and research—I focus here on four cases of egg donation politics and policy.

Although a majority of states have introduced at least one bill since 1995 concerning egg donation, it's important to this discussion to focus on state cases that are generalizable to other states, rather than on unique cases of policymaking activity. To understand how norms of femininity guide the framing of egg donation policy, it is valuable to analyze cases that can speak to broader patterns of policymaking across the country. Not all states are equally active on the topic of egg donation: only a handful of states have histories of engaging repeatedly with the topic through bill sponsorship. Moreover, state cases should be politically, demographically, and geographically diverse enough to speak to the broad differences in policymaking at the state level. Rather than selecting on the dependent variable—that is, selecting cases that conveniently fit into this book's argument about policymaking and egg donation—this chapter and chapter 3 discuss four diverse states with different political contexts, geographical locations, policy solutions, and policy outcomes. These cases provide an opportunity to test the argument that body politics and morality politics characterize egg donation for reproduction and research, and to take an unprecedented, detailed look at each state's framing process related to egg donation for reproduction and research.

Arizona, California, Louisiana, and New York serve as cases for this study because, as a group, they maximize policy activity, political context, geographical locations, policy solutions, and policy outcomes. Each of these four states introduced at least five egg donation bills between 1995 and 2010. Choosing states with a similar activity level avoids the pitfall of interpreting a single, unique state bill as a generalizable case of egg donation framing. Moreover, drawing on multiple bills in each state provides important historical context for egg donation policymaking, giving the researcher a sense of which of the actors, arguments, issue definitions, and policy solutions predate a set of policy debates

TABLE 2

Chapter 3 Case Studies

California, New York, Arizona, and Louisiana

State	California	New York	Arizona	Louisiana
Framing Strategy	Morality politics	Morality politics	Morality and body politics	Morality and body politics
Political Context[†]	48.44	42.86	48.43	73.70
Number of Egg Donation Bills, 1990–2010	17	13	8	5

† Measured by NOMINATE Score in 2006. Higher scores indicate a more conservative state legislature, on a scale of 0 to 100 (Berry et al. 2010).

under examination. While Arizona, California, and New York had no restrictions on egg donation compensation during this period, Louisiana became the first state in the nation to prohibit certain kinds of compensation for egg donation for reproduction. See table 2 for a description of the cases.

Assessing the political context of these states allows for both comparison and heterogeneity: all four legislatures are classified as full-time legislatures by the National Conference of State Legislatures, which means that a legislators' job is mostly or completely (66 percent to 100 percent) full time. This also means this type of legislature has professional staff, and each legislator collects a salary large enough to support him or her full time. Practically, professional legislatures like those in Arizona, California, Louisiana, and New York have implications for legislators and legislatures alike. Professional legislatures in general have members with longer tenures and more qualifications than their less-professionalized counterparts (Squire 2007). The legislators have more time to develop and deliberate over policy, time that is important if one is interested in examining the framing strategy related to egg donation (Squire 2007). Such legislatures are associated with stronger policy goals, less collaboration, and less inclusivity in the policymaking process (Rosenthal 1997). Considering the importance of women representing reproductive issues as legislators, professionalization makes a difference: professional legislatures are less likely to have female legislators, but women in professionalized legislatures are more likely to be highly educated and come from a higher socioeconomic class than their less professional peers—important for the representation of an issue closely related to education and privilege (Rosenthal 1997). In political science and policy studies, professionalization is a common measure for comparing the policy activities of state legislatures, particularly in relation to gendered political topics (e.g., Osborn 2012, Tolbert and Steuernagel 2001).

Although all four of these states have professionalized legislatures, the political leanings of these legislative bodies are quite different: as illustrated in table 2, the level of conservatism of the legislative body varies in each of the cases. This conservatism has been important in policymaking in response to other issues related to gender, femininity, and sexuality; some studies have noted that conservative attitudes toward gender, sexuality, and reproduction may lead to restrictive attitudes toward reproductive technologies (Jasanoff 2005, Goggin and Orth 2004, Kirkpatrick 2012). I explore the implications of these socially conservative political ideologies for egg donation politics in chapter 3.

Representing different geographical locations across the country, the cases can be paired according to demographic characteristics and political cultures in reference to issues of gender, the body, and reproduction. Compared to the rest of the country, California and New York have large, racially diverse populations, large urban centers, and a higher concentration of fertility clinics and large biotechnology firms (CDC, American Society for Reproductive Medicine, and Society for Assisted Reproductive Technology 2016). California and New York also have a historical context of policy innovation in regard to kinship, reproduction, and genetic technologies (Markens 2007). Moreover, they have been widely studied as policy entrepreneurs in the areas of reproductive technology research, commerce, and policy (e.g., Thompson 2013, Benjamin 2013, Markens 2007). California and New York are large financial and intellectual centers and have been early adopters of both reproductive technology commerce and state-funded stem cell research programs (Heidt-Forsythe 2016). Historically, both states have similarly liberal attitudes and policies toward egg-donation-related issues, such as abortion, contraception, and LGBTQ rights, which influence attitudes regarding access to reproductive technologies (Nash et al. 2017, Kirkpatrick 2012). While the two states' reproduction and technology issues are similar in many respects, California has generally been legally and politically more supportive of reproductive technologies than New York. In California, courts have repeatedly reinforced the legal parentage of donor-conceived children, even in same-sex couples (Markens 2007, Smith 2009). While important differences exist between these states, the egg donation industries in California and New York have been identified as among the largest in the country; the two states also have some of the highest consumer demand and have explicitly allowed (through law and policy) reproductive technologies to be used for reproduction and research (Thompson 2011, Benjamin 2013, Heidt-Forsythe 2016, Markens 2007).

Arizona and Louisiana are far more similar to each other in terms of population size, urbanization, and political culture. While these two states represent distinct geographical regions in the US, they are similar in having smaller, though racially diverse, populations and smaller urban centers than exist in California and New York. Arizona and Louisiana each has a much smaller concentration of fertility clinics and biotechnology firms—unlike the other two cases, Arizona and Louisiana are not considered to be major, nationally recognized locations for reproductive technology commerce or research. Their state legislatures approach policy issues of gender, reproduction, and sexuality similarly: historically, these states have constructed and enforced some of the most restrictive policies for regulating abortion, contraception, and reproductive technologies, particularly in the context of same-sex couples and single parents, compared to other states in the US (Nash et al. 2017). These conservative political attitudes about gender, sexuality, and reproduction should have a negative effect on the use and prevalence of both reproductive technologies and research in stem cells.

While the two states are similar in many ways, they exhibit some important differences in their approaches to reproductive technology policy. Like New York, Arizona has prohibited legally enforceable surrogacy contracts, while Louisiana has historically enforced marriage restrictions on reproductive technologies.[3] In terms of family law, both states failed to recognize single individuals' and same-sex couples' rights to donor-conceived children until 2015. Moreover, Louisiana was an early adopter of a ban on all compensation for egg donation for reproduction, while Arizona allows compensation for procured eggs to treat infertility, but not for research. While Louisiana's legislature is more conservative than Arizona's, they have similar political, economic, and social histories of engaging with reproductive technologies (Heidt-Forsythe 2010, 2012).

COMPENSATION, REPRODUCTION, AND RESEARCH IN FOUR STATES

After identifying the ways that compensation affects multiple stakeholders, values, and commercial interests, as well as the utility of comparing four cases of policymaking related to egg donation, I examine the specific framing processes corresponding to a major compensation bill in each of the four states, as illustrated in table 3.

These bills were selected to highlight the different ways that compensation bills seek to regulate commercial and research transactions that accompany egg donation: in California (Senate Bill 1260) and New York (Senate Bill 433B), legislators introduced compensation bills that limited monetary rewards for donating eggs for research. In contrast, Arizona's House Bill 2142 and Louisiana's Senate Bill 452 limited compensation that women could receive in reproduction and research settings. These bills were introduced in the 2006–7 legislative sessions in their respective states, which had diverse histories of introducing similar bills related to egg donation. Although these bills were introduced at the same time and had similar content concerning egg donation and compensation, each case resulted in a different outcome. While California successfully passed its bill into law, Arizona's governor vetoed its bill, and bills in Louisiana and New York died in committee. In the next section, I discuss the political contexts from which these bills emerged—what legal and political events, laws, and histories helped push egg donation to the forefront of political consciousness.

TABLE 3

Cases, Framing Strategies, and Bill Outcomes

State	California	New York	Arizona	Louisiana
Case	SB 1260	SB 433	HB 2142	SB 452
Framing Strategy	Morality (government obligation)	Morality (government obligation)	Morality (individual action) and body politics (women's health)	Morality (individual action) and body politics (women's health)
Bill Outcome	Passed: signed into law by governor	Failed: died in committee	Passed/failed: vetoed by governor	Failed: died in committee

CALIFORNIA: A "SAFE" STATE FOR
REPRODUCTION AND TECHNOLOGY

In case law, California largely protected alternative family formations and claims of legal parenthood by intended parents throughout the 1990s and the early twenty-first century. Unlike other states that have balked at the violations of traditional determinants of motherhood and fatherhood—such as genetic or gestational maternity—California protected alternative-family arrangements enabled through surrogacy in cases such as *Johnson v. Calvert* (1993), which established California as a legally safe state for recipient parents. Similarly, the group of cases in 2006 that established parental obligations equally for same-sex partners— *Elisa B. v. Superior Court, K. M. v. E. G.*, and *Kristine H. v. Lisa R.*— demonstrates that the court system conceptualizes the family in nontraditional ways (Smith 2009). Similarly, the state protects women from donor paternity claims—preventing sperm donors from establishing legal rights to an ART-conceived child, and making the state a haven for recipient parents who want legal protection to use ART in family formation (Markens 2007).

While California is one of the more liberal states regarding family policy, it has a mixed history of regulation of reproductive technology. The state is one of fifteen that have banned reproductive cloning (NCSL 2008). However, the punishment for violating this ban is less harsh than in other states, as California's law threatens medical license revocation and civil penalties if this prohibition is violated. This is in stark contrast to other states, which have established monetary penalties up to $1 million (NCSL 2008). While banning reproductive cloning, California permits nonhuman cloning in research settings, although state law regulates these practices (NCSL 2008). The state has affirmed stem cell research, going so far as to publicly fund it through Proposition 71 (2004), also known as the Stem Cell Research and Cures Bond. This was the first adopted state policy of its kind to not only endorse regenerative medicine research but also reenvision state government as having active regulatory and funding roles in stem cell research within the state.

EGG DONATION LEGISLATION IN CALIFORNIA, 1997–2004

Egg donation was identified as an important social issue between 1997 and 2004. In this period, six bills were introduced that regulated the practices of egg donation in California. These bills targeted the issues of written consent, directives, and compensation, concepts that would resurface in the regulation of egg donation in SB 1260. After 2002, the majority of legislation related to egg donation targeted the research sector. Between 2002 and 2004, Democratic senator Deborah Ortiz—who would later cosponsor SB 1260, described in the next chapter—sponsored four bills that regulated compensation, donor directives for their gametes, and research review boards. However, it was Proposition 71, an initiative that was truly the first of its kind to successfully implement state funding of stem cell research, that changed oversight of egg donation.

Proposition 71 (2004) is a unique historical event in state politics, as it represents the collision of California's unique legislative environment with its increasingly strong identity as a hub for the biotechnology sector. In 1999, the Department of Health and Human Services determined that stem cell research was exempt from the Dickey-Wicker Amendment.[4] Free to use human cells and tissue, stem cell research was not without controversy; in his presidential campaign, George W. Bush promised to ban stem cell research, a promise that was introduced in August 2001. Although Congress pushed for more relaxed rules on the use of eggs and tissue for stem cell research in 2005—primarily through the use of discarded embryos from in vitro fertilization treatments—the federal legislature refused to fund national research using assisted reproductive technology between 2001 and 2005. This lack of federal funding was the impetus for California's unique legislative opportunity to fund regenerative medicine research, through a nonlegislative initiative, Proposition 71.

Proposition 71 authorized the use of state bonds to fund stem cell research, a method of tax allocation usually reserved to finance infrastructure such as hospitals and schools. The use of these bonds for stem cell research was unprecedented, as were the goals of Proposition 71: to change the state constitution, to allocate large amounts of state funds via bonds for stem cell research, and to establish state infrastructure to oversee stem cell research and related technologies in California, infrastructure that would later become the California Institute for Regenerative Medicine. The institute created the Independent Citizens Oversight Committee, composed of citizens, lawyers, researchers, and academics, to determine how state funding would be allocated to stem cell research projects throughout the state.

California has an initiative system, by which citizens and advocacy groups can initiate state statutes without the intervention of legislative bodies in the lawmaking process. Proposition 71 was rooted in this administrative process and was backed by a wide coalition of strange political bedfellows: politicians and elected officials (again, Senator Ortiz among them), celebrities, religious groups, biotechnology companies, and mainstream women's health advocacy groups such as Planned Parenthood of California. As if to predict the politics associated with SB 1260, another strange set of alliances opposed Proposition 71. Republicans, the Conference of Catholic Bishops, pro-life groups, and bioethics groups would all later enter the debate about Deborah Ortiz's SB 1260.[5] Highly funded and well publicized, the backers of Proposition 71 gained Governor Arnold Schwarzenegger's support in October 2004. In November 2004, Proposition 71 passed by a margin of almost 3 million votes—more than a 10 percent margin in favor of state-funded stem cell research.[6]

Soon after Proposition 71's passage, the legislature—many of whose members supported the initiative—began to further regulate egg donation within the context of Proposition 71 and the California Institute for Regenerative Medicine. Between 2002 and 2006, Ortiz sponsored or cosponsored four bills that regulated egg donation.[7] In contrast, George Runner, a white Republican male senator, was a less obvious supporter of women's health policy. As a social conservative, Runner did not have a history of reproductive rights support: he had spoken out against abortion and contraception, as well as the immunization of young women with Gardasil. Despite these gender, ideological, and partisan differences, these strange bedfellows in the senate were the legislators most active in egg donation policymaking in the period leading up to the four case studies in chapter 3.

SB 1260 (the focus of the California case) was introduced on February 9, 2006, to the California State Senate and was aimed at banning compensation for egg donation for stem cell research. The bill was sent first to the Health Committee, where it received a hearing on April 19. After being amended, it passed unanimously and was then sent to the Appropriations Committee. On May 25, it was amended again and passed unanimously, and was then sent to the assembly. In the assembly, it was sent to the Health Committee (June 12) and the Appropriations Committee (August 7). After being amended in both committees, it passed in the assembly nearly unanimously on August 28; the senate concurred with the assembly amendments, and it was on Governor Schwarzenegger's desk by September 11. It was signed September 26, 2006, and remains law today—despite multiple legislative challenges.

EARLY MOVER, CAUTIOUS SHAKER: THE LONG HISTORY OF REPRODUCTIVE TECHNOLOGY IN NEW YORK

New York City is a financial, educational, and professional epicenter of reproductive technologies in the US, and it should come as no surprise that New York State has long been interested in oversight of egg donation. Since as far back as the mid-1980s, the New York Task Force on Life and the Law has worked with the state assembly and senate to create guidelines for the use of reproductive technologies in the state. Compared to California, however, New York has taken a more conservative and cautious approach to embracing reproductive-technology use. While both California and New York protect married recipients of artificial insemination from paternity claims by the donor, unmarried women in New York are not protected from such claims (Roxland 2012). In regard to surrogacy, the courts had largely come down against the legal enforceability of surrogacy contracts in cases such as *McDonald v. McDonald* (1994). While surrogacy contracts are unenforceable, New York State has historically recognized the parental rights of intended parents in legal, uncompensated surrogacy arrangements, and has decided questions of parentage and donor-conceived embryo disposition in cases such as *Kass v. Kass* (1998), *Doe v. New York City Board of Health* (2004), and *T.V. v. New York State Department of Health* (2011). Finally, New York requires insurance companies to cover infertility treatments, helping individuals with qualifying insurance coverage to afford the expense of reproductive technologies like egg donation. These divergent responses in comparable states can be attributed to the framing strategies of surrogacy in the media and in the state legislature during the late 1980s and early 1990s (Markens 2007). In the early twenty-first century, there were increasing calls for stem cell research and biotechnology development, in response to federal restrictions on fetal and embryonic research (Roxland 2012). New York, it seems, is growing into a biotechnology center that rivals the development of California.

NEW YORK AND EGG DONATION LEGISLATION, 1997–2004

In the period between 1997 and 2004, New York was a site of vigorous activity regarding issues of stem cell research and ART. New York is clearly distinct from California, given not only the volume of bills in this period that address egg donation in some way (nearly forty bills) but also the scope of these bills. The bills during this period grappled with the medical practices of egg freezing, health insurance coverage of donated eggs in fertility treatments, and reproductive cloning using donated eggs (1999–2000). These bills were introduced nearly two years earlier than comparable egg donation bills in California. There is a clear pattern in the egg donation bills proposed every session until successful passage—signaling that New York was an early site of discourse about egg donation as a political issue. For example, in the 2001–2 session, a bill that prohibited egg donation for cloning failed but was reintroduced in the next two regular sessions (2003–4, 2005–6) of the New York State Legislature. In this period, the legislature introduced bills about parentage of donor-egg-conceived children, the necessity of written directives from donors of eggs and embryos, and insurance coverage of egg donation. Given the large number of bills during this period, it is counterintuitive that bureaucracy—rather than legislation—would eventually have the last word on compensation for egg donation for research.

SB 433B was introduced on January 14, 2005, and targeted egg donation for research, proposing a statewide ban on compensation. It was immediately referred to the Senate Health Committee. It was amended in committee on March 18, 2005. While it stalled in committee for nearly a year, it was recommitted to the Senate Health Committee and amended yet again on February 3, 2006. Although Senator Liz Krueger and her cosponsors filed a motion of petition to bring the bill to a vote on March 7, they ultimately lost the motion of petition on March 21, killing the bill. While a ban on compensation for egg donation for research was never passed in the New York Assembly, only three years later a major rule went over the heads of legislators and changed the landscape of egg donation for research: on June 12, 2009, the Empire State Stem Cell Board (New York's state-funded stem cell research agency) announced that the organization would now be using state research money to pay egg donors up to ten thousand dollars for their eggs (Nelson 2009).

DEFINING PARENTS, DEFENDING
TRADITION IN ARIZONA, 2000–7

The history of regulation of egg donation in Arizona is rooted in the politics of reproductive technologies more broadly in the state. Between 2000 and 2007, Arizona's legal and statutory actions in response to reproductive technologies were a reaction to the growth of the commercial fertility sector and human embryonic stem cell research in neighboring California. Arizona—like California—has legal precedence in cases involving wrongful birth and conception (such as *University of Arizona Health Center v. Superior Court,* 1983), as well as cases involving wrongful death of embryos in contexts of reproductive technology (such as *Jeter v. Mayo Clinic of Arizona,* 2005). But in general, Arizona has not protected stakeholders in egg donation.[8] For example, Arizona has not passed the 1973 and 2002 Uniform Parentage Acts, which determine legal parentage of donor-conceived children. The acts are considered particularly important in protecting intended parents from legal claims of kinship made by egg or sperm donors; they also protect these donors from legal responsibility for a child or children who may be conceived without their knowledge through egg and sperm donation. The lack of such laws makes the state unfriendly to legal claims made by intended parents and donors alike over kinship, inheritance, child support, and donor anonymity (Crockin 2007).

Moreover, under Arizona law, surrogacy contracts may be executed but are not legal if disputed in court. This creates another layer of hostility to stakeholders using ART: as one of six states nationwide to ban legal surrogacy contracts, Arizona has made it nearly impossible to carry out legally secure surrogate pregnancies within the state. In the context of no Uniform

Parentage Act in Arizona, stakeholders such as donors, surrogates, and intended parents would find it easier to coordinate a legal birth in the neighboring states of California, Nevada, and New Mexico, although data on such reproductive travel in the region is not known. Lastly, Arizona does not have an infertility mandate in place to require insurance companies to cover or offer to cover infertility treatment. This policy context, combined with recent legislative pushes to eradicate wrongful birth and conception suits in the state, indicates that Arizona is unfriendly to ART more broadly and creates conditions that make it difficult for egg donors to anonymously donate without fear of legal ramifications (Heidt-Forsythe 2010).

THE POLITICS OF EGG DONATION
IN ARIZONA, 1997–2004

The late 1990s and early twenty-first century saw a barrage of major events that prompted Arizona lawmakers to pay attention to emerging biotechnologies: Dolly the sheep was cloned in 1996, human embryonic stem cells were derived at the University of Wisconsin 1998, and in 2002 President George W. Bush spoke directly to the American people via televised address, restricting the creation of federally funded stem cell lines. In 2005–6, Dr. Hwang Woo Suk of South Korea was indicted for falsifying stem cell research data, misuse of research funds, and accepting donated eggs from researchers in his laboratory—where he had supposedly cloned human cells, as well as created a dog from reproductive cloning (Sang-Hun 2005). The media frenzy around this discovery—along with President Bush's restrictions on stem cell research—give important political context to the reactions of Arizona. In 2005, the state legislature passed a bill that banned reproductive and therapeutic cloning through a prohibition on public funded research on cloning and, the same year, formed the Stem Cell Research Advisory Study Committee.

Republicans, particularly Republican women, were policy leaders regarding egg donation in Arizona. The committee, composed of Republicans who would later become cosponsors of Bob Stump's egg donation bill, was designated to study the impacts of stem cell research on Arizona. The legal context of reproductive technologies, plus the legislative activity on stem cell research, would come together in a series of legislative proposals aimed at egg donors. Unlike California and New York—who were also devising legislation on egg donation—Arizona would target *both* markets for reproduction and research. As a state that had previously been silent on the issue of egg donation, the Arizona legislature proposed three egg donation bills in 2006, one of them being Bob Stump's HB 2142. The other two bills, HB 2681 and SB 1097, also regulated components of egg donation for reproduction and research contexts. Four Republican women in the Arizona legislature—Pamela Gorman, Judy Burges, Trish Groe, and Karen Johnson—sponsored HB 2681, a bill that mandated informed consent for those donating eggs for reproduction and research. And although SB 1097 was a domestic violence bill at the time of introduction, it would transform into a bill regulating egg donation—and was sponsored by Republican women Judy Burges and Karen Johnson. Neither HB 2681 nor SB 1097 was ultimately successful in regulating egg donation in Arizona. However, Pamela Gorman would go on to sponsor the successful HB 2142, a bill intended to ban compensation for egg donation for reproduction and research.

After its introduction, HB 2142 was sent to the House Judiciary Committee (February 16) and the House Rules Committee

(February 21). Although the bill was debated in both committees, it was voted out of these Republican-dominated committees. After passing in the House on March 1, SB 2142 was sent to the senate, after which it was sent to the Judiciary Committee on March 13. After passing easily in the Judiciary, it was then moved to the Rules Committee (March 20), where it passed to a vote on the floor of the senate. Although the vote was split along partisan lines, the bill ultimately won enough votes to be sent back to the House, where the bill was passed on April 12, 2006. Only five days later, Democratic governor Janet Napolitano vetoed the bill. Although Arizona ultimately would not pass a ban on compensation for egg donation for reproduction, the state did eventually pass a ban on compensation for egg donation for research in 2008.

LEGISLATING FAMILY LIFE IN LOUISIANA

To better understand how different frames for the natural and unnatural use of women's bodies, reproductive labor, and egg cells create policy narratives with implications for the regulation of egg donation, we turn to Louisiana, a state that was similarly deliberating over the issue of egg donation in 2006. Historically, Louisiana has had some of the most restrictive policies in relation to reproduction in the country (Guttmacher 2018). Louisiana permits no-fault divorces but requires separation periods of six months if no minor children are involved in the divorce, and a period of a year if there are minor children involved. Like Arizona, Louisiana has additional restrictions for divorces within covenant marriage, with a minimum separation period of a year. For heterosexual couples who seek divorce and dissolution of their marriage, Louisiana is a community-property state, with "best interest of the child" and joint-custody standards in child custody cases. Louisiana had enforceable sodomy laws until 2003's *Lawrence v. Texas* and did not recognize LGBTQ adoption until 2015. While state courts have not explicitly barred visitation and custody sharing of children resulting from or involved in same-sex partnerships, two cases in the 1990s (*Lundin v. Lundin* [1990] and *Scott v. Scott* [1995]) gave fathers in each case custody of the disputed children owing to allegations of the mothers' same-sex relationships after dissolution of their heterosexual marriages.

Louisiana is one of the most restrictive states in regard to abortion liberties and access among all states (Rose 2006). Currently, Louisiana enforces a twenty-four-hour waiting period and mandatory counseling about fetal pain, and it restricts public funding of abortions except in cases of life endangerment, rape, and incest (Guttmacher Institute 2018). Abortions may be provided only by physicians within clinics that are subject to laws targeting regulation of abortion providers (Rose 2006). Minors who seek abortions must have the consent of their parents or guardians (Guttmacher 2018). This is the context for Louisiana's stance on reproductive technologies more broadly, which resembles the legislative backdrop of Arizona. Louisiana has no clear case or statutory law on surrogacy, nor has the state passed the 1973 or 2002 Uniform Parentage Act. In Louisiana, as in Arizona, the political climate and legal context make it a relatively unsafe state for stakeholders in cases of surrogacy, especially without legal parentage protections for intended parents, donors, and surrogates. While Louisiana does have an infertility mandate in place, it prohibits insurance companies from paying for in vitro fertilization. Such limits create a system whereby donation is not secure from legal parentage claims, and intended parents not only have little recourse to claim donor-conceived children as their own but also are prohibited from using insurance money to pay for certain ART procedures for which donor eggs are used. While more restrictive policies were passed late in the first decade of the twenty-first century—and are discussed at the end of this chapter—Louisiana in 2006 was not particularly friendly to egg donors or ART stakeholders in general.

LOUISIANA'S LEGISLATIVE SILENCE ON EGG DONATION, 2000–6

Before the uptick in bills about egg donation around 2005, there was little legislative interest in the subject. Only one bill regarding egg donation came before the legislature between 1999 and 2006, and it prohibited unauthorized use of ovum or sperm beyond the written consent of the donor, as well as banned use of gametes retrieved from a deceased individual without written consent.[9] While it received some opposition in the senate, it was unanimously passed after amendments regarding illegal harvesting and illegal use of eggs were adopted in the Conference Committee, and it was signed into law by Republican governor Mike Foster in August 1999. Spring of 2006 was when egg donation restrictions were next presented in the state legislature; in March 2006, two bills about egg donation were sponsored in the legislature with high levels of Republican support. While the first bill, Senator Michael Michot's SB 429 (which never made it out of committee), banned egg donation for research purposes, it established an egg donor registry in the state. Framing his bill as "protecting the ovarian health of Louisiana women," Michot proposed creating a registry for reproductive and research egg donation (SB 429, 2006). The bill established a clear frame for the use of women's eggs: the state needed to step in to prevent and track the improper use of women's eggs. In this context, policymaking had already addressed concerns over the ethical and unethical uses of women's reproductive labor long before Senator Sharon Weston Broome sponsored the "Ovarian Health Protection Law" (SB 452), a bill that proposed bans on compensation for egg donation for research.

On May 10, SB 452 was sent to the Committee of Health and Welfare, where it died. Although SB 452 never made it out of committee, a fellow Democrat, Jalila Jefferson-Bullock introduced a similar bill to ban compensation for egg donation for research, which also died in the Health and Welfare Committee. The only legislative acts related to egg donation that were successfully implemented were Jefferson-Bullock's House Study Request 11 in June 2006, which asked that the Committee of Health and Welfare study the issue of compensation for egg donation, and Broome's Senate Resolution 25 (also in June 2006), which requested a parallel study of the "sale of human eggs" and was sent to the secretary of state on June 20, 2006.

FRAMING EGG DONATION IN THE STATES

Egg donation in the US is unique compared to that of other developed nations with strong central regulation: statutes largely exist at the state level, are diverse in what they regulate, and generally follow a two-tiered system. While egg donation for reproduction is seen as a conventional, if private, choice, egg donation for research has historically been subject to public debates over first principles. If gender norms related to femininity drive US approaches to egg donation, we must understand the role that attitudes toward femininity play in framing egg donation, particularly through the frameworks of body and morality politics. Employing policy narrative analysis, the next chapter examines four cases of egg donation—legislation in California, New York, Arizona, and Louisiana to ban compensation. As observed in this chapter, these cases had diverse and rich political contexts in which egg donation legislation emerged—informing how, why, and through what means stakeholders argued for and against bans on compensation. Returning to Governor Jerry Brown's contention that "not everything is for sale," the next chapter explores how values, beliefs, and assumptions about gender, reproduction, and research have created the nation's unique, bifurcated system of egg donation (Brown 2013).

Statecraft Is Always Soul Craft

Egg Donation Politics in Four States

Appearing on a March 2006 episode of C-SPAN's *Washington Journal*, Arizona House representative Robert Stump was triumphant. His bill, HB 2142, had just passed both houses of the state legislature and was on its way to the governor for her signature. During the show, Representative Stump answered callers' questions about the bill's ban on compensation for egg donation. One particular question and response revealed the complex interactions in framing gender, reproduction, and morality in the politics of egg donation. After the caller charged Representative Stump with being "right wing" and "trying to prevent [women] from having the freedom to use their bodies for what they want," Stump quickly responded. He framed the compensation ban as feminist, evoking the women's health movement and feminist author and activist Judy Norsigian as among his allies in the bill. Moreover, he quoted George Will, well-known conservative social critic, arguing that "statecraft is always soulcraft" (*Washington Journal* 2006).

Although both individuals were employing the concept of femininity and gender in their arguments, they were using competing frames around gender. The caller evoked the bodily autonomy of women that allowed them to make reproductive choices for themselves, while conservative Representative Stump used feminist arguments to justify his introduction of the bill—ostensibly to limit access to egg donation rather than to enable free choice. In this chapter, while investigating competing arguments regarding egg donation, I examine discourse and debates in four state cases, in particular how stakeholders frame egg donation, and what the larger meanings of this discourse are for the feminist (and antifeminist) policy and politics of egg donation.

Frames about gender, particularly femininity, work differently according to the kind of egg donation being regulated. Representative Stump and the *Washington Journal* caller debated a bill banning compensation in egg donation for research and reproduction, but the cases in this chapter vary in their aims to regulate the supposed Wild West of egg donation. In the first set of cases (California and New York), stakeholders targeted egg donation for stem cell research. In these cases, state-funded infrastructure for stem cell research sparked political interest in regulating egg donation. As eggs are important biological research material in somatic cell nuclear transfer research, questions about the role of compensating egg donors as research participants emerged in both states. In the second set of cases—Arizona and Louisiana—stakeholders debated egg donation in both reproductive and research contexts. In contrast to the research development around egg donation, stakeholders in Arizona and Louisiana sought to limit what they viewed as commercial fertility *and* research markets growing out of control. While the framing strategies were different regarding egg donation for reproduction and for research, an important and counterintuitive pattern emerged across the cases: odd political alliances emerged in all of these cases—ideological and/or partisan foes joined together as strange political bedfellows in response to the issue of compensation for egg donation.

To explain the ways that egg donation is framed (that is, the ways that stakeholders define problems, diagnose causes for those problems, make judgments, and suggest policy remedies) in this chapter I examine the ways that definitions and norms of femininity guide state policymaking. Exploring four state cases through interpretive methods described in chapter 2, I analyze a series of texts related to compensation/egg donation bills: the legislative texts and bill histories, committee and floor transcripts, stakeholders' direct statements to the public (such as press releases), local press coverage, and official communications. My investigation shows that in discourses in California and New York that relate to compensation for egg donation for research, and in similar debates in Arizona and Louisiana that relate to compensation for egg donation for reproduction and research, all four cases demonstrate the attempt by stakeholders to ban payments to egg donors.

Although each of these states uses diverse interpretations of gender to frame egg donation, three major themes emerge among the case studies: gender and agency, vulnerability, and the moral duty of the state. Gender and agency, the first theme, reflects the significant scholarship around women and subjectivity in policymaking. Scholars have observed many examples where policy makers' debates characterize women as passive objects acted upon by medical doctors, researchers, and commercial interests in women's health policies (Martin 1991, Richardson 2012, Daniels and Heidt-Forsythe 2012, Jesudason and Weitz 2015). Within the four cases discussed in this chapter, language related to gender and agency emerge over and over in discourse about women: the cases demonstrate vastly different approaches, in politics and policymaking, to how women are defined as research subjects (without any mention of gender) or as hyperfeminized egg donors. On the other hand, other stakeholders depict egg donors as passive research participants or objectified women acted upon by outside forces, rather than as active subjects. This rhetoric reflects broader arguments about feminist policy—what it means to put women at the center of policy, and how such policy elevates women's equality and status in public and private spheres—and how conservative Republican lawmakers utilize feminist policy rhetoric for legislative gains (Mazur 2002, Reingold et al. 2015, Schreiber 2008, Deckman 2016).[1]

The second major theme is vulnerability. In stem cell research contexts, egg donors are defined within a bioethical framework, where research subjects are in danger of unethical exploitation if there is no proper political oversight. Women as research subjects are vulnerable and must be protected by bioethical protocols—namely, bans on compensation for egg donation for research, which prevent women from being induced to donate eggs for money. While women are portrayed in California and New York as vulnerable research subjects in the context of stem cell research, women in Arizona and Louisiana are described as especially vulnerable in the context of reproduction. Women are defined as an especially vulnerable class of people who must be protected from financial and bodily exploitation. Research subjects' vulnerability is defined more abstractly: rather than being referred to as female egg donors who may be exposed to exploitation, research subjects are stripped of any gender identity. The de-gendered research subject is vulnerable to violations of bioethical principles, like any other research participant. Before the state could achieve scientific innovation and economic growth, stakeholders argued, research subjects' bioethical vulnerability had to be addressed.

The third major theme is the moral duty of the state, or what Representative Stump (quoting George Will) calls "statecraft" as "soulcraft." If women are rendered passive (in research and reproduction) and are vulnerable to exploitation in egg donation, then it follows that the state may have a role in regulating egg donation practices. Despite the states' different aims and ideological reasons for creating policy solutions to egg donation problems, the framing processes discussed in this chapter demonstrate how the role of the state is conceived in relation to egg donation. All four cases show the ways that morality and state "duty" are evoked in policymaking. The state has a moral duty to promote what Thompson (2013) calls a pro-cures policy—the state is compelled to provide scientific cures for degenerative disease and disability. In California and New York, stakeholders believe that it is the state's role to promote scientific research that could provide cures for disease and disability. Stakeholders in Arizona and Louisiana, in contrast to the other cases, conceive the state's role as one of regulating individual behavior and protecting women against immoral exploitation. To explain the development of politics and policymaking related to compensation in egg donation in California, New York, Arizona, and Louisiana, it is necessary to discuss the four political contexts of egg donation.

REGULATING EGG DONATION IN CALIFORNIA'S RESEARCH SECTOR: SB 1260 (2006)

Senator Deborah Ortiz (D-Sacramento) spearheaded the effort to pass SB 1260, which proposed a ban on compensation for egg donation for stem cell research; the bill was cosponsored by

George Runner (R-Lancaster). The pairing of Ortiz and Runner was not politically obvious: Deborah Ortiz had an extensive history of work on stem cell and reproductive rights issues when she introduced the Reproductive Health and Research Bill. A Latina Democrat representing Sacramento, she prioritized reproductive health care during her terms as senator, such as the California Freedom of Access to Clinic and Church Entrances Act (2001), which protected individual access to reproductive health clinics from the intervention of protestors. Her cosponsor of SB 1260, Republican senator George Runner, was a social conservative with a history of sponsoring antiabortion and anticontraception legislation—and was a public opponent of stem cell research (Mclachlin 2005). Senator Ortiz, a self-described women's health advocate who "authored laws that promoted biomedical, stem cell, and cancer research while ensuring women's health was not compromised in the process," viewed bans on compensation for egg donation as a method of oversight to ultimately protect women's health (Ortiz 2016). Runner, on the other hand, saw such a ban as a way to slow down and hamper stem cell research—and the strange partnership most likely was the politically expedient solution for both senators to achieve their ideologically different goals regarding egg donation and stem cell research. The creation of strange ideological bedfellows in response to the issue of compensation for egg donation for research became a pattern seen in other cases as well.

RACING TOWARD INNOVATION IN NEW YORK: SB 433B (2006)

Between 2005 and 2006, New York's eyes were on the developments in stem cell research in California: although New York has one of the highest concentrations of biotechnology research and development firms in the nation, there had been little success in establishing legislative oversight of industry (Roxland 2012). State senator Liz Krueger was intent on changing the status quo in the case of stem cell research and egg donation. A white female Democrat representing the wealthy Upper East Side District 28 in Manhattan, Senator Krueger had been a strong and vocal supporter of abortion rights and family issues during her service to the senate. The antiabortion group New York Right to Life gave Senator Krueger a low rating, indicating that she consistently voted against abortion restrictions. In 2004, NARAL Pro-Choice New York gave Senator Krueger a positive "Pro-Choice" endorsement. In a written "Political Courage Test" produced by Project Vote Smart in 2010, Senator Krueger endorsed state funding of state stem cell research and embryonic stem cell research (Krueger 2006).[2] Senator Krueger was the sponsor and figurehead of Senate Bill 433B, a bill cosponsored by four senate Democrats (Senators Jeffrey Klein, David Paterson, Suzi Oppenheimer, and Eric Schneiderman). The bill stipulated that egg donation for research would be subject to a ban on compensation for donated oocytes in stem cell research, particularly prohibiting any "valuable consideration" that could be received for the donation of oocytes and the creation of human tissue (SB 433B, 2006).

TARGETING REPRODUCTION AND RESEARCH IN ARIZONA: HB 2142 (2006)

On January 11, 2006, Republican representative Robert Stump introduced HB 2142, a bill that prohibited any individual from selling or offering to sell, purchasing or offering to purchase, a human egg for money or any other "valuable consideration" in *either* the fertility or research context (HB 2142, 2006). Selling or purchasing eggs would be classified as a felony under the bill— targeting not only medical professionals and commercial representatives but also egg donors themselves. Representative Stump is a staunch social and political conservative who received Arizona Family Project's "Friend of the Family" Award in 2006 (Stump Legislative Website 2012).[3] Republican representative Pamela Gorman, the only woman to cosponsor HB 2142, represented District 6 until 2010.[4] "Aspiring to continue the tradition of free market principles, small government, and reduced taxation," Gorman is a member of Concerned Women for America, a group that "shares her strong socially conservative principles," according to her profile on the Arizona State Legislature web page (Arizona State Legislature 2006). Dr. Janice Shaw Crouse, the director of Concerned Women for America, has come out strongly against what she perceives as exploitation in egg donation, arguing that "no young woman should be used in procedures that jeopardize her own fertility—indeed her own life— in order to line the pockets of those who promote the infertility industry's human egg trade" (Concerned Women for America 2010). In parallel with previous studies of conservative women's activism on reproduction and motherhood issues, this organization's position echoes feminist policy rhetoric by placing women at the center of their issue position, where women should be protected from exploitation and harm inherent in the commercial interests of the fertility industry (Schreiber 2008). Despite the use of feminist rhetoric, the ban on compensation for egg donation was aimed to suppress and disincentivize paid egg donation throughout Arizona—ultimately limiting women's ability to participate in egg donation markets as donors and as consumers. In parallel to the co-optation of feminist rhetoric at the state level by conservative Republican women since the late 1990s, Concerned Women for America adopted feminist rhetoric to promote the protection of women—but for distinctly anti-feminist ends (Schreiber 2008, Deckman 2016).

PROTECTING WOMEN'S HEALTH IN LOUISIANA: SB 452 (2006)

Senator Sharon Weston Broome, an African American, Democratic woman representing Baton Rouge, introduced the "Ovarian Health Protection Law," also known as SB 452, on March 27, 2006, coinciding with Stump's appearance on *Washington Journal* (SB 452, 2006, *Washington Journal* 2006). The explicit aim of SB 452 was to "protect the ovarian health of women in Louisiana" through a ban on compensation for egg donation for research. Because Louisiana already had a statute banning compensation for egg donation for reproduction, SB 452 effectively cut off any other avenues for paid exchanges involving donated eggs.

While Senator Broome's bill is similar to Stump's bill, her racial, gender, and partisan identity could not have been more different from those of her Arizona counterpart; however, like the legislators in Arizona, she is socially conservative, particularly regarding issues of abortion and cloning. The same year she introduced her bill, Senator Broome voted for a universal state ban on abortion that would go into effect if a judicial nullification of *Roe v. Wade* were to take place, and she also voted against rape and incest exceptions to the law. In 2006, she received a 100 percent rating from the Louisiana Family Forum, a conservative organization "committed to defining faith, freedom, and the traditional family in Louisiana," indicating she voted against the liberalization of abortion laws (Louisiana Family Forum 2006). She also received accolades from Louisiana Right to Life in accordance with her stances against abortion, cloning, stem cell research, and other technologies related to fertility treatment and regenerative medical research (Louisiana Right to Life 2012). In contrast, Jalila Jefferson-Bullock, who served in the Louisiana House until 2007, had a strong pro-abortion-access voting record while in the House, voting against prohibitions on abortion. While both Broome and Jefferson-Bullock are Democratic women, who often share more ideologically liberal views on reproductive issues, they are nearly polar opposites in their ideological views on these issues—another strange partnership in pursuit of regulating egg donation.

GENDER AND AGENCY

Gender is conceptualized in diverse ways in the case of egg donation for research versus that of egg donation for reproduction. In the context of research, egg donors are rendered as research subjects, whereas egg donors in the context of reproduction are described as highly feminized, essentialized women. Gender divides each definition: in research, women are stripped of any gender identity and defined in a way similar to other clinical research subjects; while in the context of reproduction, women are solely defined by their gendered reproductive capacities and biological difference. More crucially, women in all cases have little agency. In discourse, language describes egg donors as women/research subjects who are acted upon by medical professionals, research scientists, and greedy consumers of reproductive technologies. Verbiage used by stakeholders in all the cases identifies professionals, scientists, and consumers as active subjects with strong and powerful interests in egg dona-tion, while egg donors (defined as women or as research sub-jects) are in a passive role—being enticed and encouraged to donate eggs and, in that way, exploited.

GENDER AND AGENCY: EGG DONATION FOR RESEARCH IN CALIFORNIA AND NEW YORK

California's SB 1260 and New York's SB 433B were written with similar aims: as each state developed its infrastructure for stem cell research, egg donation emerged as an important part of this research. While somatic cell nuclear transfer research—which uses donated eggs as research material—was in its early stages of development, egg scarcity is a significant barrier to such research. At the time, the federal government's reticence to fund stem cell research during the George W. Bush administration compelled California voters to pass Proposition 71 (2005), which established state-funded stem cell research institutes using taxpayer money. Other states—including New York—took notice of two aspects of this development in California: first, an emerging role for the state to fund stem cell research, and second, the problem of supplying eggs for expanded stem cell research. SB 1260 and SB 433B were introduced to deal with the multifaceted ethical and research problems inherent in egg donation for stem cell research.

In an early hearing on SB 1260 in California, several amend-ments were introduced. First, original language in the bill that targets "egg donation" was struck; it was replaced by language that depicted egg donation as egg "retrieval for research" (SB 1260, 2006b). This shift is significant: rather than describing egg donation in the lucrative fertility industry that garners thousands of dollars in compensation, committee members changed the language to resemble that of scientific research, which does not compensate donors at nearly the same level as the fertility industry. Additionally, language was added to clarify the necessary bioethical requirements of egg donation for research: in this section, protocols for egg "retrieval for research" (rather than donation) included forming an oversight group made up of scientists, ethicists, and lawyers. This oversight group would establish rules to "protect, respect, and promote human autonomy and rights in research," language that reflects bioethical concepts and protocols in research (SB 1260, 2006b). These rules also required written and oral informed consent, psychological and physiological health screenings, and the collection of demographic information about egg donors participating in research programs (SB 1260, 2006b). Finally, the bill was amended to clarify the ban on compensation for egg donation: "No payment in excess of direct, out-of-pocket expenses shall be made to any research subject to encourage her to produce human oocytes for the purposes of medical research. There shall be no reimbursement for lost wages" (SB 1260, 2006b). In these amendments, language specifically differentiated between egg donation for reproduction—which is conventionally described in often emotional, altruistic, highly gendered language about women—and egg donation for research, which reflected a focus on research subjects adhering to bioethical protocols and processes in research settings (Daniels and Heidt-Forsythe 2012). With these changes, the language shifted from targeting women, who make up the majority of egg donors in fertility treatments, to targeting individuals (identified without a gender) who donate eggs for research.

Later, SB 1260 was changed further to emphasize that the aim of the bill was to protect de-gendered research subjects: before the amendment, the bill stated that its aim was to highlight the "significant need for research [to] … understand the health effects, and formulation of standardized policies and procedures in the areas of subject protection and education … involving ovarian stimulation, [and] oocyte retrieval" (SB 1260, 2006b). After the bill was amended, language shifted: "The purposes *[sic]* of this act is to create protections for research subjects and it should not be construed to affect any other form of medical care" (SB 1260, 2006b). This language shift, from explicitly describing ovarian stimulation and egg procurement from women to referring to research subjects—bereft of any gender—continued in the Assembly. In an August 7 hearing, SB 1260's references to egg donors and egg donation were again struck from the bill, replaced by gender neutral concepts of research subjects: in the amendment, all mentions of "donor" were replaced by "subject," and the phrase "the health risks and benefits of ovarian stimulation drugs used for assisted oocyte production" was also struck from the bill (SB 1260, 2006c). Again, the language used to describe a compensated system of egg donation to treat infertility shifted to verbiage that reflects uncompensated systems in research. The terms *egg donation* and *donor* are inextricably tied to gender, as egg donors and donation are primarily connected to women; in changing the term *egg donation* to *research,* and in changing *donor* to *subject,* stakeholders delinked egg donation from women donating oocytes for fertility treatments. While effectively de-gendering egg donors, language obscures the fact that nearly all egg donors are in fact gendered subjects.

In parallel to these shifts in language, New York's SB 433B, too, focused on a de-gendered research subject who was conceptually different from female egg donors who participate in compensated market exchanges in the fertility market. Like its Californian counterpart, SB 433B aimed to create research protocols for egg donation for stem cell research—namely, banning compensation for egg donation for research as part of a wider ban on payment for fetal tissue, and any other human tissue, for research. The office of Senator Liz Krueger, the sponsor of the bill, released a statement about SB 433B in June 2006: "One important way in which New York State can encourage stem cell research is by creating an ethical policy framework to guide the development of stem cell research programs. Senator Krueger's bill would address moral issues by banning reproductive human cloning, and protect stem cell research by creating a mechanism for the transfer of unused genetic material to scientific institutions, requiring the clear and informed consent of donors" (Krueger 2006). Senator Krueger's press release uses language that identifies women as "donors" and clearly places such donation in the ethical and procedural context of the clinic and research laboratory: it is to promote stem cell research that "unused genetic material" (like human eggs) must be regulated. In the research contexts of California's SB 1260 and New York's SB 433B, egg donation is conceptually different for research than for reproduction: rather than referring to feminized egg donors, the texts and amendments of these bills are aimed at de-gendered research subjects who happen to be women. Moreover, there is no mention of the hugely successful reproductive technology sectors in each state—in 2014, California and New York had sixty-two and thirty-five clinics, respectively, that provided donor egg services.

Throughout the legislative processes of SB 1260 and the introduction of SB 433B, the boundaries between research and reproduction have been carefully drawn, so as not to invite regulation of the lucrative fertility industry in each state. Moreover, each state identifies research subjects as a largely passive group not covered by the rules of bioethical oversight, informed consent, and protection against exploitation. Even in de-gendering passive research subjects—literally stripping egg donors of their gender in discourse and debates—stakeholders in California and New York were using gender in careful ways. Norms of femininity associated with reproduction could be attached to egg donation only in fertility contexts, defining women as egg donors only in relationship to the fertility industry, which adheres to professional self-regulation. In contrast, regulation of egg donation for research is acceptable because the norms of femininity have been delinked from egg donation for stem cell research contexts, where no reproduction of humans is legal.

GENDER AND AGENCY IN ARIZONA AND LOUISIANA

Gender and agency are understood differently in the cases of Arizona and Louisiana, where their respective bills were aimed at regulating egg donation for reproduction and research. In contrast to the other cases, Arizona's HB 2142 stated that "a person shall not sell or offer to sell a human oocyte for money … and shall not purchase or offer to purchase a human oocyte in exchange for money," a prohibition that includes both reproduction and research (HB 2142, 2006). While Louisiana already had a statutory ban on compensation for egg donation, SB 452 extended the ban to any money or valuable consideration given in exchange for eggs in "experimentation or research other than the treatment of infertility" (SB 452, 2006). Not only were the bills designed to ban compensation much more widely, but they also articulated the gendered category of people who would be most impacted by these bills: women.

In a press release sent out shortly after introducing HB 2142 in the Arizona House, Representative Bob Stump stated that the bill "make[s] sure that women know about all aspects of the egg donation procedure so they can make an informed and careful decision while also increasing the penalty for criminals who traffic in human reproductive cells" (GOP press release, June 27, 2006). When the bill went to committee, House Democrats who opposed the bill likewise relied on highly differentiated, gendered categories of women and men when they argued against the bill: "[Democratic representative] Ms. Lopez stated her concern that this bill, which prohibits women from selling their eggs, does not also address men selling their sperm; she believes that this is gender discrimination" (HB 2142, 2006b). Similarly, in the Judiciary Committee, Democratic representative Steve Gallardo introduced an amendment to ban compensation for sperm donation. According to the meeting's minutes, "Mr. Gallardo ... believes this is an equality issue, and what is good for one gender is good for another." Representative Bob Stump, who was also at the Judiciary Committee meeting, responded, "The crucial question is whether to permit researchers to allow women to put their health at risk by harvesting their eggs for the purpose of engaging in human cloning research. This bill would not restrict a woman's ability to donate eggs. It would prevent the commercialization of human eggs and the ability to profit from an invasive procedure that is medically hazardous.... [My bill] is a pro-life bill and a pro-woman bill" (HB 2142, 2006b).

As the bill was voted out of the House and moved to the senate, legislators in Arizona continued to use highly gendered language to refer to the targets of HB 2142: unlike the research subjects in California and New York, women would be regulated on the basis of their sexual difference and reproductive capacities.

In a state senate Judiciary Committee hearing, Democrats and Republicans again battled over women's independence and bodily freedoms with respect to egg donation. In meeting minutes, Democratic senator Bill Brotherton argued that "the Legislature should not interfere with a woman's decision about her eggs" and voted no on the bill (HB 2142, 2006b). Gender grounds the language throughout these debates. For Republicans, a ban on compensation for egg donation would be in women's best interest because it would protect their health; while for Democrats, a ban on compensation for egg donation would treat women and men differently. Although HB 2142 implicitly tore down the firewall between egg donation for reproduction and for research, Stump and his cosponsors reassured the Judiciary Committee that women would still be able to "help" others who were infertile. In doing so, he highlighted the conceptual divide between conventional uses of donated eggs for reproduction— making families—and what he saw as the unnatural use of eggs akin to playing Dr. Frankenstein: "Representative Stump said the bill addresses the sale of human eggs in exchange for a large amount of money.... [H]e would be willing to work on that to ensure that anyone who wants to donate eggs has the opportunity to do so in order to contribute to life[,] as opposed to contributing to its destruction via cloning" (HB 2142, 2006b).

After HB 2142 passed in the House and the Senate, Stump went on C-SPAN's *Washington Journal* to discuss what would become Arizona's first ban on compensation for egg donation. When asked if his "right wing and extreme" bill prevented women from using their bodies freely and independently, Stump charged back, claiming that he had support from Judy Norsigian, one of the founding members of Boston Women's Collective (famous for publishing the feminist health guide *Our Bodies,*

Ourselves), as well as the Pro-Choice Alliance for Responsible Research (*Washington Journal* 2006). Stump argued that his egg donation ban was in fact "body politics ... from an ethical perspective" (*Washington Journal* 2006).

While such an alliance may seem strange, Stump's use of feminist rhetoric—namely, identifying women as the subjects of the bill and arguing for their protection—falls into line with previous research about the co-optation of feminist rhetoric by antifeminist political actors (Reingold et al. 2015, Jesudason and Weitz 2015). Claiming support from feminist and women's health groups and using feminist rhetoric about women's health, Stump created a narrative in which his bill was nonpartisan and garnered wide, diverse support—by employing feminist and women's health rhetoric as a justification for regulating egg donation for research and reproduction. Stakeholders in favor of the ban on compensation in Arizona argued that women were being acted upon by exploitative scientific and medical actors; in opposition to the political efforts of Stump, Democrats argued that women were the subject of unfair state restrictions based on gender and sexual difference. The language used by both sides is important: on one side, exploitative scientific and commercial interests are abusing women and threatening their health, while on the other side, the state is limiting women's abilities to make choices about their bodies. On both sides, women are described as in need of protection from outside forces—and they are largely rendered as passive, uneducated decision-makers rather than as individuals whose bodily autonomy and liberty is being protected.

Governor Janet Napolitano, a Democrat, ultimately vetoed Representative Stump's HB 2142. In her veto letter, Napolitano argued in response to this bill: "Well-meaning people can disagree about the ethical issues posed by this bill[,] ... [H]owever

I am persuaded that this bill represents an unwanted intrusion in the medical decisions of women—and only women" (Napolitano 2007). Using language highly congruous with the framing of gender and agency used by other stakeholders in Arizona, Governor Napolitano framed egg donors as a highly specialized (and highly passive) gender category facing an "intrusion" into their "medical decisions."

In similar pointed, protectionist, and feminist rhetoric about women, Louisiana senator Sharon Weston Broome introduced SB 452 in March 2006, titled the "Ovarian Health Protection Bill": "In the interest of protecting the ovarian health of Louisiana women ... it shall be unlawful for any person to intentionally or knowingly provide valuable consideration if the human eggs are being procured for experimentation or research other than the treatment of infertility" (SB 452, 2006, sec. 134). Although the bill died in committee with little attention from either party, a fascinating counternarrative emerged three months after SB 452's introduction. A fellow Democrat, Jalila Jefferson-Bullock, introduced a counterframe in her June 2006 bill about egg donation, compensation, and research: rather than referring to egg donors as women, Jefferson-Bullock proposed a bill that would ban compensation to research subjects for donating eggs for stem cell research: "No payment in excess of the amount of reimbursement of expenses shall be made to any research subject to encourage her to produce human oocytes for the purposes of medical research" (HB 1234, 2006).

There is a tension between how these Democratic women conceptualize egg donation: while Weston Broome frames egg donation as explicitly about women, Jefferson-Bullock's bill defines egg donors as de-gendered research subjects, much as stakeholders did in California and New York. Although HB 1234's regulatory purpose may be nearly identical to that of Broome's "Ovarian Health Protection Bill," as both are aimed at banning compensation for egg donation for research, HB 1234 is completely free of language related to women's health. Moreover, the alternative framing of egg donation regulation was identified as necessary for the protection of "research subjects" (HB 1234, 2006).

In a later Louisiana Right to Life video about personhood, life, and research, Sharon Weston Broome explained her political positions on egg donation, stem cell research, and human cloning (Louisiana Right to Life 2012). She contended that "women's eggs are needed for [the cloning] process," and that women are "posed with the choice of selling their eggs to the highest bidder" without being told of potential health impacts (Louisiana Right to Life 2012). Instead of identifying women as in charge of their reproductive labor, this narrative renders them as passive targets for commercial interests who are used because of their susceptibility to outside, exploitative forces.

VULNERABILITY AND RESEARCH SUBJECTS IN CALIFORNIA AND NEW YORK

Closely related to the theme of gender and agency in these cases is the concept of vulnerability. Given that California and New York framed donors as de-gendered research subjects acted upon by potentially unethical medical and scientific forces, stakeholders clarified that this was a problem because of research subjects' vulnerability in light of bioethical exploitation. Similarly, Arizona and Louisiana framed egg donors specifically as women— not just any women, but a highly feminized and differentiated category of women acted upon by unsavory commercial and research interests. This category of women is especially sensitive in light of economic exploitation—women eschewing their own health and well-being for thousands of dollars in compensation. Research subjects and the specialized, feminized category of women are not just being acted upon by outside actors but are also especially vulnerable to being damaged, exploited, or otherwise misused by these forces. Rather than thinking about these forces as greedy individual researchers, stakeholders like California's Center for Genetics and Society—a proponent of the bill and bans on compensation for egg donation for research—framed vulnerability through broad economic pressures. The Center for Genetics and Society (2006) argued that the bill would "prevent a market that influences women to provide eggs" and ultimately would be a "victory for women's health, for the protection of research subjects, and for responsible science."

Framing egg donors in research contexts, stakeholders in California and New York constructed the idea of vulnerability as connected to mitigating risk: because of their participation as research subjects, egg donors would be at risk for medical and bioethical violations. In a neoliberal context, research subjects are often assumed to accept risk once proper bioethical protocols—like informed consent—are followed (Fisher 2007, 2013). Part of the job of government is to identify these risks and put protocols in place to enable research subjects to understand and agree to individually accepting responsibility for risk, be it psychological, physical, or economic. This logic derives from a bioethical framework, where certain procedures, like informed consent, not only give information to research participants but also require the explicit approval of research participants. This explicit approval is an assumption of risk: the subject is given full information and, knowing the potentially negative consequences of research participation, can then decide whether she wants to donate eggs to stem cell research. At the same time that stakeholders in California and New York framed bans on compensation as being especially relevant to de-gendered research subjects (rather than to women who were donating eggs in similar ways for reproductive ends), stakeholders also included language about vulnerability and risk in the debates and political context around SB 1260 and SB 433B. In a hearing before the introduction of SB 1260, Francine Coeytaux from the Pro-Choice Alliance for Responsible Research used language of risk and protection when talking about women donating eggs for research:

> We are asking that mechanisms be put in place to ensure that women who provide eggs be accorded all established protections for human research subjects; that as research subjects, they be given full information in advance about the direct and indirect risks of the research; and that their recruitment never be coercive. We sincerely believe these safeguards must be put in place in order to protect the health of the research subjects, the reputations and credibility of the scientists involved, and in general to advance the promise of stem cell research. (Coeytaux 2005)

The concepts that Coeytaux uses in her testimony—particularly bioethical protocols and debate over individual risk—reemerge in SB 1260's bill text. In Section 18(a) of SB 1260, egg donors are required to read a "written summary as required ... that would include information on health risks and potential adverse consequences of the procedure," after which a state-run institutional research board would obtain "informed consent in compliance with the Protection of Human Subjects in Medical Experimentation Act" (SB 1260, 2006a). SB 1260 was later amended to state that the bill "would encourage the ICOC to take prescribed actions, including, but not limited to[,] reviewing studies concerning the health risks ... of ovarian stimulation drugs" (SB 1260, 2006c).

However, stakeholders argued about how to understand the vulnerability of egg donors in research settings. Criticizing the exploitation of poor women, Susan Fogel of the Pro-Choice Alliance for Responsible Research, framed women as vulnerable because of poverty: "How much money is enough to coerce a poor woman? And do we up the ante until they bite?" (Romney 2006). In a fascinating partnership, the Pro-Choice Alliance for Responsible Research joined the California Family Council (a subsidiary of the social conservative organization Focus on the Family) in publicly supporting SB 1260. Writing in support of the bill, the California Family Council, too, framed egg donors as vulnerable women, "believ[ing] that SB 1260 will reduce the number of women who are willing to submit their bodies to chemicals and drugs for the sole purpose of producing more embryos for research" (ICOC 2006). In a later statement reflecting on egg donation and compensation in California, Lori Arnold of the California Family Council contended, "Eggs are a foundational element for life. We support legislation that honors that. In this case, we believe it dishonors life and is subject to abuse" (Ekine 2013). While the frame of vulnerable research subjects was challenged by a counterframe of vulnerable women—stakeholders did not adopt this counterframe, continuing in bill texts, hearings, media interviews, and press releases to define egg donors as vulnerable research subjects.

In similar ways, stakeholders in New York emphasized the vulnerability of research subjects largely through the lens of individual risk in stem cell research. A 2005 press release from Senator Krueger's office announced her introduction of a legislative agenda for stem cell research and explained why legislative oversight of research was needed:

Senator Krueger's legislation creates a thorough and comprehensive set of guidelines that anticipates potential abuses of therapeutic cloning. Specific standards of informed consent are created between physicians and potential donors that both parties must agree to. In addition the legislation spells out that human genetic material is to be treated with the utmost respect and sensitivity. Her legislation would also strictly prohibit human cloning, the practice of attempting to create a new human being from raw genetic material, and strict penalties are outlined for those who do not adhere to the rules of informed consent. (Krueger 2005)

This balancing of bioethical protocols (specifically informed consent) and the assumption of individual risk—by which potential donors agree to research participation—arose in the discourse surrounding SB 433B. The last paragraph in SB 433B asserts that "New York State shall regulate this emerging technology in order to protect society from known risks," a clear message that legislative oversight provides a process by which individual and aggregate risks can be mitigated (SB 433B, Section 2452–8). Although the bill did not get much traction, owing to Republican "stonewalling," Senator Krueger continued to use the language of bioethics and, in a July 20 press release, was explicit about her intention to protect donors in stem cell research: "This legislation is not only ethically wise, but is economically sound as well. It is based on an understanding of the science associated with stem cell research, and is grounded with a thorough consideration for the bioethical concerns raised by this type of research."

Mixing legislation and bioethics, language in these bills identifies the fact that research subjects take on considerable individual risk in donating eggs; without protections such as research-informed bioethical protocols (like informed consent and conflict-of-interest requirements), research subjects are vulnerable to scientific and economic exploitation. In light of the lucrative stem cell research market, research subjects' eggs could be used with impunity in pursuit of scientific innovation and huge economic benefits. Framing research subjects as David standing against the Goliath of biotechnology research, bans on compensation in SB 1260 and SB 433B protect the most vulnerable in a research system.

VULNERABILITY IN REPRODUCTION AND RESEARCH: ARIZONA AND LOUISIANA

While stakeholders in California and New York conceptualize reproductive vulnerability through bioethical research, stakeholders in Arizona and Louisiana define reproductive vulnerability as a highly feminized, gendered concept: women are vulnerable *because* of their biological difference, namely, the health of their reproductive potential. This framing centers biological difference in definitions of egg donation and connects women's reproductive capacity with norms of femininity—particularly the idea that women are dependent, weak, and disadvantaged, easily swayed by the promises of economic gain in egg donation markets. The relationship is distinctly one-sided: outside forces use women's bodies to their own ends, ultimately against the best interests of the women themselves. Rather than seen as assuming individual risk for their participation in egg donation, women are constructed as docile bodies used by unethical, faceless entities in reproduction and research.

One of the most striking ways that stakeholders in Arizona conceptualize vulnerability is through the language of human and sexual trafficking. Promoting HB 2142, the House Republicans released a statement on the bill. In this statement, Bob Stump argued that the bill was a "firm step forward in defending life" and specified that it would increase "the penalty for *criminals who traffic* in human reproductive cells" (Arizona House Republicans 2006, emphasis added). Similar language emerged in Representative Stump's statements in the House Judiciary Committee, where he noted that the bill was a reaction to "commercial trafficking in human oocytes," language that implicitly connects the trafficking of bodies to the trafficking of body parts. Drawing a parallel between sex trafficking and commercial transactions in eggs, Stump and the Arizona Republicans framed women as passive, vulnerable bodies subject to unethical commercial forces. Mirroring this definition of egg donors as passive victims, Senator Sharon Weston Broome used similar language in the Louisiana Right to Life interview (2012). Senator Broome contended that "women are being used as research tools" in cloning research (Louisiana Right to Life 2012).

Stakeholders in Arizona and Louisiana frame vulnerability primarily through gender—indicating that women as a special category are defenseless against the commercial and research forces at work in reproduction and research—but they also rely on assumptions about gender as it interacts with age and class. Representative Stump argued that women, particularly young women, were vulnerable to the egg donation system. After being asked why egg donors shouldn't be compensated for their work, Stump replied, "I think it's troubling, again, if we propose having women go under the knife for cash and sell their eggs for a procedure which many Americans find troubling." He defended the bill, arguing that "huge financial inducements to college-aged women" could be prevented (*Washington Journal* 2006).

The focus on vulnerable women defined by their age and class is mirrored in the text of Louisiana's proposed ban on egg donation for research: "In the interest of protecting the ovarian health of Louisiana women, *especially collegians and low-income women who are disproportionately vulnerable to being monetarily induced to compromise their reproductive and ovarian health,* it shall be unlawful for any person to intentionally or knowingly provide valuable consideration" (SB 452, 2006, emphasis added). In this frame, women are vulnerable as a category, but two variables—age and socioeconomic class—increase the possibility that women will be financially induced to donate eggs. In this frame, young and poor women are passive objects of exploitation by the fertility and research industries, although they are also rendered as passive objects of regulation by the state. At no point in meeting minutes, hearings, or press releases related to HB 2142 or SB 452 did egg donors represent themselves and testify. Interestingly, the policy solutions proposed in Arizona and Louisiana are not socioeconomic or educational support policies; instead, they simply ban commercial and research practices by which women can be compensated for their bodily labor. The narrative is clear: college students and poor women need money to survive and will disregard their own health and society's morals in order to obtain money. Stakeholders who are not among the targeted group define who belongs to this category of vulnerability, creating a policy story asserting that the state must step in to protect those women who cannot protect themselves.

THE MORAL RESPONSIBILITY OF THE STATE

The third theme that emerges out of this analysis is the moral responsibility of the state, which is tightly connected to the overall policy narrative about compensation for egg donation. Across the cases, egg donors are presented as lacking subjectivity in reproductive and research contexts, rendering research subjects and women alike as vulnerable to exploitation at the hands of the reproductive market and research industry. Stakeholders' assumptions about vulnerability in research and reproduction contexts shapes policy solutions: rather than making policy that reflects objective conditions that egg donors face, stakeholders shape the definition of who is vulnerable and how best to protect women against this vulnerability. In these policy narratives, political regulation is justified by gendered and de-gendered subjects' vulnerability within research and reproduction. The policy solution to egg donors' vulnerability is for the state to be proactive, protecting egg donors (no matter whether they are defined as women or research subjects) through bans on compensation.

THE DUTY TO INNOVATION: THE MORAL RESPONSIBILITY OF THE STATE IN CALIFORNIA AND NEW YORK

In a hearing on egg donation a few months before she introduced SB 1260, California state senator Ortiz asserted that politics would not get in the way of research. In fact, legislative oversight of egg donation would create more public trust in response to stem cell research in California: "Let me reassure you all that the purpose of this hearing does not in any way jeopardize the implementation of [stem cell research].... In fact, it adds to the integrity and provides an opportunity for the public trust to be assured.... We will work together to assure that this [stem cell research] research is funded and that it's conducted in an ethical manner in the State of California" (Ortiz 2005). Instead of viewing regulation as preventing the free development of science, Senator Ortiz saw the legislature as working with research companies to create "integrity" and "public trust." At the same hearing, Senator George Runner (a cosponsor of SB 1260) added, "We need to have the best ethics regulations in place to ensure that decisions are solely made on the best interests of taxpayers, not on the best interests of stakeholders that are interested in generating potential profits" (Ortiz 2005). Francine Coeytaux, a member of the Pro-Choice Alliance for Responsible Research, further accentuated the moral duty of the state: "I'm here to urge you to use your legislative authority to demand and require the highest ethical and medical standards to protect the health of the women who will be asked to donate eggs and embryos for research purposes" (Ortiz 2005).

In New York, the state's interest in promoting scientific research was to remain economically and scientifically competitive, and regulating egg donation was an important part of this moral responsibility. Shortly after California passed Proposition 71, funding stem cell research, Senator Eric Schneiderman told the press: "If the state of New York does not recognize the competitive need, our research scientists are all going to change their tune from 'I Love New York' to 'California, Here I Come.'" David Paterson, cosponsor of SB 433B, argued that "while we congratulate the citizens of California and their leaders for what they've done, we know that the real epicenter and focus of medical research has traditionally been in New York" (Gaskell 2005). Senator Krueger followed this by explaining the need for legislative oversight: "I personally think that California, having moved its money to the table, made some mistakes in how they went forward. To be honest, they didn't build in enough government oversight and control" (McIntire 2005).

In a March 2006 press release about SB 433B, Krueger urged Republicans to stop stonewalling her bill: "In spite of New York's reputation as a world-class epicenter for medical innovation, states such as California threaten to leave New York behind in the race toward new technologies involving stem cell research" (Krueger 2006). She further argued, "When our neighbors, friends, and family members with debilitating diseases look to us for assistance, we must be able to say that we have done everything possible to help them" (Krueger 2006).

In these narratives, New York is in a stem cell arms race with California—and may lose the race, to the great detriment of suffering New Yorkers who would otherwise benefit from potential cures. Republican stonewalling on her bill is transformed into not just a political problem but also an economic and moral problem in light of the importance of stem cell research in the state. Much like the policy narrative created by Ortiz and Runner in California, Krueger's policy story is one in which the government has a moral responsibility to promote cures-centered research, as well protect individuals involved in research, implicitly assuming that individuals donating eggs for research should have the benefit of oversight (and regulations) other than that required by egg donors in reproductive settings, which do not necessitate the same protective role by the state.

REGULATING INDIVIDUAL BEHAVIOR: THE MORAL RESPONSIBILITY OF THE STATE IN ARIZONA AND LOUISIANA

Instead of describing the state as having a moral duty to promote scientific research and innovation while installing ethical protocols to protect research participants, stakeholders in Arizona and Louisiana envisioned a different moral duty. Representative Robert Stump argued that it was precisely the role of the state to intervene in difficult moral questions about egg donation, that "it's a cliché to talk about legislating morality, because that is what we do everyday" (*Washington Journal* 2006). Stump proposed that banning egg donation was justified because policymaking is always rooted in morality—and that to ignore that fact was to ignore what in his view is an essential function of government. In contrast to the narratives about morality, government, egg donation, and research found in other cases, Stump was creating a set of stakeholders, moral obligations, and social constructions of egg donation distinctly different from what is evident in other cases. Senator Broome viewed these issues as part of the greater context of her role, stating that to be a "legislator is to regulate behavior," and that her position as a pro-life Democrat was a "moral position ... a position of righteousness" (Louisiana Right to Life 2012). For these legislators, the moral duty of the state was to regulate the individual's behavior, not to promote the larger goals of scientific innovation and research. Morality is deployed differently in these four cases. In the setting of research regulation, the state must step in to provide oversight, ultimately promoting stem cell development. Ethical oversight of research, through banning compensation for egg donation, is a crucial role for the state in partnership with state-funded research. In contrast, moral leadership in Arizona and Louisiana is explicitly defined as legislating individual morality—what an individual can and cannot do according to a prescribed set of rules—in order to achieve greater ethical goals.

CONCLUSION

The politics of egg donation at the state level has long puzzled scholars for its unique and seemingly aberrant patterns of regulation. As stated earlier in this book, norms of gender are deeply important to how stakeholders think about egg donation in the US: different definitions of what is "natural" and conventional in reproduction and research shape how stakeholders define, debate, and create policy solutions to regulate egg donation. How stakeholders frame egg donation relies on the dual logics of body and morality politics: as demonstrated in California, New York, Arizona, and Louisiana, both frameworks work simultaneously (and in complex ways) to define, delineate deliberation of, and determine policy solutions to the problems associated with egg donation. The differences in framing that emerge reflect the powerful influence of assumptions about and values assigned to gender, particularly in how egg donors are defined as the target of the legislation and in the role of the state in regulating egg donation for research and reproduction. Additionally, feminist rhetoric— and the co-optation of feminist rhetoric by social conservatives from both the Republican Party and Democratic Party—is an important part of framing the story around the themes used in egg donation politics: gender and agency, vulnerability, and the moral duty of the state.

In California and New York, where bills targeted compensation for egg donation for state-funded research, stakeholder narratives consistently de-gendered egg donors. In these narratives, femininity is strongly associated with reproduction, even when assisted by egg donation. If egg donation is not used for reproductive purposes, then the link between femininity and egg donation is broken—and egg donors themselves are no longer attached to notions of femininity. In this context, stakeholders framed women as research subjects. By de-gendering women who donated eggs for research, stakeholders were able to create a dichotomy: unlike egg donation in the lucrative, compensated fertility industries in California and New York, egg donation for research could possibly be regulated by the state. Stakeholders consistently offered a narrative in which research subjects were passive participants in research and had vulnerabilities particular to stem cell research. Reflecting the language of individual risk in experimental medical research, stakeholders carved out a definition of vulnerability that hinged on the de-gendered research subject and possible exploitation in stem cell science development in violation of the norms of research ethics. To solve these problems associated with the vulnerability of research subjects in stem cell research, a motley crew of feminist, medical, professional, and religious advocates in California and New York actively argued for a ban on compensation for egg donation for research. Legislators and other stakeholders created policy solutions, framed as part of the moral responsibility of the state, to protect the integrity of stem cell research.

What results from this framing process is that conventional understandings of body politics are ignored: if femininity is delinked from reproduction, than state regulation doesn't have to follow other patterns of controlling and regulating women's reproductive capacities. Instead, we see a distinct kind of morality politics predominating in California and New York, where the moral duty of the state to protect society (particularly vulnerable research subjects) and promote science justifies state regulation of egg donation.

While the same three themes of gender and agency, vulnerability, and the moral responsibility of the state emerge in analyses of Arizona and Louisiana, the values and assumptions are distinct in these cases—because these states were limiting egg donation for reproduction and research. Stakeholders in Arizona and Louisiana defined egg donors as über-gendered, and they often used historically feminist frames to define egg donation: egg donors are first and foremost women defined by biological and reproductive difference via their eggs. As femininity is connected to reproduction across these cases, all possible reproductive materials are inextricably tied to a function of women—eggs are not meant for research because they are solely meant for reproduction; any threat to women's bodies is a threat to their reproductive health. Using feminist frames of women-centered well-being and health, conservative lawmakers further limited access to egg donation by consumers. As noted in the introduction, this co-optation of feminist rhetoric about egg donation was seen as a way to successfully change hearts and minds about egg donation. Like the women-centered, protectionist rhetoric used by Republican women and men in antiabortion policy during the late 1990s and the first decade of the twenty-first century, language used by lawmakers like Representative Stump was designed to put women at the center of egg donation policy—but it rendered women as passive objects needing protection (Reingold et al. 2015, Schreiber 2008, Deckman 2012). Political and policy actors in Arizona and Louisiana framed women as passive objects acted upon by larger, immoral forces in reproduction and research. Women are especially vulnerable *because* they are women, and their bodies and biological difference are easily exploitable. Adding to this vulnerability was age and class; stakeholders painted college-aged and poor women as especially susceptible to exploitation. With these narratives about compensation and egg donation, socially conservative stakeholders in

Arizona and Louisiana created a peculiar coalition, co-opting feminist language that described women's health and pledging partnership with women's groups to achieve their policy objective: bans on compensation for egg donation. Explicitly, stakeholders in Arizona and Louisiana saw a conservative body politics as the dominant way of understanding egg donation: in order to produce the kinds of reproduction that the state sees as morally acceptable, egg donation had to be tightly regulated—particularly to prevent the use of women's reproductive materials for nonreproductive purposes. Moreover, stakeholders recognized that some women might be using their reproductive materials improperly, or were subject to exploitation and coercion at the hands of others. Mixed with the explicit logic of body politics are the ways those stakeholders in Arizona and Louisiana used morality politics language in order to discuss solutions for the perceived problems with egg donation: it was the moral duty of the state to regulate individuals' behavior for a more ethical state culture. Debating in terms of first principles, stakeholders used the highly feminized and differentiated category of women, and women's vulnerability, as justification for state laws regulating egg donation.

These four cases reveal fascinating patterns in the regulation of egg donation at the state level. Though all four states used the dual frameworks of body politics and morality politics, stakeholders' interpretation of egg donation shifted the logic of egg donation policy: commonly connecting femininity to reproduction, California and New York rejected a body politics framework, while Arizona and Louisiana actively embraced the logic of the state regulating reproduction, bodily labor, and gender. While all four states also engaged in morality politics, the interpretation of the moral duty of the state is quite distinct in these cases: whereas in some states, the moral duty of the state is to promote cures through stem cell research, in other states it is the ethical impetus of the state to regulate individual behavior in egg donation markets. This blending of body politics and morality politics yielded strange alliances in all the cases, violating commonly held assumptions about who promotes women's health, scientific innovation, and democratic oversight—and it further reinforced the perception that egg donation for reproduction and for research exist in conceptually different spheres. In this analysis, we see the development of the two-tiered system of egg donation politics and policy at the state level: driven by certain values and by assumptions about gender, vulnerability, and the role of the state, body politics and morality politics contour the politics of egg donation at the state level—where egg donation for reproduction and research is alternatively shaped by stratified reproduction and by considerations of the moral responsibility of the state.

CHAPTER FOUR

Toward a New Gendered Partisanship

Egg Donation Politics in the States

In a conversation recorded in 1995, Republican House member Ileana Ros-Lehtinen reflected on the ways that reproductive issues often push Democratic and Republican women apart: "I think [women in Congress] have a common bond. Unfortunately, we have not paid enough attention to what unites us, and we tend to dwell on what divides us, like abortion or funding for controversial health programs.... But there are a lot of issues that we could unite and rally around, and we don't seem to pay enough attention to those family-type issues" (quoted in Carroll 2000). While abortion and other controversial health issues have divided political parties in the US for more than three decades, Ros-Lehtinen argues that these issues obscure the "family" issues that partisan women can agree on. Infertility, and treatments for infertility like egg donation, hit this sweet spot: although egg donation has historically provoked moral outrage and ethical concern, the explosion of consumer use of egg donation since the mid-1990s has normalized what was once an experimental procedure. If Ros-Lehtinen is correct in her argument—that partisan women *can* unite on family-friendly issues—how do women in politics act in unison, or as partisan women, in leadership and agenda-setting with respect to the politics of egg donation?

In this chapter, I explore and analyze the role of partisan women in agenda-setting and leadership in relation to the politics of egg donation at the state level. Given the ways that reproductive health, medicine, and family have been strongly associated with leadership and representation by female legislators in US politics, particularly Democratic women, I explain and analyze the diverse and complex roles of women in politics, specifically in egg donation politics and policymaking. Egg donation for reproduction is considered a "natural" choice for expanding one's family in a framework of body politics, in contrast with the ways that egg donation for research prompts debates over fundamental moral principles, as well as acts as an impetus for the moral action of individuals and/or governments. Bringing together research on partisan women in state legislatures, and the theoretical frameworks discussed in this book—that egg donation in the context of reproduction is framed as "natural," and that egg donation in the context of research is framed as "unnatural"—I examine these dynamics at the state level. Reflecting on the competing explanations for the politics of egg donation in body and morality politics, I first analyze the reasons why egg donation policy is created at the state level, and then analyze how partisan women play important and diverse roles in egg donation politics and policymaking. This chapter provides the first comprehensive study of egg donation politics at the state level over time (1995–2010), and it connects the divergent policy strategies related to egg donation for reproduction and research to the diverse and varied roles of partisan women in state politics.

EGG DONATION LAWS IN THE STATES

The legislative and policy context of egg donation across the states is a deeply understudied aspect of the US system of egg donation. As explained in previous chapters, there is a common belief that the US has no policy governing egg donation. Conventional wisdom states that markets and commercial interests govern egg donation in the US, in a system that is unlike the highly regulated policies that restrict egg donation elsewhere in North America and in Europe and Australia. However, this common belief obscures the ways that the politics of egg donation are in fact vibrant, if different, in the US. While not as robust as federal or unitary policies in comparative nations, state-level egg donation statutes provide important guidance to and governance over egg donors, intended parents, donor-conceived children, and medical practices in the US and have done so since the 1980s. Von Hagel (2014) observes that not only do over half of the US states have statutes governing egg donation, but these statutes are also diverse in content and expansive in the aspects of egg donation they cover. State statutes cover clinical ethics and consumer-patient protections for donors and intended parents alike. The laws govern egg donation practices by, among other ways, setting limits on compensation for donors and on modes of advertising, as well as by constraining donor recruitment. For example, the state of Connecticut has laws on the books that require informed consent, set limits on egg donor compensation and recruitment, and require that information be provided to donors about what will happen to their eggs after they are donated. They shield donors from unwanted parental obligations and clarify the legal parentage of intended mothers and fathers. Sixteen states—including North Dakota, Washington, Texas, and Colorado—protect donors from legal responsibility for donor-conceived children. Other states, like Massachusetts and New Jersey, limit the use of eggs and sperm posthumously, protecting donors (or partners) through limits on how eggs can be used after they are procured. Historically, egg donors and intended parents have been protected under the Uniform Parentage Acts, which established legal parentage, first for adopted children (in 1973), then for donor-conceived children (in 2002). The two legislative acts not only create legal definitions of the relationships between parents and their donor-conceived children but also spell out the ways that parental custody and inheritance work in the case of donor-conceived children, their parents, and donors. Table 4 illustrates the state statutory protections for egg donation for reproduction and research.

This statutory context illuminates the state laws that govern egg donation, refuting the conventional idea that the US system lacks any kind of regulation of egg donation. However, a list of state laws tells us only a partial story: egg donation statutes describe the regulations in place regarding egg donation but cannot tell us the politics behind these policies—particularly what political, economic, and gender forces are at play in the politics of egg donation. Policies on egg donation for reproduction and research reflect these stratified realities regarding reproduction and access to technologies (Heidt-Forsythe 2016, Benjamin 2013, Thompson 2013). At the same time, egg donation laws are created in a context of discourse and debates dominated by morality politics frames, as discussed in the cases of four states in chapter 3.

These dual contexts of body politics and morality politics contour the politics of egg donation. While gender framing is a major component of the ways that body politics and morality politics shape the overall regulatory logic of egg donation, there

TABLE 4

State Regulations

Egg Donors

Donor: Informed Consent	Donor: Compensation	Donor: Parental Rights	Donor: Disposition Limits	Donor: Disposition Informed Consent[i]	Research: Limits on Egg Donation / Egg Donors
AZ	AZ	AL	CA	CA	AZ
CA	CA†	AR	LA	CT	CA
CT	CT	CO	MD	FL	CT
IL	IN	CT		MA	IL
NY	LA	DE		MD	IN
	MA	FL		ND	MA
	MD	ID		NJ	MD
	NY	MN			VA
		ND			
		NM			
		OK			
		TX			
		UT			
		VA			
		WA			
		WY			

DATA sources: Von Hagel 2014, NCSL 2016.

† States that prohibit compensation in research settings but allow for limited reimbursement of medical costs, transportation, and other required activities.

[i] This category includes information requirements for egg donors.

has been scant attention to the ways that the gender and partisanship of stakeholders, particularly women in state legislative institutions, play important roles in policymaking on reproductive technology issues. Moving from the fine-grained examination of framing egg donation in chapters 2 and 3, in this chapter I engage with the broader picture of aggregate politics and policy, connecting body politics, morality politics, and gendered partisanship to egg donation governance in multiple states. Returning to Representative Ros-Lehtinen's contention that family issues could unite women in politics, I investigate in this chapter how gendered leadership and agenda-setting in egg donation policy interacts with body politics and morality politics to create a system of regulation of donor behavior, the disposition of donated eggs, and parental rights—the major categories of egg donation politics and policy in the US.

THE AIMS AND EFFECTS OF EGG DONATION POLICY

Two understudied components of egg donation legislation are the aims and effects of bills about egg donation. While there has been attention to the ways that the US regulatory system is unique in its approach to reproductive technologies, there has been little analysis of the aims and intent of regulation in the US. In what ways does egg donation policy enable, or limit, the act of and markets in egg donation? Qualitative evidence provides some clues about the complexity of an answer to this question. As demonstrated in chapter 3, egg donation policymaking can have multiple intended effects: in the cases of Arizona and Louisiana, legislation of compensation in the context of reproduction was intended to limit egg donation and monetary exchanges; in California and New York, legislation limiting compensation was mixed in its intent to limit egg donation for research. This is evidence that political partnerships between strange bedfellows can be created in the politics of egg donation, as stakeholders may work together to create a single piece of egg donation legislation for different ideological ends.

On one hand, any regulation or law limits consumers', donors', and medical professionals' participation in egg donation for reproduction and research. Without any laws limiting their ability to buy and sell human eggs, consumers, donors, and doctors could take advantage of a laissez-faire market in human eggs, where access, compensation, and participation would be free of any rules and parameters. In conventional wisdom, the Wild West of egg donation in the US operates this way, although legislative activity concerning egg donation between 1995 and 2010 tells a different story.

Egg donation policymaking is distinct from other reproductive policies, particularly abortion policy: in the US, policies that attempt to limit access to abortion services, facilities, and information stand in contrast with proabortion access policies that explicitly protect individual access to abortion services, information, and support (Kreitzer 2015). Egg donation policies work differently: while regulations on egg donation constrain purely free markets in human eggs, some of these policy categories may end up ultimately benefiting consumers, donors, and medical professionals alike (Von Hagel 2014). Policies may benefit these stakeholders by ensuring safe, healthy, and equitable experiences in egg donation—protecting donors and consumers in medical procedures, commercial exchanges, and kinship arrangements. However, policies can also possibly constrain stakeholders, limiting their bodily autonomy, economic freedoms, and ability to make independent choices about their families. In the context of research, regulations on egg donation can either support ethical research or try to stymie the development of controversial science. Unlike other reproductive policy examples, regulation of egg donation may limit some stakeholders and enable others to participate in reproduction and research—which is one reason why strange ideological partnerships have historically been a part of the politics of egg donation (Thompson 2005, 2013, Benjamin 2013).

Considering a counterfactual world without egg donation regulations may be helpful in illuminating the mixed, complex nature of egg donation politics. Unregulated egg donation could be problematic for consumers: without regulations, consumers could be caught without financial means to pay for infertility treatments, stripped of custody of donor-conceived children, or barred from exercising reproductive autonomy in light of a spouse's death or a divorce. Without egg donation rules for donors, potential and active donors could have their health and bodily autonomy put in danger by unregulated clinics and could find that they are not given full information about the donation procedure (Spar 2006). Donors' right to privacy and autonomy over the use of their cells could be put into question. A lack of rules defining legal parentage could also thrust egg donors into a position of legal custody over children conceived with their eggs. Medical professionals would also be at risk in an unregulated system: without rules and policies, medical procedures could become less safe, while medical professionals themselves could become more vulnerable to litigation; moreover, given the complex network of medical professionals who work together in highly choreographed egg donation procedures, the process could become less efficient for their customers (Thompson 2005). The only federal law that governs egg donation—the Fertility Clinic Success Rate and Certification Act of 1992—was passed in response to consumer concerns about the untrustworthy nature of fertility clinics' success-rate reporting. Although there are strong arguments for deregulation of egg donation markets, allowing the free and efficient coordination of consumers, donors, and medical professionals (e.g., Thompson 2005), the benefits of regulations and policy related to egg donation may actually outweigh the disadvantages of the limits that such policy places on free markets in egg donation (Von Hagel 2014).

EGG DONATION BILLS, 1995–2010

Examining legislation—proposed bills and passed laws—gives richer insight into the politics of egg donation that may be overlooked if one is simply observing and analyzing entrenched law. Legislative activity on an issue helps us understand why policies may succeed or fail across the US, clarifying in particular what issues are important to legislators, how they represent those issues, and ultimately how those issues get passed (or not) into statutory law, governing the social, political, and economic lives of their constituents. If norms of gender (in a system of body politics and morality politics) inform egg donation, then policies examining the effect of body and morality politics variables on egg donation legislation can verify this claim. Breaking down body and morality politics into state-level characteristics, and analyzing the effects of these attributes on policymaking regarding egg donation in the aggregate, illuminates why the US approach is unique.

The mid-1990s and the first decade of the twenty-first century saw an exponential rise in the diagnosis and treatment of infertility and involuntary childlessness; this period is also important because it witnessed the first successful cloning of an animal, as well as a rise in the development of stem cell research science. These trends are important because they both relied on donated eggs: as more individuals and couples sought medical treatment, there was a sharp increase in demand for donor eggs. At the same time, the development of somatic cell nuclear transfer increasingly relied on a (small) pool of procured eggs for expanding research sectors (Almeling 2011, Thompson 2013). During this period, there was an increase in public awareness (and use) of egg donation, increased governmental surveillance of the commercial practices of egg donation, and rapidly expanding numbers of clinics and research centers using donated eggs for reproduction and research, respectively.

The rise of consumer use of egg donation is connected to increased legislative attention to the topic of egg donation, as well as to increased political activity on the topic. Before 1995, however, legislation that focused solely on egg donation was fairly uncommon. More common was legislation that targeted insurance coverage of infertility and legal parentage laws governing children conceived through assisted reproductive technologies, not just egg donation (such as the Uniform Parentage Law revisions that were implemented across the states). Between 1989 and 1994, where data is available, only seven states introduced bills to regulate any part of egg donation.[1] These bills entailed either donor compensation, informed consent, or disposition limits, a total of four donor-related (disposition, informed consent, or compensation) bills and eleven parental rights bills. Despite the relatively high number of parental rights bills during this period, these bills covered not just egg donors but also sperm donors and intended parents. Owing to the relative rarity of legislative action on egg donation before the mid-1990s, as well as the 1995 implementation of the Fertility Clinic Success Rate and Certification Act of 1992,[2] this chapter examines a period of increased attention to, and legislative activity related to, egg donation at the state level, between 1995 and 2010.

To capture the increased level of politics related to egg donation in the US from 1995 to 2010, this analysis addresses state-level bills introduced during this period that were related to egg donation for reproduction and research. These bills cover four major categories: donor, disposition, parental rights, and commercial practices. Donor bills include *informed consent* bills, which require egg donors to give permission to clinics to procure eggs once they have read a description of risks and possible consequences of egg donation; limits on the amount of *compensation* a donor may receive from egg procurement; and *parental rights* restrictions, which indicate that egg donors are not the legal mothers of donor-conceived children and do not have legal responsibility for donor-conceived children in pregnancy or after they are born.

The next category, disposition, refers to what happens to eggs after they are donated—how they can be used or how they must be disposed of. Disposition bills include *informed consent* bills, which, again, require donors to give permission for how their eggs may be used by third-party fertility clinics in the future. Disposition bills also may enforce *limits* on how the eggs many be used in the future. For example, they specify whether the eggs may be used posthumously and how many families may receive eggs from a single donor.

In the third category, *parental rights* bills ensure that intended parents are the legal custodians of donor-conceived children.[3] This type of policy is particularly important in the context of egg donation, as many states have historically defined legal parenthood through biological motherhood; while adoption law has clarified the legal status of adopted children, these laws can be unclear for donor-conceived children. Although a set of Uniform Parentage Acts was passed by states to clarify the legal parentage of donor-conceived children, these laws are not universal. As a result, states have stepped in to address questions of legal parentage of egg-donor-conceived children, clarifying that the donor-conceived child's mother, rather than the egg donor, is the intended mother.

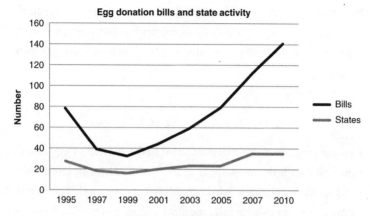

Figure 1. Egg donation bills and state activity, 1995–2010.

The final category of legislation is *research*, where bills regulate the use of donated eggs in cloning and stem cell research only.[4] As discussed in chapter 3, states have stepped forward to regulate their growing stem cell research industries; many states treat research oversight as distinct from reproductive oversight. Bills in this category cover three major themes: restrictions on cloning research, bans on chimeras,[5] and limits on funding for somatic cell nuclear transfer and/or research on human embryonic stem cell lines that involves human eggs. Twenty-four states introduced at least one bill about research between 1995 and 2010.

Forty-nine states have introduced legislation regarding some aspect of egg donation practices in reproduction or research,[6] for a total of 808 bills introduced in state legislatures between 1995 and 2015. In patterns of state policymaking, it is common to see states introduce bills to revise egg donation policies that have been put in place; for example, states have passed parentage bills and then revised them in later bills (Von Hagel 2014, Heidt-Forsythe 2013). Figure 1 illustrates how the number of bills proposed each year increased over time, as did the number of states that proposed an egg donation bill between the years 1995 and 2010.[7] On average, states introduced at least one bill by 2003.

THEORIES AND EXPECTATIONS

Considering the complexity attached to the politics of egg donation—particularly the ways that regulation can simultaneously limit some stakeholders while enabling others—in this chapter I examine the state-level bills regulating donor behavior, disposition, parental rights, and research, and the bills' potentially different outcomes. In bills regulating donor behavior (through informed consent, compensation, and parental responsibilities), one can expect the policies to be aimed to protect donors themselves. Stakeholders, as evidenced in previous chapters, argued that women needed state intervention to guard against commercial and research exploitation, financial inducement, and undue dangers to women's health. While stakeholders have different reasons for advocating legislation or arguing against it, the politics at play reflect the intervention of the state in issues of gender, reproduction, and bodily autonomy—all issues relevant to body politics. Given the findings in chapter 3, however, we may expect morality politics to play a lesser role in such bills.

In contrast, bills that target the disposition of donor eggs speak to what happens to eggs after they are donated for reproduction and research. Difficult questions about the importance of informed consent, and legal limits on donated eggs, are addressed in disposition bills. Because these bills reflect their proponents' values and beliefs about bodies and their parts, we may expect morality politics to play a more important role in the production of disposition bills.

Policies governing parental rights and responsibilities may be driven by a different logic than other kinds of egg donation bills. These bills describe, clarify, and legalize new and emerging forms of parenthood in establishing legal kinship between donors, intended parents, and donor-conceived children. Parental policies protect vulnerable individuals who go unrecognized by traditional norms of parenthood (particularly lesbian, gay, queer, and single parents) in the context of egg donation. The state's role in defining and protecting parents fits into a framework of body politics, where intervention of the state reinforces certain ideologies about gender, sexuality, reproduction, and kinship. Given the importance of traditional family structures to debates in morality politics—as evidenced by language and debates discussed in chapter 3—we may expect this category of egg donation to be influenced in some ways by morality politics.

Finally, in line with the role of debates about moral and ethical issues in past scholarship on stem cell research and cloning, we may expect morality characteristics to play a positive and influential role in predicting legislation about research. Since in many cases these issues are clearly delineated from reproduction, morality characteristics variables, rather than body politics variables, will most likely have a stronger role in determining agenda-setting in relation to research issues.

Considering the mixed political forces at work in egg donation, table 5 illustrates the expected relationships between body politics variables, morality politics variables, and egg donation policy categories.

TABLE 5

Morality Politics, Body Politics, and Egg Donation Bills

Policy Area	Restrict or Enable?	Morality or Body Politics?
Donor Behavior	Restrict	Mixed effects
Disposition	Restrict	Body politics
Parental Rights	Enable	Mixed effects
Research	Restrict	Morality politics

BODY POLITICS AND EGG DONATION POLICIES

Previous studies have demonstrated the important linkages between the presence of women in political and economic spheres and body politics issues in the US. As women enter spheres formerly inhabited only by men, "private" matters of reproduction and regulation transform into matters of public concern. This is a generally positive influence; historically, women in the public sphere have liberalized attitudes and policies toward a battery of reproductive issues, from pregnancy to abortion. Moreover, the presence of women in public life has often highlighted the inequalities experienced by women in the context of reproduction and family formation. Increased representation of women in the political sphere—particularly Democratic women—is associated with the representation of policies that increase access to reproductive health technologies like abortion and contraception (e.g., Wolbrecht 2000). The presence of more women in the social and economic spheres is similarly associated with reproductive policies that allow women to delay marriage and childbirth, such as abortion (Mooney and Lee 1995). Multiple studies have shown that women from many walks of life are increasingly delaying pregnancy and childbirth, increasing the demand for maternal-age-related infertility services like egg donation (e.g., Mamo 2008, Thompson 2005, Markens 2007, Traister 2016).

There is considerable evidence that the presence of women in legislatures at the national and state levels has substantial impact on the type of bills that are proposed and debated (Wolbrecht 2000). Female legislators are more likely to introduce and cosponsor legislation that enables reproductive choices (Osborn 2012, Wolbrecht 2000). Not all women in state legislatures act the same: party identification creates variance in how women in state legislatures represent reproductive issues. Although Democratic and Republican women are quite different in how they lead, set agendas, and represent issues like abortion and contraception, this analysis indicates that Representative Ileana Ros-Lehtinen may in fact be correct: that women across the aisle will work together in relation to egg donation. In this analysis, the *percentage of Democratic female legislators* in each state legislature by year and the *percentage of Republican female legislators* in each state legislature by year are tested. Given the argument that women in state legislatures can collaborate on issues regarding family formation—for Democratic women, such issues play to their base, while Republican women may frame the issue as pronatal—there is likely to be a positive association between the presence of women in political spheres and state intervention in egg donation, reflecting the logic of body politics. Republican women may be more active on egg donation issues than on other reproductive issues, as noted in chapter 3. Republican women in states like Arizona, Maryland, Michigan, and North Dakota have been cosponsors of egg donation legislation and have been crucial to the development of policies related to egg donation for reproduction and research. Politically, the presence of women in legislatures is associated with fewer reproductive limitations; in this category of body politics variables, we may expect *reproductive restrictions* to play a negative role in the presence of egg donation policies.

If body politics are driving egg donation politics in the US, then one may expect to see a parallel between the presence of women in economic spheres and a particular type of egg donation policy, reflecting the ways that the intervention of the state determines who can and cannot access reproductive technologies in a body politics framework. Women in the workforce have been a significant predictor of the presence of reproductive policies such as access to contraception and abortion (Mooney and Lee 1995). As the delay of childbearing owing to workforce participation is an important reason why women and men turn to reproductive technologies for reproduction, I would expect the increased *percentage of women in the workforce* to be positively associated with the introduction of egg donation bills that enable safe, healthy, and equitable use of egg donation. All of these variables—the *percentage of Democratic female legislators* in state legislatures, the *percentage of Republican female legislators* in state legislatures, *reproductive restrictions,* and the *percentage of women in the workforce*—are crucial to a body politics framework, as they directly influence the ways the state intervenes in questions of gender, reproduction, and uses of the body, and they can significantly alter policy outcomes. These variables should have a positive effect on donor behavior and parental rights, as these policies may be most affected by body politics.

MORALITY POLITICS AND EGG DONATION POLICIES

Morality politics have a strong role in egg donation, as evidenced by the diverse interpretations of the moral responsibility of the state toward egg donors in the four cases discussed in chapters 2 and 3. Moral concerns about life, marriage, and the definition of family enter into a debate over egg donation; ethical arguments about state intervention in reproduction and research have been an important part of the political landscape regarding egg donation since the late 1990s (Nisbet et al. 2003). To test the role of morality politics in state governance, two measures capture the ways that state culture and citizen religiosity shape the emergence of morality politics.

The first determinant, *moralist* culture, is from Elazar's (1966, 1980) study of state cultures. I have coded each state for the presence of a moralist political culture as defined in Elazar's study.[8] In *moralist* state cultures, the government is expected to protect the public good and promote public welfare; I would expect *moralist* states, compared to states with nonmoralist cultures, to be enthusiastic about intervening in ethical issues like egg donation.

The second variable, the *percentage of Christians,* reflects the importance of fundamental moral values related to religious belief, specifically a Christian belief that values specific definitions of life, family, and intimate relations. The percentage of a state's population that identifies as Christian affects legislation about controversial issues that figure in the faith's moral debates about life, personhood, and family (Meier 1994). Christian religiosity is an important indicator in studies of various morality policies connected to reproduction and kinship, such as abortion and gay rights (Mooney and Lee 1995, Rose 2006, Mucciaroni 2011). I expect higher *percentages of Christians* to be associated with egg donation bills that restrict the use of egg donation for reproduction and research. The morality politics variables— *moralist* state culture and *percentage of Christians*—should have a positive effect on bills that concern egg donation disposition.

ECONOMIC AND STATE CONTEXT VARIABLES

Other variables outside of body and morality politics may influence the likelihood that a state will introduce a bill on egg donation. These variables are connected to a state's partisan context and economic interests. Democratic control of government increases the likelihood that reproductive issues, as well as broader women's health issues, make it onto the legislative agenda (Aldrich and Rohde 2001, Tolbert and Steuernagel 2001, Swers 2016). To account for the expected positive relationships between party and egg donation, I use the measure *unified Democratic government* to capture the presence of Democratic control of both houses in the legislature from Carl Klarner (2015) and the annual *Book of States* between 1995 and 2010. Policy scholars highlight the importance of intergovernmental influence, also known as diffusion—especially for legislation that can economically benefit a state (Berry and Berry 1990). *Diffusion* is defined as the influence of states on neighboring or like states in the proposal and passage of public policy (Walker 1969). Recent studies have shown, however, that the learning-and-emulation effect of state neighbors is not as strong regarding legislation about morality issues (Karch 2007). Other studies of morality policies regarding sex and reproduction reinforce the idea that diffusion of policy from neighboring states may not increase legislative activity (Sharp 2005), but that states may instead look to "like" states—those states that are similar in state culture, innovation, and ideology. To measure the influence of diffusion, I employ *emulate proposal*, which is calculated as the percentage of states neighboring a given state that proposed, or had in place, any egg donation legislation in the previous year. It is likely that geographical diffusion effects will not have a significant impact on the chances egg donation will be put on the agenda.

Attention has been paid to the ways that fiscal interests shape public perceptions of reproductive technology use (Markens 2007, Thompson 2005). A measure of industry strength is the number of *clinics* per state per year per hundred thousand residents as reported by the Centers for Disease Control, an agency that has surveilled clinics since 1995. Another important measure of reproductive technologies is the number of individuals seeking fertility treatment (Thompson 2005). Finally, because economic resources influence access and use of reproductive technology, I accounted for the *median income* for each state (Markens 2007, Roberts 2009). Income is important owing to the high cost of egg donation (among other treatments) in fertility medicine, which makes the technologies often unreachable for those who are not insured (or, alternatively, whose insurance companies do not pay for fertility services) and cannot pay thousands of dollars for an ovum. For a description of all variables in this analysis, please see appendix 2.

METHODS AND MODELING STRATEGY

I use event history analysis in this chapter to clarify how body politics, morality politics, and economic variables affected egg donation policymaking between 1995 and 2010. Event history analysis of policymaking has been used extensively in political science to explain the importance of the passage of time when analyzing public policy[9]—particularly for bills introduced and passed at the state level (Berry and Berry 1990, 1992, Mooney and Lee 1995, Box-Steffensmeier and Jones 1997). Event history analysis is a highly regarded method for studying public policies such as those concerning egg donation, as the method allows researchers to see how time-varying *and* time-independent variables affect policies introduced over a long period of time, a clear advantage over other statistical methods, such as multiple regression. Moreover, our information about egg donation policy is incomplete: because there is only limited archival data on bills about egg donation, event history analysis allows the researcher to account for missing and incomplete data.[10] Event history analysis is ultimately a flexible method, allowing the researcher to understand how variables representing body politics, morality politics, and state context may increase or decrease the probability of bill introduction over a period of fifteen years.[11] The unit of analysis is state/year among forty-nine states—totaling 808 bill introductions in the categories of donor behavior, disposition, and parental rights. To discover how body politics variables, morality politics variables, and state context variables affect the introduction of egg donation bills, this analysis begins by observing all state bill introductions, beginning in 1995 and ending in 2010.[12] In this analysis, we look for the significant predictors that increase or decrease the chances that any bill about egg donation will be introduced during this period. To illuminate the different factors at work in egg donation legislation, this analysis uses multilevel modeling of event history analyses of the data to examine, first, all bills about egg donation, and then donor behavior bills, disposition bills, and parental rights bills separately. These models not only allow us to understand the factors at play in the politics of egg donation overall but also allow us to examine the political, social, and economic nuances that influence individual categories of policy. For a description of data collection, see appendix 3.

BODY POLITICS, MORALITY POLITICS, AND
THE ROLE OF WOMEN IN POLITICS

Looking at all bills that target some aspect of egg donation, this analysis finds broad support for the idea that relationships exist between egg donation legislation and both morality politics and body politics (particularly the role of women in political and economic life). In table 6, the analysis of fifteen years of legislation in forty-nine states demonstrates that within morality politics, a higher *percentage of Christians* slightly increases the chances that any kind of egg donation bill will be introduced. However, that a state is *moralist* has no effect on egg donation bills as an entire category. Despite the many conventional assumptions that religiosity is connected to the regulation of reproductive technologies, it has only a small effect on egg donation bills overall.

The presence of women in the public sphere—and their access to reproductive liberties—makes much greater difference in the politics of egg donation. As predicted, the *percentage of women in the workforce* is a significant influence in increasing the chances of an egg donation bill. Owing to the growing demands of education and career on women, this positive relationship is not surprising; if egg donation legislation increases the access to, safety of, and legality of egg donation, then demand for legislation would naturally increase with the demands for reproductive technology by working women.

Women in the political sphere are also significant in the introduction of egg donation bills overall. Increased numbers of *Democratic* women in state legislatures improve the chances that a state will have some kind of politics related to egg donation. As Democratic women are policy leaders in women's health care issues (particularly reproductive issues), such a relationship fits

TABLE 6

Morality and Body Politics Effects on Agenda-Setting, 1995–2010
All Egg Donation

Covariates	All Egg Donation[†]
Morality	
Moralist	−.442 (.173)
Percentage Christian	.034 (.007)***
Body Politics	
% Democratic Women in Legislature	.025 (.015)**
% GOP Women in Legislature	.029 (.018)
% Women in the Workforce	.039 (.019)**
Reproductive Restrictions	−.099 (.021)***
State Context	
Clinics per 100,000	.098 (.052)*
Median Income	−.000 (.000)***
Unified Democratic Government	−.224 (.215)
Diffusion	−.004 (.000)
Observations	643
Events	248
Wald Chi	.000
Log Pseudo-likelihood	−1284.6992
Single-Tailed Tests,	

† Estimated coefficients.
* p<.10, ** p<.01, ***p<.001

into existing scholarship on partisanship, gender, and reproductive policy. Additionally, states that are more permissive regarding *reproduction*—allowing women to more freely access reproductive services like contraception and abortion—are also more likely to have policies related to egg donation during this period.

Overall, some aspects of the economic side of egg donation are relevant to state legislation during this period: as the number of fertility *clinics* in a state rises, there is a greater chance that a legislator will introduce a bill on some aspect of egg donation. In this broad measure, we see the dual roles of morality and body politics—with a positive, if expected, role of Democratic women in agenda-setting regarding the broad category of egg donation.

Breaking down egg donation policy into subcategories is necessary to understand the politics involved. As discussed earlier in this chapter, the politics at play concerning different topics within egg donation—such as bills that target egg donors, legislation that seeks to regulate how to dispose of eggs after they have been donated, and parental rights—may vary. In table 7, egg donation is broken down further into four different categories: bills that target donor behavior (informed consent, compensation, and parental responsibilities), disposition of eggs after they have been donated (limits and informed consent), parental rights (of the intended parents and the egg donor), and research.

DONOR BEHAVIOR

Donor behavior in reproduction and research can be regulated in three major ways. First, egg donors may be required to read and sign informed-consent forms, which outline the risks and benefits of donation for reproduction and/or research. Second, donors may be restricted in the kinds of compensation they receive. As described in chapters 2 and 3, legislators throughout this period debated the positive and negative ways that a monetary exchange affects egg donors. Third, egg donors are relieved of maternal responsibilities, and legal parentage of donor-conceived children,

TABLE 7

Morality and Body Politics Effects on Agenda-Setting, 1995–2010 Donor Behavior, Disposition, Parentage, and Research

Covariates	Donor Behavior	Disposition Limits	Disposition Informed Consent	Parentage	Research
Morality					
Moralist	−.843 (.204)*	.367 (.253)	−.408 (.310)	−.682 (.251)***	−.832 (.260)***
Percentage Christian	.061 (.008)***	−.027 (.013)*	−.006 (.012)	.030 (.010)***	−.018 (.012)
Body Politics					
% Democratic Women in Legislature	.027 (.017)	.106 (.025)***	−.002 (.024)	.053 (.021)***	.007 (.020)
% GOP Women in Legislature	.061 (.021)***	.016 (.028)	−.072 (.030)**	−.019 (.025)	.011 (.024)
% Women in the Workforce	.085 (.027)***	.014 (.038)	.004 (.043)	.103 (.031)***	−.003 (.037)
Reproductive Restrictions	−.173 (.031)***	.182 (.046)***	.035 (.044)	−.017 (.036)	−.006 (.008)
State Context					
Clinics per 100,000	.150 (.056)***	−.008 (.135)	−.070 (.111)	.013 (.099)	.172 (.061)***
Median Income	−.001 (.001)**	−.001 (.001)**	.001 (.001)	−.001 (.001)**	−.000 (.000)

Unified Democratic Government	.246 (.257)	−.614 (282)	−.179 (.380)	.237 (.310)	.132 (.266)
Diffusion	−.003 (.002)	.990 (.003)***	.010 (.004)*	−.004 (.002)	.006 (.004)*
Observations	643	643	643	643	643
Events	191	104	83	135	121
Wald Chi	.000	.013	.031	.000	.000
Log Pseudo-likelihood	954.801	−566.233	−433.48462	−692.561	−578.057
Single-Tailed Tests					

* p<.10, ** p<.01, *** p<.001

through anonymity, consent, and legal regulations related to egg donation. We may expect mixed results from the evidence of framing around compensation for egg donation—that is, we may expect morality and body politics to play a role in agenda-setting.

The politics that influence donor behavior are in fact different from those that govern egg donation as a whole, as partisanship and gender in politics emerge as significant in policymaking. As described in table 7, body and morality politics produce mixed results. Non*moralist* states, as well as states with larger *Christian* populations, are more likely to have introduced a bill regulating donor behavior. However, there are robust relationships between gender, partisanship, and agenda-setting regarding egg donors. States that restrict *reproductive liberties* are less likely to have introduced bills about egg donors; and, as a general rule, the *percentage of Democratic female legislators* does not significantly impact the probability of egg donor behavior bills being introduced.

However, the presence of *Republican female legislators* increases the likelihood that a bill about egg donor behavior will be introduced—an interesting twist to our expectations about the role of partisanship and gender in women's health legislation. Examining relationships among variables in individual policy categories (donor informed consent bills, compensation bills, and parental responsibility bills) yields the information that gender and partisanship are in fact important parts of the politics of egg donation: the presence of Republican women in the aggregate dramatically increases the chances that informed consent, compensation, and parental responsibility bills about egg donors will be introduced. Even in a context where morality and body politics variables have mixed effects in the politics of egg donation, gender and partisanship play an important role in egg donor bills, both in aggregate and when analyzed separately.

DISPOSITION OF DONATED EGGS

The data about bills that provide rules for disposition expose a diverse and sometimes contradictory politics at work. Disposition bills are important in both reproduction and research for regulating what happens to eggs after they are procured—for regulating everything from legal inheritance rights, to posthumous reproduction, to testing of eggs for disease.

The results regarding disposition limits reveal that states with more *reproductive restrictions* are likely to have introduced a bill limiting the future of donated eggs, as are states with larger *Christian* populations. Despite the clear role of social conservatism in the politics of egg-donation disposition limits, the presence of *Democratic female legislators* also increases the chances that a disposition limit will be introduced in the legislature, although Democratic women are not as powerful a force on policymaking as other state characteristics. Informed consent seems to be subject to different forces, as a lower *percentage of Republican female legislators* in a state legislatures decreases the chances that a bill about informed consent in egg disposition will be introduced. It seems that diffusion among neighboring states in fact makes a difference: states are more likely to *emulate* their neighbors in this respect.

PARENTAL RESPONSIBILITIES

Legal parentage ensures that women and men who intend to become parents will have legal responsibility for their donor-conceived children. For this category of bills, there seems to be a mix of morality politics and body politics at work: both the presence of larger *Christian* populations and more women in the workforce increase the chances there will be a parental responsibility bill introduced in the state legislature. However, a higher *percentage of Democratic female legislators* also increases the chances that a legal parentage bill will be introduced—potentially connecting Democratic women's expertise and leadership in family issues to the topic of egg donation.

RESEARCH

The category of research bills includes all legislation that seeks to limit egg donation in the context of somatic cell nuclear transfer or research on human embryonic stem cell lines only, particularly bills that target cloning, chimeras, and funding for stem cell research. These bills are targeted at egg donation only within these categories, as opponents argue that egg donation is immoral and unethical within these research areas. As predicted, morality politics play an important role in agenda-setting in the context of research using donor eggs, as described in Table 7. *Moralist* states are more likely to introduce a research bill, as are states with a larger *percentage of Christians* in the population, although religiosity is slightly less strong relative to research bills, among other morality variables. Interestingly, state context also matters: as the number of *clinics* per hundred thousand people rises, there is an increased likelihood that research will be regulated. Moreover, states are more likely to *emulate* each others' legislation related to research. Also, as predicted, body politics variables do not have a significant effect on the likelihood that a research bill will be introduced.

The results we see across policy categories are striking, revealing the nuances of the politics of egg donation during this period. At the outset of this analysis, donor behavior and parental rights seemed to be especially vulnerable to body politics variables. This turned out to be true: the presence of Republican and Democratic women in political life, reproductive liberties, and women in the workforce are all associated with the presence of more bills regulating egg donation in general, especially egg donor behavior and parental responsibilities. Disposition bills, on the other hand, are more likely to be influenced by both morality and body politics, with a larger Christian population and restrictive laws about reproduction increasing the chances that a disposition bill will be introduced across the states. Moreover, the absence of women in public life—particularly Republican women—improves the chances that a disposition bill will be put on the agenda. While body politics and morality politics both contribute to the politics of egg donation at the state level, results about the role of gender and partisanship are surprising: rather than revealing women working together on family issues, this analysis reveals the diverse and divergent ways that party identification and gender work in agenda-setting related to egg donation, particularly according to different policy categories.

WHOSE BODY, WHAT POLITICS? GENDER, PARTISANSHIP, AND AGENDA-SETTING IN THE CONTEXT OF EGG DONATION

The findings of the first half of this chapter seem counterintuitive: while the overall percentage of Democratic women in state legislatures in the aggregate increases the probability that egg donation bills will be introduced in state legislatures, Democratic women do not have the expected positive effect on egg donation policymaking across individual policies. Given the significant research on gender, partisanship, and leadership on women's issues, how can this pattern be explained? While Democratic women have long been policy leaders in bill introductions related to women's health policy, the role of Republican women is important to the story of egg donation in the US. Egg donation policies demonstrate the diverse and varied roles of partisan women in state politics, particularly with respect to reproductive issues outside of the contentious politics of abortion. Diving deeper into current debates about conservative women in politics and reproductive policy, the rest of this chapter examines an unfolding question of gender, partisanship, and policy leadership in relation to egg donation: what if Republican women are driving bill introductions regarding this topic?

GENDER AND PARTISAN POLITICS

Central to understanding this broad question are the ways that gender, partisanship, and institutional context interact in policy leadership. Women's leadership on "women's issue" bills is well established by decades of research on the behavior of women in national and state legislatures: colleagues and constituents expect female legislators of both parties to be policy experts on issues that disproportionately affect women, children, and families, such as health care and reproduction. Women step up to be what are called "policy entrepreneurs" on issues like health care. They claim health as an area of expertise and lead policymaking efforts in health, so this entrepreneurship is carefully calculated. Like any other reelection-seeking legislator, women of both parties have strategic concerns related to policy leadership and expertise: they weigh policy leadership in light of partisan and constituent demands, as well as the ways that policy leadership may affect their professional reputations. Moreover, the partisan setting—for example, what party controls the chamber, whether the female legislator is in the majority or minority party, and whether the party has an agenda for an issue—may modify women's influence on agenda-setting in the context of women's issues (Osborn 2012). Women in legislatures have to navigate not only gender and party but also increasing political polarization. Many argue that since the 1990s, new types of partisan women have emerged in state legislatures (Dodson 2006, Swers 2002, Frederick 2009). In particular, Republican women in legislatures are more socially conservative than in decades past (Frederick 2009)

While women in legislatures are more likely than their male counterparts to introduce and sponsor health bills, partisanship shapes women's policy solutions (Swers 2002, Osborn 2012, Tolbert and Steuernagel 2001, Caiazza 2004). For Republican women, this can mean a conflict: while they engage in women's health care issues, they must find solutions that differ from the dominant policy solutions introduced by Democratic women, as well as an alternative to the dominant feminist narrative of women's health issues. Republican women are less likely their male colleagues to introduce women's health bills (Osborn 2012). When Republican women do introduce women's health bills, their policy leadership reflects gender and partisanship: while Republican women in state legislatures are likely to restrict abortion and contraception in women's health bills, they are also likely to introduce bills that remedy women's health problems (Osborn 2012). Most interestingly, the examples of Republican women who introduced the health bills discussed in Tracy

Osborn's (2012) study of ten state legislatures reflect a concern over maternal health. For example, Republican women introduced bills that promoted breastfeeding in the workplace and insurance coverage of lactation support for new mothers. In her study of women in the conservative organizations Concerned Women for America and the Independent Women's Forum, Ronnee Schreiber (2008) found that advocates promote solutions to women's health issues as an alternative to Democratic and feminist rhetoric on women's health. For example, she finds that these groups reject the idea of "women's health" as a feminist category of policy; instead, they advocate the protection of women's health through restrictions on abortion and contraception (Schreiber 2008). Among self-identified conservative and libertarian Tea Party women, Melissa Deckman (2016) found similar results: Tea Party advocates often engage (and co-opt) feminist frames around reproductive rights. However, she discovered that many Tea Party women propose an alternative frame of "freedom feminism" that supports a softening of traditional gender norms in the pursuit of reproductive empowerment, free from government intervention (Deckman 2016, 189). While Republican women and conservative advocates promote policy entrepreneurship on women's health issues, the policy solutions reflect a commitment to partisan and ideological goals on the political Right.

Although studies have examined motherhood as an important issue for conservative movements in the US, one that guides overall political strategy related to gender, sexuality, and reproductive issues, the role of motherhood as a conservative concept and Republican political strategy has not yet been connected to reproductive technologies like egg donation. While gender and partisanship mediate Republican women's leadership on women's health issues, advocating the adoption of certain visions of motherhood is an important political strategy for conservatives in general. When these findings on gender, partisanship, and policy leadership on women's health issues are examined together, what may account for partisan women's interest in egg donation is the centrality of motherhood to conservative politics. Moral maternalistic politics—whereby women's claims to motherhood are connected to their moral and ethical reform of the political sphere—is a common political and rhetorical thread joining women's suffrage, the temperance movement, the Red Scare and anticommunism movements, Phyllis Schlafly's activism against the Equal Rights Amendment, and the "hockey moms" and "Mama Grizzlies" of the modern Republican Party (Deckman 2016). Using political rhetoric related to motherhood to appeal to conservative women and men throughout the twentieth century and in the twenty-first, Republicans (and conservative advocates) distinguished themselves from feminists in their divide between "good" and "bad" motherhood (Schreiber 2008, Deckman 2016). Although Republicans' description of what constitutes "good" motherhood changed as they switched from a vibrant defense of stay-at-home motherhood to a more flexible vision of working, "empowered" motherhood, they have historically contrasted a positive, moral vision of motherhood against a model of immoral, chaotic motherhood (such as that of welfare recipients or those who have subsidized reproductive health care) that is too deeply intertwined with a paternalistic, interventionist government (Schreiber 2008, Deckman 2016). Importantly, conservative and libertarian women in politics argue that motherhood and family life should be private— secluded from the immoral meddling of the state. Unlike feminists' responses to motherhood, conservative women react to maternal and family issues in a far different way: conservative women view motherhood and the family as extensions of social and economic values of small government and laissez-faire markets (Deckman 2016).

Conservative rhetoric related to motherhood and gender roles has shifted since the 1990s. As Schreiber (2008) and Deckman (2016) observe, there has been a softening of the position on motherhood in conservative political circles. While conservative women such as Phyllis Schlafly argued for the elevation and protection of women as homemakers, modern conservative women's groups more thoughtfully balance a high regard for stay-at-home motherhood with the economic realities of modern womanhood and family formation. Concerned Women for America largely defends homemaking as a natural choice for mothers, whereas libertarian women acknowledge that the norms of mothers who do not work are outdated. The practical realities have touched all women in the US: the delay of marriage and childbearing owing to educational attainment, career ambition, and the rigors of dual-income parenting require the conservative movement to reject old-fashioned norms of motherhood and instead focus on "empowering" working mothers (Deckman 2016). This increased flexibility of gender roles in the conservative worldview is important, ceding room for women to have increased autonomy over the timing and method of starting families. Although conservative and libertarian women still strongly defend motherhood and women who care for children in lieu of wage-earning work, Republicans acknowledge that their ideologies of motherhood and gender roles must be more flexible to capture potential female voters (Deckman 2016). These potential voters are often white, suburban women who have attended college and are likely to balance work and motherhood (Swers 2013).

Despite their acknowledgement that social change has shaped motherhood and gender roles, conservative political narratives about motherhood are rooted in naturalized biological essentialism. Conservative women advocates and legislators claim that motherhood is an innate, natural difference between women and men (Schreiber 2008, Deckman 2016). While conservatives' promotion of motherhood clearly dovetails with the uses of egg donation to create parents, the ways that motherhood is connected to biological difference is important to the issue of egg donation. Motherhood as a characteristic of biological difference between women and men is reinforced by egg donation, a technology of procuring and manipulating women's biological material. At a cellular level, egg donation reinforces the different biological, genetic contributions of women versus men. More broadly, egg donation and reproductive technology may help address infertility and involuntary childlessness, reinforcing norms of motherhood and the nuclear family as a natural, conventional choice. Although the implications of egg donation are problematic for social conservatives—for example, egg donation can aid gay couples as easily as heterosexual couples—egg donation reinforces socially conservative norms regarding natural biological difference and motherhood.

Returning to the central inquiry, gender and partisanship are significant in the politics of egg donation. As motherhood, particularly working motherhood, is of major importance to conservative actors, egg donation may be viewed as pro-woman and pro-family. The biological essentialism of conservative motherhood claims is reinforced, rather than rebuked, by egg donation: women's sex cells, the very building blocks of biological difference, are procured, fertilized, and implanted for reproduction. While policymaking regarding egg donation is in tension with conservative values of limited government and laissez-faire markets, these policies may benefit potential mothers and fathers more than harm them in their efforts to have children. Even the increased flexibility of gender norms of femininity and reproduction in conservative ideology are potentially reinforced by egg donation: given the availability of reproductive technology, women can achieve both economic stability and traditional nuclear families.

As Osborn (2012) notes in her study of partisan women in state legislatures, agenda-setting can be a strategic opportunity for women to claim issue expertise: if there are no party agendas on egg donation, for example, partisan women may be able to claim egg donation as their priority. In the case of Republican women in legislature, it is feasible that in the absence of a strong partisan stance on egg donation, they can modify how egg donation is perceived and the potential solutions to problems surrounding the technology. Rather than being a symbol of sexual liberation, blurred gender roles, and LGBTQ family formation, egg donation could be claimed as a modern technique to both help couples achieve traditional families and produce more "good" motherhood.

EGG DONATION BILL SPONSORS: GENDER AND PARTY

To further investigate the ways that gender and partisanship affect egg donation politics, I examined the gender and party of primary sponsors of a sample of egg donation bills during this period. Using a random sample of egg donation bills from the central data set, I coded each bill introduction with the gender and party of its primary sponsor. In this sample, Republican women introduced thirty-four bills, while Democratic women

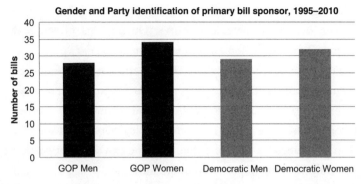

Figure 2. Gender and party of primary bill sponsors, 1995–2010.

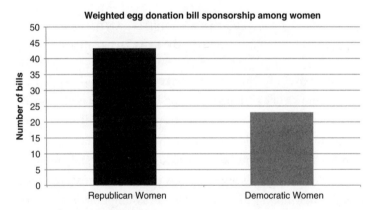

Figure 3. Weighted bill sponsorship among women in state legislatures, 1995–2010.

introduced thirty-two bills, and Republican men and Democratic men introduced twenty-eight and twenty-nine bills during this period, respectively. This is illustrated in Figure 2.

In considering gender and party identification in bill sponsorship, it is important to take into account the large differential in the composition of state legislatures: in this period, there were significantly more Democratic women than Republican women overall in state legislatures. During this fifteen-year period, Republican women composed, on average, 37 percent of female state legislators, while Democratic women composed about 66 percent of state legislators. After weighing the number of bills introduced by Republican and Democratic women according to their composition in state legislatures,[13] I found a clear difference between the women of the two different parties: Republican women proposed more bills about egg donation than Democratic women did in proportion to their representation in state legislatures, as illustrated in Figure 3.

GENDER, PARTISANSHIP, AND THE STATE POLITICS OF EGG DONATION

As the analyses in this chapter make clear, not only is there a robust politics of egg donation in the US, but there is also active policymaking at the state level in response to the diverse issues of egg donation. While conventionally the US system of regulation has been characterized as lackluster at best, and absent at worst, the findings discussed in this chapter directly challenge this way of thinking, disputing both the assumption of inactivity on the issue of egg donation, and common explanations for US policy. In terms of statutes, slightly over half of all state legislatures have passed laws that directly protect stakeholders, such as intended parents, medical professionals, and egg donors (Von Hagel 2014). However, examining original data in this chapter reveals that nearly all states have introduced bills attempting to regulate some aspect of egg donation for reproduction or research. This demonstrates that while there is a lack of federal regulation of egg donation, this quality of the US system obscures the policymaking activity regarding egg donation in nearly all states. Unlike the common characterization of the US as disinterested in the difficult political debates on egg donation, egg donation is a subject of state political interest and action.

This chapter illuminates how social, political, and economic state measures associated with body and morality politics predict agenda-setting in the context of egg donation. Testing these frameworks, body politics variables—those variables that represent the ways that women in economic and political life represent egg donation as a political issue—significantly drove the introduction of egg donation bills between 1995 and 2010. While the presence of women in public life (for example, in politics and in the workplace) increased the chances that a state's legislature had introduced an egg donation bill more generally, there is a counterintuitive finding: although Democratic women are generally associated with introducing women's health bills in legislatures, they did not have the same positive effect on egg donation bills. Instead, the overall percentage of women in state legislatures had a positive effect. A puzzle emerges in these findings: although gender and representation proved to be a significant aspect of egg donation policymaking, it was not in the same way that we see gender and partisanship playing a role in abortion or contraception. While the percentage of women in state legislatures overall increased the chances of bills about egg donation being introduced, the percentage of Democratic women had a negative effect. A closer examination of bill sponsors and the overall representation of partisan women at the state level shows that Republican women disproportionately introduce egg donation bills.

Egg donation may be perceived as a gendered reproductive issue reflecting conservative ideologies of family formation. It subverts in many ways our perceptions of how gender, partisanship, and body politics interact: egg donation is not like the representation of abortion in state legislatures, which is generally associated with increased representation by Democratic women. Instead, it may be a "safe" reproductive issue for Republican women, where pronatalism is communicated through traditional maternalistic and pro-family policy—despite the potential moral and ethical objections to egg donation. My analysis of egg donation politics reveals that, rather than working together on "family issues," as Representative Ros-Lehtinen suggests, Democratic and Republican women are influencing different aspects of egg donation policy in a highly polarized context. Illuminating the dark spaces of conventional thinking about egg donation in the US, the findings in this chapter suggest that body and morality politics are working in complex and nuanced ways regarding the identities of gender, partisanship, and family values.

Conclusion

Gazing out of the window of his laboratory, Dr. Frankenstein muses about the future of his abject monster. After considering a female mate for his lonely creation, Frankenstein is struck by the reproductive and scientific implications of what he has done: "One of the first results ... would be children, and a race of devils would be propagated upon the earth who might make the very existence of the species of man a condition precarious and full of terror. Had I right, for my own benefit, to inflict this curse upon everlasting generations? ... I shuddered to think that future ages might curse me as their pest, whose selfishness had not hesitated to buy its own peace at the price, perhaps, of the existence of the whole human race" (Shelley [1818] 1999, 222). The dark reflections of Dr. Frankenstein, who was tortured by his thirst for knowledge, plagued by his desire for creation, are similar to our own worries: what is life, what is research, and what does stretching the limits of each mean for the future? Existing in a dark space between Frankenstein and the imagery, discourse, and politics of families, egg donation has immense power to end involuntary childlessness, and has vast potential as a building block of regenerative medical research. Although Mary Shelley wrote about the intersecting humanity and horror inherent in the scientific processes of her "modern Prometheus" two centuries ago, these anxieties linger in the modern politics of egg donation in the US.

Despite the potential of egg donation for kinship, medicine, and financial gain, there has been little reflection on how this reproductive technology is defined, debated, and regulated in the unique US system of politics and policymaking. Rather than throwing up our hands and leaving all activity to the marketplace—or recoiling in ethical and moral horror at the "curse upon everlasting generations"—we can engage squarely with the idea that our attitudes, beliefs, and values with respect to identity shape the politics and policy of egg donation (Shelley [1818] 1999, 222). Competing ideas about gender, race, and class contour the US political system, whereby beliefs about state intervention in reproduction come up against debates rooted in fundamental, ethical principles. In this system, body politics and morality politics create logics for regulating egg donation. Moreover, body and morality politics gain and lose power (and often, gain power again) as policymaking frames placed around the history of egg donation in the US. In this book, I examine these processes through four state cases and a broad analysis of policymaking by state legislatures in the period of egg donation politics from 1995 to 2010.

FEMININITY AND THE POLITICS
OF EGG DONATION

With the view that egg donation can be defined as a "natural" act of the body in reproduction, the US system of regulation reifies gender norms of femininity, particularly of reproductive labor. Feminist scholars have long studied reproductive labor as assigned to the private sphere—labor associated with and defined by norms of femininity in relation to reproduction and childrearing, as well as in relation to domestic care tasks. While the idea of reproductive labor is not always associated with the labor of producing eggs for reproduction, scholarship has linked the bodily processes and the work that goes into donating eggs for one's own fertility purposes or for others' use for family formation (Harwood 2007, Almeling 2011, Daniels and Heidt-Forsythe 2012, Thompson 2005, 2013, Waldby and Cooper 2014, Spar 2006). The US system of egg donation supports a feminized definition of reproductive labor. Egg donors and egg recipients alike are not only expected to adhere to but also to perform normative femininity as patients and consumers (Thompson 2005, Almeling 2011, Daniels and Heidt-Forsythe 2012). Normative practices of femininity in relation to reproduction are repeatedly emphasized in the US system: egg donors are young and hyperfertile in a market that compensates them for their reproductive labor; but this market also asks egg donors to comply with feminine norms of altruism. Not only are certain bodies the "natural" sources of reproduction, but also these bodies act in accordance with feminine gender norms about labor and reproduction. However, these definitions of femininity and reproduction are situated in stratified reproduction, which defines whose reproduction is valued and encouraged, and whose reproduction is diminished and prevented (Colen 1986).

The enforcement of ideologies that define "good" versus "bad" motherhood extends to the individuals involved in egg donation. In this system, "good" fertile bodies of third-party egg donors are chosen through the selection of phenotypic and social traits that reflect stratified definitions of race, gender, and class (Daniels and Heidt-Forsythe 2012). Egg donors are more likely to be white, more highly educated, taller, and thinner than the average woman between the ages of eighteen and twenty-nine (Daniels and Heidt-Forsythe 2012). In another study, scholars hypothesized that a two-tiered egg donation market would emerge out of this division between "good" phenotypical bodies who donate eggs for third-party reproduction, and "unfit" phenotypical bodies who donate eggs for research purposes (Waldby and Cooper 2008, 2011, Roberts 2009). Commercial egg donation banks place limits on what is considered a body "good" for donating eggs: generally, women who are younger than thirty; are prohibited from drinking, smoking, and using drugs; and are screened for psychological and physiological disability and disease (Almeling 2011, Daniels and Heidt-Forsythe 2012). "Unfit" fertile bodies—such as those that are too large or are disabled, not educated enough, or not altruistic enough—are excluded from the reproductive egg donation market but are freer to donate for research purposes (Almeling 2011, Waldby and Cooper 2014). Consumers and intended parents are subject to similar judgments about their reproductive value in light of their race, class, sexuality, and gender identities; the division between able and disabled bodies is sharply drawn in the stratified access to egg donation in the US (Roberts 1998, 2009, Garland-Thomson 2002). The intervention of state politics and policy is intended to enforce this stratification of bodily labor and reproduction within a logic of body politics. Since the 1990s, egg donation for reproduction has increasingly reflected body politics frames in politics and policymaking.

Violating the idea that women's bodies, sexuality, and reproductive labor are meant to create families, egg donation for research has recently been framed as morally and ethically suspect in the public sphere. Linked to cloning, chimeras, and frightening futures in a brave new world, egg donation for research evokes the horror of creating a potential monster. Gender norms of femininity are upended and challenged in the de-gendered context of research using human eggs. The division between the private and public spheres becomes even less clear as traditionally private parts of the body—human eggs—are used in brave new ways for controversial research, research far away from the use of donated eggs for reproduction. The framework of morality politics, used by political science and policy studies to understand the moral and ethical tenor of many controversial issues and their politics, not only helps contextualize ideological debates about egg donation for research but also best explains the increased deliberation and attention to egg donation for research.

COMPETING FRAMES: THE HISTORY AND POLITICS OF EGG DONATION IN THE US

In the US, the first child conceived using a third-party donor egg was born in 1984. Soon after, the demand for eggs grew, particularly among women who yearned to use the relatively new and revolutionary technology of IVF but whose own eggs could not be used for conception owing to age, cancer, or other physiological problems. During this period, feminist and religious groups often pushed back against these technologies on the basis of fundamental moral principles: egg donation, among other reproductive technologies, had troubling implications for feminist and orthodox definitions of the body, reproduction, family, and power (Corea 1981). The media often characterized egg donation within a morality-politics frame, a practice in parallel with the moralistic discourse used by political actors during the 1980s and early 1990s (Bonnicksen 1989, Thompson 2005). However, in response to lobbying, technological change, and shifts in consumer demand, the power of morality-politics frames began to lose traction by the mid-1990s.

Throughout the decades that followed, there was an explosive transformation in medical practices that address infertility and involuntary childlessness, in which clinical techniques became more sophisticated and consumer demand for donor eggs grew. The number of clinics providing egg donation services swelled, as did the demand for egg donors. Lobbying by Resolve, the ASRM, and the American College of Obstetricians and Gynecologists also helped shift how political actors and the public viewed egg donation: rather than a terrifying technology that threatened to pull apart what it meant to be human, these reproductive technologies were simply another weapon in an arsenal against involuntary childlessness (Jesudason and Weitz 2015). Additionally, legislatures such as the California and New York State Assemblies began to pay increasing attention to the ways that politics and egg donation intersected, focusing on making the infertility industry more friendly, safe, and accessible to consumers. Political rhetoric from state legislatures, as well as public perceptions of egg donation, reflect this increasing normalization over the mid-1990s and early in the twenty-first century: rather than egg donation being solely a matter of moral values, it became associated with private notions of family formation. Rather than regulating matters of morals and ethics, the state instead was regulating (or not regulating) reproduction. By the first decade in the twenty-first century, the burgeoning, mass commercial practices related to reproductive technologies; increasingly detailed ethical guidelines; and new applications and manipulations of egg donation for the mass market all contested the conventional meanings of gender and reproduction (Almeling 2011, Thompson 2005, Ginsburg and Rapp 1995, Franklin and Ragoné 1998). In the popular imagination and in popular discourse, reproductive technologies became more visible: celebrities joked about putting their eggs in the freezer, hoping to undergo IVF with their future spouses (Saad 2013). One can search the Internet for "egg donors" and find hundreds of egg banks with extensive online profiles of women willing to donate eggs (Daniels and Heidt-Forsythe 2012). Feminist scholars have been predicting the normalization of egg donation during the last twenty years, and the explosion and relative acceptance of egg donation as a way to create families, not Frankenstein, reinforces the forward thinking of feminists concerning egg donation (Ginsburg and Rapp 1995, Ikemoto 2009, Thompson 2005).

In concert with the shifts in thinking about morality and body politics related to reproduction over three decades, debates about egg donation have shifted with the creation of new forms of life through human embryonic stem cell research in the late 1990s. In a realization of hopes (and fears) about the potential of human cells to regenerate, the development of human embryonic stem cells in a laboratory setting created a new potential use for human eggs beyond family formation—the treatment of degenerative disease and disability. As donor eggs began to be used to help create blastocysts from which human embryonic stem cells are derived, the world of reproduction collided with that of regenerative medical research: the financial, scientific, and medical potentials that exist in human eggs mean that we can create not just children but also cures (Waldby and Cooper

2008, 2014, Franklin 2013, Thompson 2013). In sharp contrast with the slippage in morality and body politics frames in political institutions and the popular culture of egg donation for reproduction, the explosion of research innovation related to stem cells and somatic cell nuclear transfer (or "reproductive cloning") has been framed consistently in both spheres as a moral issue. Egg donation for stem cell research is characterized by dramatic and conflict-oriented stories in the press and morality politics in legislatures, connecting the research to moral arguments in the scientific, religious, and public communities (Nisbet et al. 2003). As Lisa Ikemoto (2009) argues, the development of egg donation for research created a new paradigm for egg procurement: rather than reflecting a concern about state intervention in reproduction, egg donation for research prompted a concern about ethical and moral research in genetics and embryology (see also Thompson 2005). Debates about the meaning of life and personhood are embedded in the discourse about egg donation—specifically, the ethics of fetal and embryonic research and cloning (Thompson 2005, Goggin and Orth 2004). There are also considerable moral concerns about the commodification of intimate relationships within the family, the use of reproductive materials in the marketplace, and alternative kinship formations enabled by egg donation, despite its being a pronatal practice (Thompson 2005, Spar 2006, Satz 2010).

Even though the peak of egg donation use seems to have been reached, technological development in egg donation procedures have created new sources of demand and supply, and new sites of debate and contestation. In 2013, the largest professional organization of fertility experts recommended that cryopreservation of eggs should no longer be considered "experimental" (Pfeifer et al. 2014). Previously available only to oncology patients, egg-freezing technologies had improved throughout the second decade of the twenty-first century, creating better pregnancy outcomes than observed in egg-freezing experiments in the 1990s and in the early years of the twenty-first century. Major organizations, from the ASRM to the American College of Obstetricians and Gynecologists, recommended egg freezing for the wider public even though it is a less successful procedure than the traditional use of IVF with nonfrozen eggs (ACOG 2014). Like clockwork, media stories emerged, such as those describing older parents paying the egg-freezing costs for their marriage- and family-delaying daughters—a financial investment in their daughters' future families (Gootman 2012). Alongside egg cryopreservation, the "three parent" in vitro fertilization, uterine transplant, and development of induced pluripotent stem cells are all poised to further shape the demand in, supply of, and market for human eggs. Yet again, new technologies have revived old debates about the norms of femininity in reproduction as stakeholders struggle over the ways that femininity is inextricably linked to reproduction and research.

FRAMING EGG DONATION IN FOUR STATES

In response to these exciting and challenging new developments of the 1980s to the present, other nations across the globe created sophisticated and centralized regulatory structures that highly restricted egg donation. While egg donation is extremely visible in public life, the politics of egg donation seems to never accompany these public displays, instead remaining in the shadows of the huge commercial market. Unlike nations across the globe, the US appears to literally not have anything *but* laissez-faire commerce in eggs. Although other reproductive options and life course decisions (such as abortion or contraception) made by women have been regulated by the state, the US appears apolitical when it comes to the issue of egg donation. According to conventional wisdom, the US refuses to take on the political challenges brought about by the privatization of egg donation in the public sphere, because the controversial and polarizing politics of abortion have precluded debate on egg donation, and because the US has not had the democratic capacity to debate bioethical issues. While these characterizations do help explain the US's unique approach to egg donation, in this book I forward the idea that the rich politics and policy of egg donation at the state level reveal additional truths about how debates are constructed and governance is created. In this book I explore the alternative paths of the politics of egg donation through two major areas: how stakeholders frame egg donation, revealing the underlying beliefs, attitudes, and values of politics and policy; and the ways that gender and partisanship shape the unique US system.

Framing is a dynamic process by which an issue and its problems are defined, debates about the issue are established, and policy solutions are created. In an analysis of how reproduction and research are framed, the politics of egg donation begins to be illuminated. Using policy narrative analysis of texts generated by stakeholders in California, New York, Arizona, and Louisiana, I trace, in chapters 2 and 3, three major themes that emerge from framing processes: gender and agency, vulnerability, and the moral responsibility of the state. These themes shape the ways that egg donation for reproduction and research is defined and debated and how policy is created at the state level.

With the absence of federal funding for early stem-cell research in the twenty-first century, California and New York became laboratories of democracy in funding their own state stem cell research initiatives. This work relied on the use of human eggs as the raw material for research, thrusting these states into the role of procuring eggs in parallel to commercial markets for fertility treatment. In these coastal states, egg donation for research was framed as a conceptual issue distinctly different from egg donation for reproduction. Unlike donors in the vibrant commercial market for eggs used for reproduction that exists in California and New York (states that were leaders in the reproductive market), egg donors for the research market were conceptualized and defined significantly differently, as research subjects whose reproductive labor should be protected much like that of subjects in clinical trials. De-gendering the egg donor allowed California and New York to create a policy narrative about donors' vulnerability to violations of bioethical standards. This definition of egg donors also created the state's moral obligation to protect and promote research that would lead to cures for devastating diseases and disability; moreover, each of the two states constructed a policy solution that entailed a ban on compensation to further cement how egg donation for research was distinct from egg donation for reproduction. While prompting debates based on fundamental principles of the moral role of the state, and on justice, equality, and protecting vulnerable individuals from risk, the morality politics that took shape in California and New York reflects a narrative in which the moral obligation of the state is to protect the potential health and well-being that can come from human embryonic stem cell research. The division of egg donation—into donation for reproduction and donation for research—creates policymaking contexts where there is a profound invisibility of egg donation for reproduction and, thus, justifies the creation of regulations that treat the same medical procedure (egg donation) in drastically different ways depending on the purpose of the egg procurement.

In Arizona and Louisiana, distinctly different frames and policy narratives were constructed around egg donation, and these relied on body and morality politics to shape the framing process. Framing egg donation for research *and* for reproduction as unconventional and risky processes that potentially damaged women's reproductive potential, political stakeholders used the concepts of fundamental principles of health, risk, bodily labor, and gender equality to create metanarratives about the moral duty of the state to protect women's bodies from coercive egg donation practices. Moreover, policy narratives in Arizona and Louisiana co-opted feminist rhetoric from women's health and feminist advocacy to describe the moral obligation of the state to protect the vulnerable—not only from exploitative commercial interests but also from their own bodily actions. Incorporating the rhetoric of state control over reproductive and bodily labor—such as sex work—the policy narratives created in Arizona and Louisiana demonstrate the blurring of body politics and morality politics that occurs when states create policies that target egg donation for reproduction and research. While the policy narratives reflect morality politics, these narratives expose the heterogeneity of morality politics: as others have noted about reproduction and sexuality issues, diverse politics can arise out of a singular issue like egg donation. Instead of rendering egg donation for reproduction and research as distinct and thus subject to different politics, the cases of Arizona and Louisiana demonstrate the ways that debates rooted in fundamental values, religiosity, and moralism can co-opt feminist rhetoric within body politics, creating policy that justifies the regulation—and silencing—of egg donors and consumers.

A NEW GENDERED PARTISANSHIP IN
THE POLITICS OF EGG DONATION

Looking only at policies on egg donation for reproduction—bills that propose some regulation of commercial or clinical practices related to egg donation, or that establish rules for legal parentage—we may expect that body politics frameworks will play an important role in explaining why policymaking occurs. Thinking more critically about body politics and what these politics mean for legislative processes, we can see that body politics frames center policy on women and their bodily experiences. Given the historical role and importance of gender and partisanship in the representation of women's health and reproductive issues, we may expect the presence of women and partisanship to play a more significant role in policymaking related to egg donation for reproduction. Employing event-history analysis, in this book I test morality variables, such as state culture and religiosity, against gender and representation variables in predicting agenda-setting in relation to egg donation for reproduction. The results demonstrate that women in public life make a significant difference in agenda-setting related to egg donation for research. However, unlike historical findings about the significance of Democratic women in agenda-setting with respect to women's health and reproductive issues, I conclude that Republican women are leading the charge in setting agendas related to egg donation for reproduction. This finding lends support to gender and politics scholarship that finds Republican women, while active in women's issues, are often constrained by partisanship (Osborn 2012). The Republican Party has increasingly regulated abortion and contraception; egg donation for reproduction may be one issue that serves both women's bodily choices regarding reproduction and pronatal ideologies concerning the nuclear family that are entrenched in the Republican Party. While the ways that Republican women conceptualize, define, and frame egg donation for reproduction need further study, these findings suggest that a new partisan body politics is emerging out of the fact that egg donation has been made a conventional or natural choice for reproduction.

THE LADY (IN POLITICS) VANISHES: GENDER, POLITICS, AND FEDERALISM IN EGG DONATION

Although people who produce cells and tissues for the purposes of the reproductive and research markets are essential for the continued medical and financial successes of the infertility and regenerative research markets, Donna Dickenson (2006) observes that "the lady vanishes" in debates about these technologies. She argues that the human labor essential to reproductive technologies and biomedical research is often rendered invisible, particularly when women are performing this labor. Women who donate eggs for reproduction and research go through weeks of hormone therapy, clinical appointments, and outpatient surgery for egg procurement, but they are absent from bioethical debates; moreover, in these debates, it is rare for stakeholders to acknowledge that women who are egg donors should have ownership over the products they have labored to produce (Dickenson 2006). While other individuals (such as infertility patients, medical professionals, scientists, and religious leaders) are often central in bioethics debates and legal decrees, the "clinical labor" of women is often marginalized at best and invisible at worst (Dickenson 2006, Waldby and Cooper

2014). The central actor—the "lady" who donates eggs—is simply absent in debates between bioethicists. This observation seems particularly true when reflecting on the past thirty years of media coverage and popular cultural conceptions of egg donation for reproduction and research in the US: often, political narratives focus on those who experience disease and disability; moreover, these narratives have a pro-cures orientation and privilege academic and medical elites rather than testimony from donors (Thompson 2013, Benjamin 2013).

What is striking is that as the "lady vanishes" from discussions of egg donation, so does her connection to the political world. Moreover, other individuals involved—such as women in the political sphere—are invisible in debates about egg donation. I argue that the lady *in politics* vanishes in discussions of egg donation in the US. Egg donors are not recognized as political subjects, and there is little visibility or acknowledgment of feminist policy and gendered representation regarding egg donation in the US context. Finally, I argue that the benefits and drawbacks of policymaking in a federal system, where the crucial role of the states in the politics of egg donation has long been ignored, deserve more attention.

EGG DONORS AS POLITICAL SUBJECTS

First, egg donors are not acknowledged as individuals with political efficacy and specific political interests. Although egg donors have largely been rendered as silent participants in egg donation markets, people who donate eggs have an interest in the politics and policy created about them. These politics engage directly with egg donors' experiences as autonomous participants in medical treatments, in economic exchanges between donors and intended parents, and as genetic relations to donor-conceived children. All of these experiences are debated and discussed in the political sphere, as chapters 2 and 3 demonstrate—however, rarely do we see egg donors speaking about their own experiences.

Lived experiences in the US system underpin the need to shift our thinking about egg donation as a private issue; as the feminist adage warns, the personal is in fact political. Egg donors and consumers have "unruly bodies"—bodies that are constantly managed, often by perceived professionals who measure bodily labor in terms of the "normal and abnormal" (Bridges 2011, 76; see also Petersen 2017). While individuals with these unruly bodies are subject to state and professional control and regulation, little is known about their own political desires, interests, issues, and preferences.

I argue that women—both potential donors and consumers—are socially constructed as policy targets that are silent, disenfranchised subjects in politics (Schneider and Ingram 1993). As demonstrated by framing processes in various states, women are often marginalized (through gender, assumptions about agency, and labels of vulnerability) by their experiences of stratified reproduction and norms of femininity. Women sidelined by egg donation markets are so often excluded from politics and policy that they may find it hard to even identify themselves as political actors with important interests in egg donation, much like other marginalized groups who have failed to see their own political agency (Piven and Cloward 1978, Gaventa 1980, Mink 2001). Their interests are defined as private and ultimately burdensome on public goods. But even those who are socially constructed as silent targets of egg donation policy have important interests: health, sexuality, cultural and religious values, scientific innovation, and family formation are all tied to access to fair and egalitarian reproductive and research systems (WHO 2016).

Stakeholders often speak for egg donors, framing donors' experiences in specific ways to advance and set a legislative agenda about egg donation. Even when advocating on behalf of egg donors, stakeholders often fall into the trap of framing egg donors as passive, vulnerable objects acted upon by outside economic and social forces. Importantly, not all donors have the same experience; while we can hypothesize that there may be shared interests among donors based on the ways that women are screened by medical professionals, there is important heterogeneity among donors in their intentions, feelings, and physical experiences related to egg donation.

Donors should be seen as belonging to what Iris Marion Young (1994) calls a "series": rather than a group united by common experiences and identities, individuals with heterogeneous identities and experiences are linked together through an external process like egg donation. Each member of the series has a partial perspective on this external process of egg donation, which in turn determines what issues are relevant to them (Young 1997, 2000, Weldon 2011). Issues like informed consent, compensation, disposition, and legal parentage all emerge as particularly relevant to the interests of those who donate eggs, because potential donors have a vested stake in the disclosure of medical risks, and an interest in the financial obligations and benefits of donation, in how their eggs will be used in the future, and in whether their genetic linkage to donor-conceived children has implications for issues like child support. This book makes clear that there are gaps in the knowledge about donors as stakeholders in egg donation politics and policymaking. Talking directly to donors about their experiences as political subjects, governed by state laws and subject to political debates about reproduction, research, and state intervention, would begin to fill this gap. As narratives of infertility and involuntary childlessness have grown more diverse, complex, and nuanced in relation to experiences of race, sexuality, and class, the experiences of donors—and the connection of these experiences to political action—deserve equal hearing. Whether in the form of feminist interest and advocacy groups, individual testimony, or donors' groups, increased participation in the political process is rooted in recognition of egg donors as political subjects.

FEMINIST POLICY AND GENDERED REPRESENTATION

Focusing on egg donation politics through the frame of the invisible woman (in politics), the findings of this book—from the ways that norms of femininity shape how body and morality politics are used over time as political frames, to the importance of diverse women in politics—demonstrate the need to rethink not only conventional perceptions of feminist reproductive policy issues but also the very nature of gendered, partisan representation at the state level. These findings push the limits of how reproductive issues are conceptualized in gender and policy studies, complicating the ways that policies reinforce feminist or antifeminist goals. Moreover, these findings suggest new avenues for understanding how women, particularly women constrained by party identification, can represent these complex issues that exist at the intersection of reproduction, technology, and medicine.

Egg donation demonstrates the limits of conventional thinking about feminist and antifeminist reproductive issues, as egg donation policies at the state level are not always clear in their intent to limit or enable the use of egg donation for reproduction and research. As demonstrated by the analysis of microlevel framing processes in California related to egg donation compensation, political actors may have very different reasons for supporting an egg donation bill. While Deborah Ortiz self-identified as a Democratic woman's health advocate, her cosponsor, Republican George Runner, had historically blocked feminist proposals for increased abortion access and human papillomavirus vaccines in the state. Their bill was less clearly feminist or antifeminist, since obviously there are different interpretations of banning compensation for egg donation in research: in Ortiz's view, she was protecting egg donors from financial and medical exploitation, while Runner was motivated to curtail egg donation on the basis of moral concerns about the research involving human embryos. Such a bill could promote the safe and equal treatment of women in research, but it could also be interpreted as part of a larger project of curtailing women's bodily autonomy.

This complexity and lack of clear feminist and antifeminist policy boundaries reflects historical feminist debates about reproductive technologies—namely, whether oppression or liberation is inherently a quality of egg donation. For some feminists, reproductive technologies are not inherently oppressive (although they can be used for such a goal), as they allow women increased autonomy and decision-making power regarding motherhood. Moreover, egg donation can be understood as another form of women's bodily labor. For others, reproductive technologies like egg donation are inherently oppressive: egg donation segments and commodifies the body and its processes; egg donation may enforce, rather than resist, norms of motherhood; egg donation in the US is a process of objectification and exploitation of women, particularly donors. Mirroring these arguments, egg donation policy can serve both antifeminist and feminist goals: for example, bans on egg donation compensation can act to reduce women's choices and autonomy in relation to their bodies, research, and reproduction. However, bans on egg donation compensation may also put in place important safety and ethical protections that actually ease the process by which women donate eggs for reproduction and research, and by which others use those eggs to start families or stem cell lines. Unlike other reproductive policy issues that have a clear intent—curtailing abortion use through such barriers as waiting periods, targeted regulation of abortion providers, and twenty-week bans—egg donation adds important complexity to how scholars and stakeholders conceptualize feminist and antifeminist policies.

The invisibility of women in egg donation can also be understood through the lens of gendered representation. Scholarly and popular discussions of the politics of egg donation have largely ignored the importance of women representing women in the US political system—not only do women as donors vanish (alongside their political interests), but also the power of representing gendered interests is rendered invisible. Egg donation is connected to the gendered health issues, particularly infertility and involuntary childlessness. An important segment of the egg donation market experiences infertility and involuntary childlessness as intended parents. Although men and women experience infertility at nearly equal rates, infertility has been socially constructed as a women's issue: women are disproportionately affected by infertility compared to men (Greil et al. 2016). Heterosexual women experience, on average, higher levels of external and internal stigma and more medical interventions than their male partners when dealing with infertility. Queer women, broadly defined, also experience negative stigma and psychological impacts when dealing with social infertility (as opposed to medical infertility). Culturally, infertility has been narrowly defined through women's sexual and biological characteristics, and dominant imagery, medical interventions, and social practices reflect this disproportionate focus on women's infertility. Yet infertility is not universally recognized by political stakeholders as a health issue that affects women in different ways than men; infertility is often ignored among other reproductive justice issues, such as abortion and contraception.

Additionally, there may be reason to consider regenerative medicine as an issue particularly relevant to women. Since many women are caregivers—particularly for aging and infirm family members—health issues in general have been historically categorized within women's interests. With the promises and potential of stem cell and cloning research, we may expect these issues to disproportionately affect those who give care to dependents experiencing disease or disability. Egg donation within the contexts of research also may be considered an issue of particular importance and relevance to the lived experiences of women.

Women legislators have historically represented women's issues, particularly health issues, at the state legislative level: women are not only more likely to put such issues on the legislative agenda, they are also more likely to speak out in support of such bills and vote for them. In particular, Democratic women have historically represented these issues more than their counterparts have, Democratic men and Republican women alike. Seen as vanguards of women's health issues, Democratic women have been historically identified as the gendered, partisan representatives of women's health in the public sphere. Yet egg donation is rarely grouped with these issues, and the split between feminist and antifeminist policy is less clear. My findings from the state cases, as well as my broad analysis of egg donation politics at the state level, support a slightly different argument: that while gender and party are important in the representation of women's health issues, it was Republican women who were the egg donation agenda-setters during the 1990s and the middle of the first decade of the twenty-first century.

These findings shift how we think about what it means for female legislators to represent issues that disproportionately affect women: while Democratic women often appeal to the Democratic base by representing women's health issues, Democrats have also historically sought protectionist legislation for women and labor (Freeman 1987). There is a different pattern behind the prominence of Republican women's representation of egg donation: Republican women, in highly polarized and partisan state legislative contexts, view egg donation as a contemporary issue through which to promote motherhood in politics. As Melissa Deckman (2016) and Ronnee Schreiber (2008) observe, motherhood is an identity essential to conservative women's organizations historically; however, given that most contemporary nuclear families are no longer reliant on just one breadwinner, conservative women must fit into motherhood *and* are required to work outside the home. As a result, modern solutions to the very real contemporary experiences of delaying marriage and childbirth in order to get an education and pursue a career are needed—and potentially, reproductive technologies like egg donation fit into this evolving conception of the modern woman, wife, and mother among conservative women in the US.[1]

"LABORATORIES OF DEMOCRACY":
EGG DONATION POLICY IN A FEDERAL SYSTEM

The third major area of empirical and theoretical development reflects the US model of federalism. States are famously "laboratories of democracy": they are locations of policy experimentation, particularly for reproductive and research issues relevant to egg donation. One of the primary reasons why the US is seen as lawless on the subject of egg donation is precisely because of this federal system: while most comprehensive regulations governing egg donation are centralized, the US distributes political power differently. Given the Tenth Amendment powers of the state (as well as historical positions on the administrative role of states in interpreting and implementing federal laws), egg donation politics exist primarily at the state level.[2] Policymaking regarding women's health and scientific research, particularly since early twenty-first century, has been especially subject to devolution to subnational governance. Multiple concerns and traditions play a role in state policymaking on women's health issues and scientific issues more broadly. A lack of comprehensive reproductive health care and access, where maternity care and pediatric care are seen as a privilege, not a right, shapes this system. Health care more broadly is seen as a federal issue that also requires state interpretation and intervention. On the research side of egg donation, scientific research funding at the national level has been subject to highly contentious, polarized, and partisan politics. Given the political power that controls federal funding of controversial research, many states—such as California and New York, as described in Chapters 2 and 3— have stepped in to provide the research funding and infrastructure that is unavailable at the national level.

This political arrangement has both benefits and drawbacks. States may be sensitive to their unique populations, to their health and research needs, and be responsive to these needs in ways that the federal government cannot. As technologies are constantly changing, policy experiments could help cope with these changes on a smaller, state scale. As evidenced by state entrepreneurs in egg donation, state legislatures in California and New York have experimented with and developed policies at a much faster rate than we may imagine could occur in Congress. Political polarization and gridlock in national government makes the innovation and entrepreneurship of state-level politics appealing (Bonnicksen 2007, 2002). However, clear problems exist with a state-centered politics and policymaking model. Inequalities run rampant when policies exist on a state level: as evidenced by the cases of California and Arizona, donors and consumers alike are subject to vastly different ideological and partisan positions on egg donation, resulting in clear differences in the day-to-day experiences of these actors. Policies that unduly surveil, regulate, and constrain donors and consumers are likely to be found in a system where other reproductive choices are similarly limited. States may be vulnerable to a "race to the bottom," where state competition for policy creates a context of negative spillover effects (Shipan and Volden 2012).

While centralization of egg donation policy seems to be the better choice among the options for governance in the US, we may approach this idea with caution. Increased polarization and a lack of party agendas on reproductive technologies means that progress may be slow on these issues; while markets for reproduction and innovation in science continue, movement toward additional national policy is likely far away. Historically, the bureaucracy that exists around bioethics issues (such as the

Presidential Bioethics Commission) has been advisory. Centralization of egg donation policy would require a rethinking of the relationships between states and the federal government, as well as of the role of the federal government in issues where reproduction and research blur together. For policy change to occur, a countermovement must be established to challenge the status quo of policy, and political opportunity must exist; public opinion about an issue can open up debate about policies (Tatalovich 2017). Given states' entrepreneurship regarding egg donation, as well as increased public attention and political organizing, we might expect states like California and New York to provide a model for national policy. However, the speed at which such political and policy change will happen is very much up in the air. For the time being, it may be easier to focus further attention on making state policies that achieve feminist goals for social justice than to create these massive national changes.

BETWEEN FAMILIES AND FRANKENSTEIN

Although egg donation is a naturalized, highly visible reproductive technology in the US—a topic of tabloids and university newspaper advertisements, as well as a way of achieving parenthood—it also is the source of bioethical controversy, religious objections, and contentious debates rooted in fundamental principles. Donating eggs for reproduction and research are identical processes, but the future of procuring eggs is framed in a far different manner. Egg donation is mutable over time, and this single process has been situated between the dominant narratives of the family and the horrors of Dr. Frankenstein's monster. Over time, these frames, reflecting body and morality politics, have gained and lost traction, shaping the ways that egg donation politics and policy have unfolded at the state level. Rather than being the Wild West, the US system of egg donation is the source of vibrant politics and policymaking, exposing our assumptions about femininity and the body, and our attitudes toward fundamental values in science. Moreover, this reproductive technology challenges how we think about fundamental issues in politics and policy. Illuminating this dark space, this book presents a diverse picture of the actors, policies, and processes that make up the unique system of egg donation in the US, and I explain the ways that the US system has developed. Moreover, I offer a new vision: that egg donation doesn't inherently reflect families or Frankenstein but carries the promise of a new future sensitive to the innovation and dynamic change embedded in reproductive technologies. Egg donation has the potential to create life and cures, as well as a more just, democratic, and equitable political future—for donors, intended parents, scientists, and patients alike.

MEDICAL AND PSYCHOLOGICAL PRACTICES AND RISKS OF EGG DONATION

Egg procurement for personal use in IVF, cryopreservation, third-party reproduction, and stem cell research is based in one medical procedure, although preparation for that procedure varies. If a third party plans to produce eggs for others, she will first go through a battery of tests for sexually transmitted infections and blood type per guidelines from the Centers for Disease Control and the primary organization for infertility professionals, the American Society for Reproductive Medicine. Once these have been completed, a potential egg donor will experience medical and psychological interviews and tests, complete with extensive interviews and surveys that detail her medical, educational, religious, and social background. Noting the importance of the commercial aspects of egg donation markets in the US, many have observed that egg donors are often interviewed and screened for "sellable" qualities, such as a potential donor's altruism, motivation, financial status, and personality characteristics (Almeling 2011, Daniels and Heidt-Forsythe 2012, Ikemoto 2009). Depending on results from these tests, an egg bank coordinator, physician, or genetic counselor may require more extensive genetic testing of a potential donor. Such tests may not be necessary or relevant for egg procurement for immediate, personal IVF or cryopreservation. In cases of egg sharing, where women undergoing personal egg procurement have an excess of eggs, a woman may donate her "leftover" eggs to others. In these cases, tests for sexually transmitted infections and for blood type, recommended by the Centers for Disease Control and American Society for Reproductive Medicine, are performed.

The road to egg donation starts with the reproductive cycle before a woman's eggs will be retrieved. She begins with a daily schedule of three injected doses of a gonadotropin-releasing hormone medication, often Lupron. Once she begins menstruation, she will add a daily intramuscular injection of a gonadotropin medication (follicle-stimulating hormones or human menopausal gonadotropin) to her doses of Lupron. The two sets of medications will continue for a week or a week and a half, during which she will submit to frequent transvaginal ultrasound tests and blood draws as her physicians observe her estradiol levels. These levels communicate to what extent her egg follicles are developing and maturing for the best chances of fertilization in vitro. Once her follicles are at an optimal maturation, the donor gets an injection of human chorionic gonadotropin, which will trigger ovulation in thirty-five to forty-eight hours. At this time, retrieval is completed through transvaginal ultrasound aspiration while the donor is fully anesthetized. This is a procedure whereby a long, thin needle is inserted through the vagina into the ovary and applies suction to the follicles, retrieving the matured eggs. A donor's retrieved eggs will usually be inseminated the same day and then transferred to the intended mother (or surrogate) three days after retrieval. If the eggs are intended for the self, either for personal

IVF or cryopreservation, eggs are either inseminated the same day or immediately frozen without being fertilized, respectively.

MEDICAL AND PSYCHOLOGICAL RISKS

Despite the lack of long-term studies on the effects of egg donation procedures on women's reproductive health and fertility, there are known risks to women's health. Women may experience minor, moderate, or severe ovarian hyperstimulation syndrome (OHSS), which can result in bloating, feelings of heaviness and discomfort, headaches, and mild nausea or vomiting. For most patients, these reactions subside soon after they are done donating eggs. More serious OHSS conditions are rare among egg donors and are usually indicated by high blood pressure, rapid weight gain, and difficulty breathing. At its most severe, OHSS can cause renal failure, hemorrhage, blood clots, or even death (Pfeifer et al. 2016). Mild forms of OHSS are common and affect about a third of all women who donate eggs for themselves or for others. Moderate forms of OHSS—which require monitoring by a physician and sometimes hospitalization—affect between 3 and 6 percent of all donors. The most dangerous forms of OHSS affect only a tiny percentage of donors, between .1 and 2 percent (Corbett et al. 2014). While mild forms of this syndrome are reported by many patients, there is consensus that severe impacts on patient well-being are rare and that preventative measures can be taken to reduce the risk of OHSS (Corbett et al. 2014). In one survey of egg donors, a majority of women knew about potential medical risks of egg donation but underestimated how severe OHSS can be (Kenney and McGowan 2010).

Outside of physiological impacts, there are potential psychological impacts, and tests have been designed that try to prevent potential psychological problems in egg donors. In one study of commercial egg banks, comprehensive psychological tests of potential donors lasted on average ninety minutes (Almeling 2011). These tests screen for mental illness and donor motivation in an attempt to screen out donors who may have a risk of not completing the procedure or may have a negative reaction to egg donation. However, despite the fact that nearly all clinics administer psychological tests to donors, there is often no psychological follow-up after an egg donation procedure. Psychological risks to donors and others who go through egg procurement are not well-documented, again owing to the lack of long-term studies on the psychological health and well-being of donors and others who have undergone egg procurement procedures. Mood swings and mild depression have been reported in association with donors taking hormone medication during egg procurement. Outside of these reactions, donors may feel regret, loss, or anguish over children born as a result of egg donation. Other risks include anxiety over the medical procedure or legal agreements concerning donor anonymity (Kalfoglou and Geller 2000, Kenney and McGowan 2010). In surveys and interviews about their experiences, a majority of donors reported positive and altruistic feelings about their donation, with few negative responses (Kenney and McGowan 2010). In contradiction to the expectation that egg donors may feel like their genetic contribution to a donor-conceived child creates kinship, Almeling (2011) observes that the majority of egg donors do not feel like mothers after donation. However, there is much research to be completed—both in the short term and in the long term—before we can understand the full effect of egg donation procedures on donors' physical and psychological well-being.

MEASURES IN CHAPTER 4

TABLE 8

Predictor Variables

Morality Variables	
Moralist	Static variables, coded 1/0. There are three types of cultures: traditionalist, moralist, and individualist. In the data set, *traditionalist* is the omitted category. There is no value for the District. (Data from Crowley et al. 2012, Elazar 1967, 1980.)
Reproductive Restrictions Score	Measure of overall state support or suppression of abortion access; scores range from −6 to 10, with higher scores indicating more restrictive state policies on abortion. (Data from Rose 2006, scores calculated by author.)
Percentage of Christians	Percentage of Christians by the decade. (Data from Crowley et al. 2012.)
Percentage of Democratic Female Legislators	Percentage of Democratic female legislators by state and year, 1995 to 2010. (Data from the Center for American Women and Politics 2018.)

(continued)

TABLE 8

continued

Morality Variables	
Percentage of Republican Female Legislators	Percentage of Republican female legislators by state and year, 1995 to 2010. (Data from the Center for American Women and Politics 2018.)
Percentage of Women in the Workforce	Percentage of women in the workforce (both part time and full time) by state and year. (The 1995–2010 data is from Bureau of Labor Statistics 2013.)

State Context Variables	
Emulate Proposal	Diffusion variable; % of neighboring states that proposed any ART legislation in the previous year. (Data from Erin Heidt-Forsythe 2013, calculated by same.)
Median Income	Median income by state and year, 1995–2010. (Data from US Census Bureau 2010.)
Clinics per 100,000 residents	Number of reporting clinics in a state per year, for 1995–2010. (CDC 2013; population calculated from US Census Bureau 2010.)
Unified Democratic Government	(Data from Klarner 2003.)

TABLE 9

Egg Donation Policy Categories and Definitions

Policy Category	Subpolicies	Definition
Egg Donor (All)	Compensation, informed consent, disposition informed consent, disposition limits, parental responsibilities (donor and intended parent)	Additive measure of all bills targeting egg donation; 1 = presence of bill, 0 = absence of bill.
Donor Behavior	Informed consent, compensation, parentage responsibilities	Additive measure of all bills targeting egg donors and egg donor activities. 1 = presence of bill, 0 = absence of bill.
Disposition	Disposition limits, disposition informed consent	Policies that limit or enforce informed consent on disposition of donated eggs. 1 = presence of bill, 0 = absence of bill.
Parental Rights	Intended parental responsibility	Policies that regulate who are parents and guardians in relation to egg donations. These are policies that relate to the legal relationships and legal rights in regard to the relationships between "intended parents" and donor-conceived children. 1 = presence of bill, 0 = absence of bill.
Research	Cloning, chimeras, funding	Policies that restrict egg donation in the context of cloning and/or chimeric research. Includes restrictions on funding for nonreproductive research involving donated eggs. 1 = presence of bill, 0 = absence of bill.

DATA COLLECTION OF EGG DONATION BILLS, 1995–2010

Research in chapters 2, 3, and 4 relies on original data on egg donation bills collected at the state level. Unlike previous studies, this project examines egg donation legislation at the agenda-setting stage, providing crucial insight into the interest, activity, and framing of reproductive technologies and relevant political, social, and economic issues (Bonnicksen 2007). The methods employed in this project initially used online searches of state legislative archives in 2012, and the results were cross-checked with a Lexis-Nexis State Capital legislative search in 2015 using the same search terms (table 10). In the original data set, I collected data on a universe of bills that reflected legislative activity related to assisted reproductive technologies. This universe encompassed the following categories of bills: egg donation, surrogacy, parentage, somatic cell nuclear transfer, and insurance coverage of ART. In the second round of data collection and data checking, I isolated all bills immediately relevant to egg donation.

For the search terms used in online legislative website search engines and LexisNexis State Capital, see table 11. While this

TABLE 10

Search Terms

In vitro fertilization
Gamete
Infertility
Oocyte
Ovum
Assisted reproductive technologies
Assisted reproduction
Reproductive technology
Reproductive cloning
Somatic cell nuclear transfer
Donation
Embryo
Biotech

study uses unique methods to collect legislative data on ART, search terms were derived from research on similar studies of ART policy, specifically from passed ART bills and studies of surrogacy (Bonnicksen 2007, Markens 2007, Heidt-Forsythe 2010, Von Hagel 2014). Lastly, Boolean operators were used to capture ART bills in legislative website searches—for example, I searched for "assisted repro*" alongside "assisted reproduction." Searches were done for regular sessions of the House and Senate in each state.[1] House and Senate versions of bills were collected as separate bills.

After searches were completed, introduced versions of bills were analyzed by two coders, who read each bill. First, bills were coded according to their aim, reproduction or research. Bills could be coded in both categories. Then, bills were coded in each

TABLE II
Egg Donation Bill Categories

Donor informed consent

Donor compensation

Donor parental responsibilities

Disposition limits

Disposition informed consent

Intended parental responsibilities

Business

Research cloning

Research chimeras

Research funding

category (reproduction and research) according to their substantive focus. The categories of egg donation bills are in Table II.

While this search collected bills unrelated to egg donation (such as surrogacy or cloning), bills were coded according to best fit—the overall subject of the bill. If this was in question, paragraphs were counted in the introduced version of the bill. For example, if there was a bill in which the majority of the text (measured in paragraphs) was devoted to egg donation, and a minority of the text was devoted to surrogacy, the bill was coded as an egg donation bill. After the bill was coded, it was entered into a spreadsheet where the bill number, year, category of policy, and outcome (signed into law, vetoed) were recorded. If searches could not be completed for the entire 1995 to 2010 period, this data was noted and data entry began on the first year available for searching on each legislative website. In total, these methods culled over eight hundred bills in five categories, among forty-nine states, between 1995 and 2010.

NOTES

INTRODUCTION

1. James Thompson and his team from the University of Wisconsin successfully created the first human embryonic stem cells from human blastocysts in 1998 (Thomson et al. 1998). Stem cells are "pluripotent" cells, meaning that they can generate any kind of cell. This potential means that pluripotent cells have incredible medical and technological applications; degenerative disease and disability may someday be treated by stem cell research technologies, allowing people to regenerate neural, bone, and muscle cells. Additionally, human eggs can be used for somatic cell nuclear transfer research (also known as "reproductive cloning), where a nucleus of a differentiated cell is placed inside of a donated oocyte (Robinton and Daley 2012, Roxland 2012). The process is still in its nascent stages of development. Moreover, alternatives to human eggs exist: in 2006, induced pluripotent cells were developed, which created pluripotent cells without oocytes (Takahashi and Yamanaka 2006). These cells are not perfect replacements for human embryonic stem cell lines, and more research is needed to determine how induced pluripotent cells can be used for regenerative medicine (Robinton and Daley 2012). As these substitutions are imperfect, donated human eggs are still necessary for

research on human embryonic stem cell lines and somatic cell nuclear transfer (Roxland 2012, Deuse et al. 2015).

2. The Center for Genetics and Society is a "nonprofit social justice organization that works to create an equitable future where human genetic and reproductive technologies benefit the common good" (Center for Genetics and Society 2017). The center produces scholarship and, in the public sphere, discusses issues of biomedicine, reproduction, stem cell research, identity, bioethics, and politics; the center is particularly active in California politics with respect to reproductive technologies, which I discuss in chapter 3.

3. This image of egg donation in the US as the Wild West—where libertarian, laissez-faire access to complex reproductive technologies prevails—is in sharp contrast to other reproductive issues in the US. While egg donation is seemingly ungoverned by politics, other reproductive issues have been a source of contentious and vigorous policymaking. Abortion and contraception have been tightly regulated throughout the nineteenth, twentieth, and twenty-first centuries at the state and national levels, with acceleration of antiabortion policy implementation, in particular, at the state level since 2010 (Nash et al. 2017).

4. There are exceptions to this claim—Charis Thompson's (2013) and Ruha Benjamin's (2013) excellent work on the case of California demonstrates a careful consideration of the public deliberation and policymaking related to stem cell research, although these works are not solely focused on egg donation.

5. The sex/gender system is the relationship that is often assumed between biological sex and gender; in this system, female or male biological sex is permanently fixed to notions of femininity and masculinity. In dominant ideologies about the sex/gender system, for example, female biological sex is seen as inextricably connected to feminine expression and behavior. The sex/gender system has been highly criticized by radical and postmodern feminist scholars, who argue that the relationship between biological sex and gender is subjective and mutable.

6. This language is also rooted in the concept of the gift transaction found in blood and organ donation, best known from Richard Tit-

muss's groundbreaking book on the intersection of altruism and blood donation, *The Gift Relationship* (1997). However, while this gift language is present in egg donation markets (where norms of femininity prevail), it does not exist in sperm donation markets—gifts, altruism, and care are more highly valued in the egg transaction. For further discussions of altruism and compensation in gamete and organ donation, see Michele Goodwin (2006, 2010) and Almeling (2011).

7. Other studies of feminist policy measure it like any policy in the wide category of women's issues that is not explicitly antifeminist, arguably a broader measure (Bratton 2002, Bratton and Haynie 1999). Despite this broad measure, findings related to the gender gap in policy leadership are the same as for more narrow measures of feminist policy.

8. For example, abortion and contraception are often studied through the lens of feminist policy (e.g., Reingold et al. 2015, Bratton 2002, Saint-Germain 1989), and policies can be delineated by (1) promoting equality and the status of women as a group and/or (2) not being explicitly antifeminist. In the case of abortion and contraception, access to these technologies is considered to be feminist, as it promotes women's reproductive and bodily autonomy (which is connected to social, economic, and political liberty and independence). Blocking such access would be considered antifeminist policy. In the case of egg donation, access versus blocking access does not necessarily define policy as feminist or antifeminist, as discussed in this chapter and chapter 4.

9. Reingold et al. (2015) found that, during this period (1997–2012), other factors also enabled and encouraged conservative Republican women to be policy leaders on antifeminist, antiabortion legislation: increasing numbers of conservative Republican women in state legislatures, Republican legislative control in many states, the prominence of abortion as a cornerstone political issue for the GOP, and increased women-centered advocacy in the antiabortion movement all contributed to this pattern.

10. One such website is We Are Egg Donors (www.weareeggdonors .com), which is connected to a restricted Facebook group for approved donors and women interested in egg donation.

CHAPTER ONE. DREAM OR NIGHTMARE?

1. In this early period of assisted reproductive technology, people of color, non-Christians, and same-sex couples struggled to find clinics that would serve their infertility needs without discrimination by, for example, banking donor eggs and sperm from nonwhite donors (Roberts 1998, Daniels and Heidt-Forsythe 2012).

2. After this period of rapid growth in consumer use of egg donation in the mid-1990s, there was another shift, in the gendered experience of reproduction and access to technology in a stratified system. Technological innovation—such as the explosion in genetic testing available to parents, donors, and children conceived through assisted reproductive technologies—shaped the concepts of health and medicine. Called *biomedicalization,* biomedical and pharmaceutical development and research enabled new ways to define human experiences of infertility and involuntary childlessness (Clarke et al. 2010). Rooted in the idea of medicalization—in which common human problems and conditions are defined as treatable medical conditions—people experience illness, health, and medicine according to identities of gender, race, and class, which alleviate or aggravate access to medical care in a system of biomedicalization (Clarke et al. 2010, Mamo and Fosket 2009).

3. Some states did cover infertility treatment via public insurance until the 1980s; however, these policies were completely disbanded in parallel with stronger restrictions on social welfare provisions, including policies like Family Caps, aimed to reduce reproduction by recipients (King and Meyer 1997, Roberts 1998).

4. *Griswold v. Connecticut* (1965) is a Supreme Court decision that defined contraception (at least among married, heterosexual couples) as an individual choice protected by Constitutional definitions of marital privacy, effectively overturning contraceptive bans that had been put into place by the Comstock Acts in the nineteenth century. In 1971, this sphere of privacy was extended to single and unmarried individuals by the Supreme Court decision in *Eisenstadt v. Baird* (1972).

5. *Roe v. Wade* (1973), one of the most infamous Supreme Court decisions of the twentieth century, protected limited abortion access,

particularly in the first trimester of pregnancy and with the advice of a medical professional.

6. Some scholarship in the morality politics literature defines morality policy as a form of redistributive policy—that is, legislators shift resources among the population according to changes in moral values (Haider-Markel and Meier 1996, Meier 1994, Mooney and Lee 1995, Schroedel 2000).

7. Morality policy issues allow for high levels of citizen participation in debates and deliberation; moreover, political actors are highly responsive to citizens and religious interest groups on morality issues (Camobreco and Barnello 2008, Cohen and Barrilleaux 1993, Cook, Jelen, and Wilcox 1992, Norrander and Wilcox 2001).

8. In a similar vein, LGBTQ rights issues are often labeled as a monolithic morality policy, when subissues (such as same-sex adoption policy) vary in how they adhere to the characteristics of morality politics (Mucciaroni 2011).

9. The ASRM has since abandoned recommendations for compensation limits owing to their settlement in the antitrust case *Kamakahi v. ASRM* (ASRM 2016).

10. See for example Smith (2009).

CHAPTER TWO. FRAMING EGG DONATION AT THE STATE LEVEL

1. For a full description of data sources for the policy narrative analysis of my four cases, please see appendix 3.

2. The process of framing egg donation as a political issue is mediated by the concept of salience: in a framing process, certain information is highlighted as more relevant and important than other information (Entman 1993, 53). In the process of framing egg donation as a social and political issue, elite political actors and those who want to claim ownership over egg donation make certain parts of egg donation more noticeable, poignant, or meaningful to fellow elites, consumers, and the broader public. This often means omitting certain realities about egg donation in order to promote particular images, messages, and symbols. Salience and omission play important roles in

defining egg donation as an issue worth deliberating; moreover, the processes of salience and omission are crucial in understanding the US regulation of egg donation for reproduction versus egg donation for research.

3. Louisiana passed these restrictions in 2016; while in conflict with Supreme Court decisions in *United States v. Windsor* (2013) and *Obergefell v. Hodges* (2015), the law has not been challenged, as of this writing.

4. The Dickey-Wicker Amendment, signed into law by President Bill Clinton, barred federal research money from funding Department of Health and Human Services research that would destroy any embryo, regardless of the origin of the embryo.

5. The bioethics groups involved were the Center for Genetics and Society and the Pro-Choice Alliance.

6. Proposition 71 is notable for how it symbolizes a strong state response to federal reluctance about stem cell donation, and how it signals California as a consumer-friendly state for stem cell research, egg donation in the research setting, and the biotechnology industry in general. As the first state to commit tax money to stem cell research and infrastructure, California was distinct. Although Massachusetts had passed a similar stem cell law, it did not have the same infrastructure and funding ramifications as Proposition 71.

7. Ortiz cosponsored SB 18 (2005) with George Runner. It was passed by the legislature, only to be vetoed by Governor Gray Davis.

8. Wrongful conception claims are those claims made by individuals who may "wrongfully" conceive after a medical procedure.

9. HB 214 was introduced in February 1999 by Representative Rob Marionneaux Jr. (D-District 18) and was signed into law by Governor Mike Foster in July of that year.

CHAPTER THREE. STATECRAFT IS
ALWAYS SOUL CRAFT

1. As discussed in the introduction, what constitutes feminist policy—defined according to Mazur's (2002) core tenets regarding targeting women as a group, advancing women's rights, and reducing gender-based inequalities—is complex in the case of egg donation, as

there have been heterogeneous feminist policy responses to the reproductive technology (Jesudason and Weitz 2015, Daniels and Heidt-
Forsythe 2012). However, this chapter and the next examine how
diverse stakeholders (including Republican men and women) utilize
and co-opt feminist rhetoric of gender, protection, and women's health
to frame the issue of egg donation in the state legislative sphere.

2. Project Vote Smart, http://votesmart.org/candidate/political-
courage-test/55235/liz-krueger/#.UO2TmIVm_7A.

3. The Arizona Family Project is a conservative pro-life group
started by Republican political consultant Constantin Querard in
2003. The primary function of the Arizona Family Project is to bestow
the "Friend of the Family" awards (always given to Arizona pro-life
Republicans), which are conferred yearly.

4. While Stump was the figurehead of HB 2142, the other cosponsors were not just demographically similar to Stump but also ideologically indistinguishable from Stump. Cosponsors Robert Yarbrough
and Steven Blendu, for example, received "Friend of the Family"
awards for their "strong commitment to strengthening Arizona's families [and] promoting pro-family values and ideals" (Arizona Family
Project 2012). Like Stump, Yarbrough and Blendu also received a 100
percent rating from Arizona Right to Life and the Center for Arizona
Policy (Project Vote Smart 2012).

CHAPTER FOUR. TOWARD A NEW
GENDERED PARTISANSHIP

1. Legislative data on egg donation before 1995 is more difficult to
obtain; while data in this chapter was found through scraping Lexis-
Nexis State Capital, and by secondary research of state legislative
websites, not all states in the data set (n = 49) provided results for the
1989–94 time period, according to the Boolean search I used for this
chapter. Pre-1989 data is generally not available across a wide sample
of state legislatures. Although the data in this chapter is left-censored,
down-weight effects of independent variables on bill introductions
and passage are not of great concern, owing to both the rarity of legislation before this time period and the common pattern of multiple bill

introduction and revision related to egg donation policy. According to a pilot study (Heidt-Forsythe 2012), among a sample of forty states, only three states (Illinois, California, and New York) introduced multiple egg donation bills per session during the period 1990 to 1998.

2. While the Fertility Clinic Success Rate and Certification Act was passed in 1992 with the intent to immediately collect data on the economic and clinical activities of fertility clinics across the states, it was not immediately funded to do so. Not until 1997 did the Centers for Disease Control, along with the Society for Assisted Reproductive Technology, release the first report describing fertility clinic data about reproductive technologies. The fact that the data has been collected and reported only since 1995 is a data limitation; however, considering the hypothesized relationship between the economic demands of the fertility clinic industry and egg donation legislation, as well as the increased attention to egg donation after 1995, this chapter examines egg donation legislation during the period of fertility clinic surveillance by the CDC.

3. Additionally, some states enforce *marriage* statutes that require intended parents to be legally married before they can access egg donation. This prevents single individuals (and before the federal legalization of same-sex marriage in 2015, same-sex couples) from using egg donation in fertility treatments. Since not all marriage statutes are clear about the use of donated eggs, I omitted this category of policy from my study.

4. This category excludes legislation that covers both reproductive and research contexts, which is classified in the other dependent variable categories in this study.

5. A chimera is an animal/human hybrid.

6. Nebraska has been excluded from my analysis of gender and partisanship owing to the nonpartisan legislature in that state.

7. In this sample of egg donation bills, I am interested in legislative events—the introduction of bills on egg donation per year, between 1995 and 2010. For each state/year, I include the first introduction of a bill on egg donation. Once a state has introduced a bill for a given year, it is coded as 1. If a state has not introduced a bill in a given year, it is

coded as 0. Once a state introduces a bill, future observations of bill introduction are dropped from the analysis.

8. Elazar's studies organized states into three categories: *moralist, individualist,* and *traditionalist* cultures—reflecting political culture of the individual versus society, the perceived role of government, and the roles political leaders play in state politics. Using Elazar's data, I have coded each state that has a moralist political culture as 1; I have coded each state that does not have a moralist political culture (defined as either individualist or traditional) as 0.

9. Survival analysis is defined as an analysis of *hazard rates* (the probabilities) of *failure or death* (a legislative event occurring) among a *risk set* (a set of states that are at risk of introducing a bill) during a *risk period* (the period of observation time in a study, also called a *spell*). From this information, this study can describe the probabilities of a state "surviving" (or not passing a bill) over a period of time, also known as a *survivor function.*

10. Among different types of event history analysis, the Cox proportional hazards regression model (a type of semiparametric modeling) is a flexible method used in political science studies when the authors do not make an assumption about the relationship between time and the hazard rate. While the researcher can assume that risk is dependent on time, the researcher does not need to specify if the hazard rate increases, decreases, or does both. As previous literature on the proposal and passage of egg donation legislation at the state level has not clearly established the relationship between policy proposal and/or passage and time, the Cox proportional hazards regression model is most useful for the analysis. A hazard rate greater than 1 indicates an increased risk of a public policy event occurring, while a hazard rate less than 1 indicates a decreased risk of a public policy event occurring. The proportionality assumption is tested through Schoenfeld and Scaled Tests (Cleves et al. 2004).

11. Event history analysis has the capacity to analyze diverse types of variables over time, a clear advantage of the method over OLS regressions and logistic regressions: the method can handle both time-dependent and time-independent covariates as well as incomplete

data. The Cox model assumes that each covariate has a proportional and constant effect on the risk of a public policy event occurring. This quality of survival analysis is especially useful when looking at independent variables in this study that vary with time and may be significant in increasing the risk that a state may introduce an egg donation bill, such as the percentage of all state legislators who are women. Additionally, survival analysis can deal with data that is "censored," meaning that incomplete information exists about the data owing to the constrained observation period. This too is an advantage of this methodology, as data on egg donation bills (and independent variables) are limited by data availability.

12. As noted earlier, 1995 to 2010 was a significant period for the development of the politics of egg donation. It was in 1995 that the Centers for Disease Control began to survey and gather data about the operation of fertility clinics, including donor egg services. Moreover, this period was one of explosive growth of consumer use of egg donation and increases in compensation for, advertising for, and recruitment of egg donors (Almeling 2011). Finally, this was a significant period for the development of stem cell and cloning research, which rose sharply in the late 1990s after the cloning of Dolly the sheep.

13. To weigh partisan women's bill introductions, I divided the number of bills introduced by Republican and Democratic women, respectively, by the proportion of each group in the legislature.

CONCLUSION

1. This view of egg donation as a Republican women's issue is not without critique, however. As evidenced by the case of Arizona's Representative Robert Stump, Republican men have also adopted the issue in state legislatures, co-opting women's health rhetoric to further restrict reproductive options for infertility patients and bodily autonomy for egg donors. The boundary between imposing a conservative vision of empowered motherhood and adopting restrictions on the reproductive behavior and labor of women (as an extension of abortion and contraception restriction) is porous. Republican women

joined Representative Stump in cosponsoring Arizona's 2006 bill to ban compensation for egg donation and were mostly silent while others advocated acceptance of the bill. Other studies have noted that conservative rhetoric related to abortion restriction is similar to rhetoric used to justify restrictions on reproductive technologies (Jesudason and Weitz 2015, Thompson 2005; see chapter 4 of the present volume).

2. Particularly since the 1980s and 1990s, there has been a pointed attempt by both parties in the US to devolve policy, especially social and health policy (Shipan and Volden 2012). Other examples of this policy devolution are social welfare and education, where federal authority has given way to increasing state governance.

APPENDIX 3

1. As Nebraska is the only state with a unitary legislature, information on egg donation bills was collected but the state was not considered in case selection.

WORKS CITED

ACOG (American College of Obstetricians and Gynecologists). 2014. "Oocyte Cryopreservation." Committee Opinion no. 584: 221–222. www.acog.org/Clinical-Guidance-and-Publications /Committee-Opinions/Committee-on-Gynecologic-Practice/Oocyte-Cryopreservation.

Adashi, Eli, and Laura Dean. 2016. "Access to and Use of Infertility Services in the US: Framing the Challenges." *Fertility and Sterili*ty 105 (5): 1113–1118.

Aldrich, John H., and David W. Rohde. 2001. "The Logic of Conditional Party Government: Revisiting the Electoral Connection." In *Congress Reconsidered*, edited by Lawrence Dodd and Bruce Oppenheimer. Washington, DC: CQ Press.

Almeling, Rene. 2007. "Selling Genes, Selling Gender: Egg Agencies, Sperm Banks, and the Medical Market in Genetic Material." *American Sociological Review* 72 (3): 319–340.

———. 2009. "Gender and the Value of Bodily Goods: Commodification in Egg and Sperm Donation." *Law and Contemporary Problems* 72 (37): 37–59.

———. 2011. *Sex Cells: The Medical Market for Eggs and Sperm*. Berkeley: University of California Press.

Arizona Family Project. 2012. "Friend of the Family Awards." http://azproject.org.

Arizona House Republicans. 2006. "House Legislation Protects Human Egg Donors." February 27. Press release in the possession of the author.

Arizona State Legislature. 2006. "Pamela Gorman: Member Page." www.azleg.gov/MembersPage.asp?Member_ID=20&Legislature=47&Session_ID=83.

ASRM (American Society for Reproductive Medicine). 2007. "Financial Compensation of Oocyte Donors." *Fertility and Sterility* 88:305–309. The Ethics Committee of the American Society for Reproductive Medicine wrote this brief.

———. 2014. "State Infertility Insurance Laws." November 12. www.asrm.org/insurance.aspx.

———. 2016a. "Financial Compensation of Oocyte Donors." *Fertility and Sterility* 106 (7): 15–19. www.reproductivefacts.org/globalassets/asrm/asrm-content/news-and-publications/ethics-committee-opinions/financial_compensation_of_oocyte_donors-pdfmembers.pdf.

———. 2016b. "Ovarian Hyperstimulation Syndrome: Fact Sheet." www.asrm.org/awards/detail.aspx?id=10274.

———. 2016c. "State Infertility Insurance Laws." www.asrm.org/detail.aspx?id=2850.

Associated Press (AP). 1987. "Clinic in Ohio Starts Egg Donor Plan." *New York Times,* July 15, 1987. www.nytimes.com/1987/07/15/us/clinic-in-ohio-starts-egg-donor-plan.html?pagewanted=print.

———. 2006. "Disgraced Korean Cloning Scientist Indicted." *New York Times,* May 12, 2006. www.nytimes.com/2006/05/12/world/asia/12korea.html.

Banchoff, Thomas. 2005. "Path Dependence and Value-Driven Issues: The Comparative Politics of Stem Cell Research." *World Politics* 57: 200–230.

Barrett, Michele. 1980. *Oppression Today: Problems in Marxist Feminist Analysis.* Verso: London.

Baumgartner, Frank, Jeffrey Berry, Marie Hojnacki, David Kimball, and Beth Leech. 2009. *Lobbying and Policy Change: Who Wins, Who Loses, and Why.* Chicago: University of Chicago Press.

Baumgartner, Frank R., and Bryan D. Jones. 1993. *Agendas and Instability in American Politics.* Chicago: University of Chicago Press.

Baumgartner, Frank, and Beth Leech. 1998. *Basic Interests: The Importance of Groups in Politics and Political Science.* Princeton, NJ: Princeton University Press.

Beckwith, Karen. 2011. "Interests, Issues and Preferences: Women's Interests and Epiphenomena of Activism." *Politics and Gender* 7 (3): 424–429.

Bell, Ann V. 2009. "It's Way Out of My League: Low-Income Women's Experiences of Medicalized Infertility." *Gender and Society* 23 (5): 688–709.

———. 2010. "Beyond (Financial) Accessibility: Inequalities within the Medicalisation of Infertility." *Sociology of Health and Illness* 32 (4): 631–646.

———. 2014. "Diagnostic Diversity: The Role of Social Class in Diagnostic Experiences of Infertility." *Sociology of Health and Illness* 36 (4): 516–530.

———. 2015. "Overcoming (and Maintaining) Reproductive Difference: Similarities in the Gendered Experience of Infertility." *Qualitative Sociology* 38:439–458.

———. 2016. "The Margins of Medicalization: Diversity and Context through the Case of Infertility." *Social Science and Medicine* 156 (2016): 39–46.

Benjamin, Ruha. 2013. *People's Science: Bodies and Rights on the Stem Cell Frontier.* Stanford, CA: Stanford University Press.

Berry, Frances, and William Berry. 1990. "State Lottery Adoptions as Policy Innovations: An Event History Analysis." *American Political Science Review* 84:395–416.

Berry, William D., Richard C. Fording, Evan J. Ringquist, Russell L. Hanson, and Carl Klarner. 2010. "Measuring Citizen and Government Ideology in the American States: A Re-appraisal." *State Politics and Policy Quarterly* 10:117–135.

Bitler, Marianne, and Lucie Schmidt. 2006. "Health Disparities and Infertility: Impacts of State-Level Insurance Mandates." *Fertility and Sterility* 85 (4): 858–865.

———. 2012. "Utilization of Infertility Treatments: The Effects of Insurance Mandates." *Demography* 49 (1): 125–149.

Blake, Valarie, Michelle McGowan, and Aaron Levine. 2015. "Conflicts of Interest and Effected Oversight of Assisted Reproduction Using Donated Oocytes." *Journal of Law, Medicine, and Ethics* 43 (2): 410–424.

Blanchfield, Bernadette, and Charlotte Patterson. 2012. "Utilization of Infertility Treatments: The Effects of Insurance Mandates." *Demography* 49 (1): 125–149.

———. 2015. "Racial and Sexual Minority Women's Receipt of Medical Assistance to Become Pregnant." *Health Psychology* 34 (6): 571–579.

Boffey, Phillip M. 1987. "The Vatican's Doctrine: Ethics Concern; Doctrine Follows Years of Debates on Procedures." *New York Times.* March 12.

Bonnicksen, Andrea. 1989. *In Vitro Fertilization: Building Policy from Laboratories to Legislatures.* New York: Columbia University Press.

———. 2002. *Crafting a Cloning Policy: From Dolly to Stem Cells.* Washington, DC: Georgetown University Press.

———. 2007. "Oversight of Assisted Reproductive Technologies: The Last Twenty Years." In *Reprogenetics: Law, Policy, and Ethical Issues,* edited by Lori P. Knowles and Gregory E. Kaebnick, 64–86. Baltimore: Johns Hopkins University Press.

Book of States. 2010. "Book of States Archive." http://knowledgecenter .csg.org/kc/category/content-type/bos-archive.

Box-Steffensmeier, Janet, and Brian Jones. 1997. "Time Is of the Essence: Event History Models in Political Science." *American Political Science Review* 41 (4): 336–383.

———. 2004. *Event History Modeling: A Guide for Social Scientists.* Analytical Methods for Social Research Series. Cambridge: Cambridge University Press.

Bratton, Kathleen. 2002. "The Effect of Legislative Diversity on Agenda Setting: Evidence from Six State Legislatures." *American Politics Research* 30 (2): 115–142.

Bratton, Kathleen, and Kerry Haynie. 1999. "Agenda Setting and Legislative Success in State Legislatures: The Effects of Gender and Race." *Journal of Politics* 61 (3): 658–679.

Bridges, Khiara. 2011. *Reproducing Race: An Ethnography of Pregnancy as a Site of Racialization.* Berkeley: University of California Press.

Brown, Edmund G., Jr. 2013. Veto letter for AB-926. www.gov.ca.gov /docs/AB_926_Veto_Message.pdf.

Browner, Carole, and Carolyn Sargent. 2011. *Reproduction, Globalization, and the State: New Theoretical and Ethnographic Perspectives.* Durham, NC: Duke University Press.

Brozan, Nadine. 1988. "Rising Use of Donated Eggs for Pregnancy Stirs Concern." *New York Times,* January 18. www.nytimes.com/1988 /01/18/us/rising-use-of-donated-eggs-for-pregnancy-stirs-concern .html?pagewanted=1.

Bureau of Labor Statistics. 2013. *Geographic Profile of Employment and Unemployment, 1995–2010.* Compiled by Brian Hannon, BLS. Washington, DC: Bureau of Labor Statistics. www.bls.gov/opub/gp /laugp.htm.

Caiazza, Amy. 2004. "Does Women's Representation in Elected Office Lead to Women-Friendly Policy? Analysis of State-Level Data." *Women and Politics* 26 (1): 35–70.

Cammisa, Anne, and Beth Reingold. 2004. "Women in State Legislatures and State Legislative Research: Beyond Sameness and Difference." *State Politics and Policy Quarterly* 4 (2): 181–210.

Camobreco, John F., and Michelle A. Barnello. 2008. "Democratic Responsiveness and Policy Shock: The Case of State Abortion Policy." *State Politics and Policy Quarterly* 8 (1): 48–65.

Carey, John, Richard Niemi, and Lynda Powell. 1998. "The Effects of Term Limits on State Legislatures." *Legislative Studies Quarterly* 23 (2): 271–300.

Carmines, Edward, and James Stimson. 1980. "The Two Faces of Issue Voting." *American Political Science Review* 74 (1): 78–91.

Carroll, Susan J. 1992. "Women State Legislators, Women's Organizations, and the Representation of Women's Culture in the United States." In *Women Transforming Politics,* edited by Jill Bystydzienski. Bloomington: Indiana University Press.

———. 2000. *Impact of Women in Public Office.* Bloomington: Indiana University Press.

CDC (Centers for Disease Control). 2013. "ART Success Rates: Archived ART Reports and Spreadsheets." www.cdc.gov/art/reports/archive .html.

————. 2014. *Centers for Disease Control 2014 Assisted Reproductive Technology Fertility Clinic Success Rates Report.* www.cdc.gov/art/reports/2014/fertility-clinic.html.

————. 2017. "Archived ART Reports and Spreadsheets." www.cdc.gov/art/reports/archive.html.

CDC, American Society for Reproductive Medicine, and Society for Assisted Reproductive Technology. 2016. *ART Success Rates: 2015 ART National Summary Report.* Atlanta, GA: US Department of Human Services. www.cdc.gov/art/reports/2015/national-summary.html.

Ceballo, Rosario. 1999. "'The Only Black Woman on the Face of the Earth That Cannot Have a Baby': Two Women's Stories." *Women's Untold Stories: Breaking Silence, Talking Back, Voicing Complexity,* edited by Mary Romero and Abigail Stewart. Routledge: New York.

Ceballo, Rosario, Antonia Abbey, and Deborah Schooler. 2010. "Perceptions of Women's Infertility: What Do Physicians See?" *Fertility and Sterility* 93 (4): 1066–1073.

Ceballo, Rosario, Erin Graham, and Jamie Hart. 2015. "Silent and Infertile: An Intersectional Analysis of the Experiences of Socioeconomically Diverse African-American Women with Infertility." *Psychology of Women Quarterly* 39 (4): 497–511.

Center for American Women and Politics. 2018. "Fact Sheet Archive: Women in State Legislatures, 1975 to 2016." www.cawp.rutgers.edu/fact-sheet-archive-women-state-legislatures.

Center for Genetics and Society. 2006. "California Enacts Law to Reduce Risks to Women Who Provide Eggs for Stem Cell Research." September 9. www.geneticsandsociety.org/press-statement/california-enacts-law-reduce-risks-women-who-provide-eggs-stem-cell-research.

————. 2017. "About CGS." www.geneticsandsociety.org/about-us.

Chang, Wendy, and Alan H. DeCherney. 2009. "The History of Regulation of Assisted Reproductive Technology (ART) in the USA: A Work in Progress." *Human Fertility* 6 (2): 64–70.

Clarke, Adele, Laura Mamo, Jennifer Ruth Fosket, Jennifer Fishman, and Janet Shim. 2010. *Biomedicalization: Technoscience, Health, and Illness in the U.S.* Durham, NC: Duke University Press.

Cleves, Mario, William W. Gould, Roberto G. Gutierrez, and Yulia Marchenko. 2004. *An Introduction to Survival Analysis Using Stata.* 2nd ed. College Station, TX: Stata Press.

Coeytaux, Francine. 2005. Joint Informational Hearing. http://shea.senate.ca.gov/sites/shea.senate.ca.../PROP_71_OVERSIGHT_TRANSCRIPT.doc.

Cohen, Jean, Alan Trounson, Karen Dawson, Howard Jones, Johan Hazekamp, Karl-Gosta Nygren, and Lars Hamberger. 2005. "The Early Days of IVF outside of the UK." *Human Reproduction Update* 11 (5): 439–459.

Cohen, Jeffrey E., and Charles Barrilleaux. 1993. "Public Opinion, Interest Groups and Public Policy Making: Abortion Policy in the American States." In *Understanding the New Politics of Abortion,* edited by M. Goggin, 203–221. Newbury Park, CA: Sage.

Colen, Shellee. 1986. "Stratified Reproduction: The Case of Domestic Workers in New York City." Paper presented at a meeting of the American Ethnological Society, Wrightsville Beach, NC.

————. 1995. "'Like a Mother to Them': Stratified Reproduction and West Indian Childcare Workers and Employers in New York." In *Conceiving the New World Order: The Global Politics of Reproduction,* edited by Faye Ginsburg and Rayna Rapp. Berkeley: University of California Press.

Concerned Women for America. 2010. "Eggsploitation Documentary Reveals Secrets of the Infertility Industry." https://concerned-women.org/eggsploitation-documentary-reveals-secrets-of-infertility-industry/.

Connell, R. W. 1987. *Gender and Power.* Cambridge, UK: Polity Press.

Cook, Elizabeth A., Ted G. Jelen, and Clyde Wilcox. 1992. *Between Two Absolutes: Public Opinion and the Politics of Abortion.* Boulder, CO: Westview Press.

Corbett, Shannon, Doron Shmorgun, and Paul Claman. 2014. "The Prevention of Ovarian Hyperstimulation Syndrome." *Journal of Obstetrics and Gynaecology Canada* 36 (11): 1024–1033.

Corea, Gina. 1981. *Man-Made Women: How Reproductive Technologies Affect Women.* Bloomington: Indiana University Press.

Cowell-Meyers, Kimberley, and Laura Langbein. 2009. "Linking Women's Descriptive and Substantive Representation in the United States." *Politics and Gender* 5 (4): 491–518.

Crockin, Susan L. 2007. "Overview of Reproductive Genetics and the Law." Genetics and Public Policy Center, August. www.dnapolicy.org.

Crowley, Elise, Jocelyn, Radha Jagannathan, and Galo Falchettore. 2012. "The Effect of Child Support Enforcement on Abortion in the United States." *Social Science Quarterly* 93 (1): 152–172.

Daniels, Cynthia. 1993. *At Women's Expense: State Power and the Politics of Fetal Rights.* Cambridge, MA: Harvard University Press.

———. 2006. *Exposing Men: The Science and Politics of Male Reproduction.* New York: Oxford University Press.

Daniels, Cynthia, and Erin Heidt-Forsythe. 2012. "'Gendered Eugenics' and the Problematic of 'Free Market' Reproductive Technologies: Sperm and Egg Donation in the United States." *Signs* 37 (3): 719–747.

Darcy, R., Susan Welch, and Janet Clark. 1994. *Women, Elections, and Representation.* New York: Longman.

Deckman, Melissa. 2016. *Tea Party Women: Mama Grizzlies, Grassroots Leaders, and the Changing Face of the American Right.* New York: NYU Press.

Deuse, T., D. Wang, M. Stubbendorff, R. Itagaki, A. Grabosch, L. Greaves, and S. Schrepfer. 2015. "SCNT-Derived ESCs with Mismatched Mitochondria Trigger and Immune Response in Allogenic Hosts." *Stem Cell* 16 (1): 33–38.

Dickenson, Donna. 2006. "The Lady Vanishes: What's Missing from the Stem Cell Debate." *Journal of Bioethical Inquiry* 3 (1–2): 43–54.

———. 2007. *Property in the Body.* Oxford: Oxford University Press.

Dodson, Debra. 2006. *The Impact of Women in Congress.* New York: Oxford University Press.

Dodson, Debra, and Susan J. Carroll. 1991. *Reshaping the Agenda: Women in State Legislatures.* New Brunswick, NJ: Center for the American Woman and Politics.

Dresser, Rebecca. 2000. "Regulating Assisted Reproduction." *Hastings Center Report.* November.

Edelman, M. 1964. *The Symbolic Uses of Politics.* Champaign: University of Illinois.

Egg Donation Center of Dallas. 2017. "Requirements for Donors." www.eggdonorcenter.com/donor_requirements.html.

Ehrenreich, Barbara, and Deirdre English. 1978. *For Her Own Good: Two Centuries of the Experts' Advice to Women.* New York: Anchor.

Eig, Jonathan. 2014. *The Birth of the Pill.* New York: W. W. Norton.

Ekine, Jon. 2013. "Progressives Abandon Idea That Women Control Their Own Bodies." *Forbes* (July 31). www.forbes.com/sites/jonentine /2013/07/31/progressives-abandon-stand-that-women-control-their-own-bodies-and-eggs/#6351e2d6a0c8.

Elazar, Daniel. 1966. *American Federalism: A View from the States.* New York: Crowell.

———. 1970. *Cities of the Prairie.* New York: Basic Books.

———. 1980. "Afterword: Steps in the Study of American Political Culture." *Publius* 10 (2): 127–139.

Ellison, B., and J. Meliker. 2011. "Assessing the Risk of Ovarian Hyperstimulation Syndrome in Egg Donation: Implications for Human Embryonic Stem Cell Research." *American Journal of Bioethics* 11 (9): 22–30.

Entman, Robert. 1993. "Framing: Toward a Clarification of a Fractured Paradigm." *Journal of Communication* 43 (4): 51–58.

Farquhar, Dion. 1996. *The Other Machine: Discourse and Reproductive Technologies.* New York: Routledge.

Feree, Myra Marx, William Gamson, Jurgen Gerhards, and Dieter Rucht. 2002. "Four Models of the Public Sphere in Modern Democracies." *Theory and Society* 31 (3): 289–324.

Fisher, Jill. 2007. "Coming Soon to a Physician Near You: Medical Neoliberalism and Pharmaceutical Clinical Trials." *Harvard Health Policy Review* 8 (1): 61–70.

———. 2013. "Expanding the Frame of 'Voluntariness' in Informed Consent: Structural Coercion and the Power of Social and Economic Context." *Kennedy Institute of Ethics Journal* 23 (4): 355–379.

Franklin, Sarah. 1995. "Postmodern Procreation." In *Conceiving the New World Order: The Global Politics of Reproduction,* edited by Faye Ginsburg and Rayna Rapp. Berkeley: University of California.

———. 2013. *Biological Relatives.* Durham, NC: Duke University Press.

Franklin, Sarah, and Helene Ragoné. 1998. *Reproducing Reproduction: Kinship, Power, and Technological Innovation.* Philadelphia: University of Pennsylvania Press.

Frederick, Brian. 2009. "Are Female House Members Still More Liberal in a Polarized Era? The Conditional Nature of the Relationship between Descriptive and Substantive Representation." *Congress and the Presidency* 36 (2): 181–202.

Freeman, Jo. 1987. "Who You Know versus Who You Represent: Feminist Influences in the Democratic and Republican Parties." In *The Women's Movements of the United States and Western Europe: Feminist Consciousness, Political Opportunity, and Public Policy,* edited by Mary Katzenstein and Carol Mueller, 215–244. Philadelphia: Temple University Press.

Gamson, W.A., and A. Modigliani. 1987. "The Changing Culture of Affirmative Action." *Research in Political Sociology* 3: 137–177.

Garland-Thomson, Rosemarie. 2002. "Integrating Disability, Transforming Feminist Theory." *NWSA Journal* 14 (3): 1–32.

Gaskell, Stephanie. 2005. "Pols Urge State to Hike Stem Cell Research $$." *New York Post.* http://nypost.com/2005/01/17/pols-urge-state-to-hike-stem-cell-research/.

Gaventa, John. 1980. *Power and Powerlessness.* Champaign: University of Illinois Press.

Ginsburg, Faye, and Rayna Rapp. 1995. *Conceiving the New World Order: The Global Politics of Reproduction.* Berkeley: University of California Press.

Goggin, Malcolm, and Deborah Orth. 2004. "The United States: National Talk and State Action in Governing ART." In *Comparative Biomedical Policy: Governing Assisted Reproductive Technologies,* edited by Ivar Bleiklie, Malcolm Goggin, and Christine Rothmayr. London: Routledge.

Goodwin, Michele. 2006. *Black Markets: The Supply and Demand of Body Parts.* New York: Cambridge University Press.

———. 2010. *Baby Markets: Money and the New Politics of Creating Families.* Cambridge: Cambridge University Press.

Gootman, Elissa. 2012. "So Eager for Grandchildren, They're Paying the Egg-Freezing Clinic." *New York Times.* May 13. www.nytimes

.com/2012/05/14/us/eager-for-grandchildren-and-putting-daughters-eggs-in-freezer.html.

Gordon, Linda. 2004. *The Moral Property of Women*. Champaign: University of Illinois Press.

Gormley, William. 1986. "Regulatory Issue Networks in a Federal System." *Polity* 18:595–620.

Greil, Arthur L., Julia McQuillan, Karina M. Shreffler, Katherine M. Johnson, and Kathleen S. Slauson-Blevins. 2011. "Race/Ethnicity and Medical Services for Infertility: Stratified Reproduction in a Population-Based Sample of U.S. Women." *Journal of Health and Social Behavior* 52:493–507.

Greil, Arthur L., Kathleen Slauson-Blevins, Stacy Tiemeyer, Julia McQuillan, and Karina M. Shreffler. 2016. "A New Way to Estimate the Potential Unmet Need for Infertility Services among Women in the US." *Journal of Women's Health* 25 (2): 133–138.

Guttmacher Institute. 2018. "January 2018 Fact Sheet: State Facts about Abortion: Louisiana." www.guttmacher.org/fact-sheet/state-facts-about-abortion-louisiana.

Haider-Markel, Donald P., and Kenneth J. Meier. 1996. "The Politics of Gay and Lesbian Rights: The Case of Legislative Voting on Lesbian and Gay Issues." *Policy Studies Journal* 27 (4): 735–749.

Hamilton, Rebecca. 2010. Debate Transcript, HB 3077. Oklahoma State House of Representatives. www.oklegislature.gov/BillInfo.aspx?Bill=HB3077&Session=1000.

Harwood, Karey. 2007. *The Infertility Treadmill*. Durham, NC: University of North Carolina Press.

Hawkesworth, Mary. 1997. "Confounding Gender." *Signs: Journal of Women in Culture and Society* 22 (3): 649–685.

Hecht, Alexander. 2001. "The Wild Wild West: Inadequate Regulation of Assisted Reproductive Technology." *Houston Journal of Health Law and Policy*. 1:227–261.

Heidt-Forsythe, Erin. 2010. "ART and the State: Federalism and the Regulation of Assisted Reproductive Technologies." Presented at the annual meeting of the Midwest Political Science Association, Chicago, IL.

————. 2012. "Reproducing a State: Morality, Economics, and the Politics of Location in Assisted Reproductive Technology Legislation, 1990 to 2010." Presented at the annual meeting of the Western Political Science Association, Portland, OR.

————. 2013. "Reconceiving the State: Morals, Markets, and State Regulation of Assisted Reproductive Technologies." PhD diss., Rutgers University.

————. 2016. "You Can Go Your Own Way: Oocyte Donation in California and New York." *BioSocieties* 11 (4): 476–496.

Holland, Suzanne. 2007. "Market Transactions in Reprogenetics." In *Reprogenetics: Law, Policy, and Ethical Issues,* edited by Lori P. Knowles and Gregory Kaebnick. Baltimore: Johns Hopkins University Press.

House Bill 2142a. 2006. Arizona State Legislature. https://apps.azleg.gov/BillStatus/BillOverview?billnumber=HB2142&Sessionid=83.

House Bill 2142b. 2006. Rules Committee Meeting Minutes. February 21.

Huddy, Leonie, and Nayda Terkildsen. 1993. "Gender Stereotypes and the Perception of Male and Female Candidates." *American Journal of Political Science* 46 (3): 503–525.

Ikemoto, Lisa. 2009. "Eggs as Capital: Human Egg Procurement in the Fertility Industry and the Stem Cell Research Enterprise." *Signs: Journal of Women in Culture and Society* 34 (4): 763–781.

ICOC (Independent Citizens Oversight Committee). 2006. CIRM meeting transcripts. www.cirm.ca.gov/sites/default/files/files/agenda/transcripts/06–02–06.pdf.

Inhorn, Marcia, and Michael Fakih. 2009. "Arab Americans, African Americans, and Infertility: Barriers to Reproduction and Medical Care." *Fertility and Sterility* 85 (4): 844–852.

Jackson, Chantal. 2008. "State Pulls Back on Stem Cell Funding." NJ.com. www.nj.com/newark/index.ssf/2008/06/state_pulls_back_on_stem_cell.html.

Jasanoff, Sheila. 2005. *Designs on Nature: Science and Democracy in Europe and the US.* Princeton, NJ: Princeton University Press.

————. 2011. *Reframing Rights: Bioconstitutionalism in the Genetic Age.* Cambridge, MA: MIT Press.

Jelen, Ted G., and Clyde Wilcox. 2003. "Causes and Consequences of Public Attitudes toward Abortion: A Review and Research Agenda." *Political Research Quarterly* 56 (4): 489–500.

Jesudason, Sujatha, and Tracy Weitz. 2015. "Eggs and Abortion: 'Women-Protective' Language Used by Opponents in Legislative Debates over Reproductive Health." *Journal of Law, Medicine, and Ethics* (Summer 2015): 259–269.

Kaempffert, Waldeman. 1934. "This Week in Science: Rabbits Born in Glass." *New York Times,* May 13.

Kalfoglou, Andrea L., and Gail Geller. 2000. "A Follow-Up Study with Oocyte Donors Exploring Their Experiences, Knowledge, and Attitudes about the Use of Their Oocytes and the Outcome of the Donation." *Fertility and Sterility* 74 (4): 660–667.

Kalfoglou, Andrea L., and Joel Gittelsohn. 2000. "A Qualitative Follow-Up Study of Women's Experiences with Oocyte Donation." *Human Reproduction* 15 (4): 798–805.

Kalfoglou, A. L., J. Scott, and K. Hudson. 2008. "Attitudes about Preconception Sex Selection: A Focus Group Study with Americans." *Human Reproduction* 23 (12): 2731–2736.

Karch, Andrew. 2007. "Emerging Issues and Future Directions in State Policy Diffusion Research." *State Politics and Policy Quarterly* 7 (1): 54–80.

Keehn, Jason, Eve Holwell, Rugayyah Abdul-Karim, Lisa Judy Chin, Chend-Shiun Leu, Mark Sauer, and Robert Klitzman. 2012. "Recruiting Egg Donors Online: An Analysis of IVF Clinic and Agency Websites' Adherence to ASRM Guidelines." *Fertility Sterility* 98 (4): 995–1000.

Kenney, Nancy, and Michelle McGowan. 2010. "Looking Back: Egg Donors' Retrospective Evaluations of Their Motivations, Expectations, and Experiences during Their First Donation Cycle." *Fertility and Sterility* 93 (2): 455–466.

King, Leslie, and Madonna Harrington Meyer. 1997. "The Politics of Reproductive Benefits: US Insurance Coverage of Contraceptive and Infertility Treatments." *Gender and Society* 11 (1): 8–30.

Kirkpatrick, Kellee J. 2010. "Pathways to Parenthood: The Impact of State Law on Surrogate Parenting." Paper presented at the 2010 annual meeting of the Midwest Political Science Association.

———. 2012. "Pathways to Parenthood: Regulating Assisted Reproductive Technologies in the United States." PhD diss., University of Kansas.

Klarner, Carl. 2003. "Measurement of the Partisan Balance of State Government." *State Politics and Policy Quarterly* 3 (Fall): 309–319. www.indstate.edu/polisci/klarnerpolitics.htm.

———. 2015. "State Partisan Balance Data." www.indstate.edu /polisci/klarnerpolitics.htm (November 12, 2014).

Klitzman, Robert, and Mark Sauer. 2015. "Kamakahi v. ASRM and the Future of Compensation for Human Eggs." *American Journal of Obstetrics and Gynecology* 213 (2): 186–187.

Kolata, Gina. 1999. "$50,000 Offered to Tall, Smart Egg Donor." *New York Times,* March 3. www.nytimes.com/1999/03/03/us/50000-offered-to-tall-smart-egg-donor.html.

Kreitzer, Rebecca. 2015. "Politics and Morality in State Abortion Policy." *State Politics and Policy Quarterly* 15 (1): 41–66.

Krueger, Liz. 2005. "State Senator's Liz Krueger and David Paterson to Introduce Dual, Comprehensive Stem Cell Research Legislation." Press release. www.lizkrueger.com/pressreleases/stemcellpr.htm.

———. 2006. "State Senator Liz Krueger Calls on Senate Majority to Bring Stem Cell Research Bill to Floor." March 22. Press release. www.nysenate.gov/newsroom/press-releases/liz-krueger/state-senator-liz-krueger-calls-senate-majority-bring-stem-cell.

Lasagna, Louis. 1962. "Heredity Control: Dream or Nightmare?" *New York Times,* August 5.

Lawrence, William. 1939. "First Step Shown in Human Creation." *New York Times.* April 28.

———. 1944. "Notes on Science: Test Tube Fertilization of Ova— Double-Purpose Vaccine." *New York Times.* August 6.

Levine, Aaron. 2006. *States and Stem Cells: The Policies and Implications of State-Funded Stem Cell Research.* Princeton, NJ: Policy Research Institute, Woodrow Wilson School at Princeton University.

———. 2010. "Regulation, Compensation, and the Ethical Recruitment of Oocyte Donors." *Hastings Center Report* 40 (2): 25–36.

Lewin, Tamar. 2015. "Egg Donors Challenge Pay Rates, Saying They Shortchange Women." *New York Times,* October 16. www.nytimes

.com/2015/10/17/us/egg-donors-challenge-pay-rates-saying-they-shortchange-women.html?src=me&_r=1.

Li, Shan. 2012. "Asian Women Command Premium Prices for Egg Donation in U.S." *Los Angeles Times.* May 4. http://articles.latimes.com/2012/may/04/business/la-fi-egg-donation-20120504.

Louisiana Family Forum. 2006. "Louisiana Family Forum Legislative Scorecard: Senate 2006." http://lafamilyforum.us/docs/2006senate.pdf.

Louisiana Right to Life. 2012. *Live with the Legislators: Broome.* Video. www.prolifelouisiana.org/127.html.

Lowi, Theodore. 1964. "American Business, Public Policy, Case Studies, and Political Theory." *World Politics* (July).

———. 1972. "The Four Systems of Policy, Politics, and Choice." *Public Administration Review* (July–August).

———. 1998. "Forward: New Dimensions in Policy and Politics." In *Moral Controversies in American Politics: Cases in Social Regulatory Policy,* edited by Raymond Tatalovich and Byron Daynes. Armonk, NY: ME Sharpe.

Luker, Kristin. 1984. *Abortion and the Politics of Motherhood.* Berkeley: University of California Press.

Lyerly, A.D., E.E. Namey, B. Gray, G. Swamy, and R.R. Faden. 2012. "Women's Views about Participating in Research While Pregnant." *IRB Ethics and Human Research* 34 (4): 1–8.

MacDonald, Ryan, and Erin O'Brien. 2011. "Quasi-Experimental Design, Constituency, and Advancing Women's Interests: Reexamining the Influence of Gender on Substantive Representation." *Political Research Quarterly* 64 (2): 472–486.

Mamo, Laura. 2007. *Queering Reproduction: Achieving Pregnancy in the Age of Technoscience.* Durham, NC: Duke University Press.

———. 2008. *Queering Reproduction: Achieving Pregnancy in the Age of Technoscience.* Durham, NC: Duke University Press.

———. 2013. "Queering the Fertility Clinic." *Journal of Medical Humanities* 34:227–239.

Mamo, Laura, and Jennifer R. Fosket. 2009. "Scripting the Body: Pharmaceuticals and the (Re)making of Menstruation." *Signs: Journal of Women in Culture and Society* 34:925–949.

Markens, Susan. 2007. *Surrogate Motherhood and the Politics of Reproduction*. Berkeley: University of California Press.

Martin, Emily. 1987. *The Woman in the Body: A Cultural Analysis of Reproduction*. Boston: Beacon Press.

———. 1991. "The Egg and the Sperm: How Science Has Constructed a Romance Based on Stereotypical Male-Female Roles." *Signs* 16 (3): 485–501.

Mazur, Amy. 2002. *Theorizing Feminist Policy*. Oxford: Oxford University Press.

McIntire, Mike. 2005. "Fearing New York May Fall Behind, Senator Proposes Stem Cell Institute." *New York Times*. http://query.nytimes.com/gst/fullpage.html?res=9900EED61538F934A25752C0A9639C8B63.

Mclachlin, Malcolm. 2005. "Stem Cell Research: Cutting Edge Science or Corporate Subsidies?" *Capitol Weekly News* (September 15).

Meier, Kenneth. 1994. *The Politics of Sin: Drugs, Alcohol, and Public Policy*. Armonk, NY: M.E. Sharpe.

Mink, Gwendolyn. 2001. *Welfare's End*. Ithaca, NY: Cornell University Press.

Mintrom, Michael. 2009. "Policy Entrepreneurs and the Diffusion of Innovation." *American Journal of Political Science* 41 (3): 738–770.

Mooney, Christopher Z. 2000. "The Influence of Values on Consensus and Contentious Morality Policy: US Death Penalty Reform, 1956–1982." *Journal of Politics* 62 (February): 223–240.

———. 2001. "The Public Clash of Private Values." In *The Public Clash of Private Values,* edited by Christopher Z. Mooney. New York: Chatham House.

Mooney, Christopher Z., and Mei-Hsien Lee. 1995. "Legislating Morality in the American States: The Case of Pre-Roe Abortion Regulation Reform." *American Journal of Political Science* 39:599–627.

Mooney, Christopher Z., and Richard G. Schuldt. 2000. "The Influence of Values on Consensus and Contentious Morality Policy: US Death Penalty Reform, 1956–1982." *Journal of Politics* 62 (February): 223–240.

———. 2008. "Does Morality Policy Exist? Testing a Basic Assumption." *Policy Studies Journal* 36 (2): 199–218.

Mucciaroni, Gary. 2011. "Are Debates about 'Morality Policy' Really about Morality? Framing Opposition to Gay and Lesbian Rights." *Policy Studies Journal* 39 (2): 187–216.

Nachtigall, Robert, Martha Castrillo, Nina Shah, Dylan Turner, Jennifer Harrington, and Rebecca Jackson. 2009. "The Challenge of Providing Infertility Services to Low-Income Immigrant Latino Populations." *Fertility and Sterility* 92 (1): 116–123.

Napolitano, Janet. 2007. HB 2142 veto letter.

Nash, Elizabeth, Rachel Benson Gold, Zohra Ansari-Thomas, Olivia Cappello, and Lizamarie Mohammed. 2017. "Policy Trends in the States: 2016." Guttmacher Institute. January 3. www.guttmacher .org/article/2017/01/policy-trends-states-2016.

NCSL (National Conference of State Legislatures). 2014. "Insurance Coverage for Infertility Laws." June. www.ncsl.org/research /health/insurance-coverage-for-infertility-laws.aspx.

———. 2016. "Embryonic and Fetal Research Laws." June. www.ncsl .org/research/health/embryonic-and-fetal-research-laws.aspx.

Nelson, Libby. 2009. "New York State Allows Payment for Egg Donation in Research." *New York Times*. June 29, 2009. www.nytimes .com/2009/06/26/nyregion/26stemcell.html.

New York State Task Force on Life and the Law. 1989. *Assisted Reproductive Technologies.* www.health.ny.gov/regulations/task_force/reports_ publications/execsum.htm.

Nisbet, Matthew, Dominique Brossard, and Adrianne Kroepsch. 2003. "Framing Science: The Stem Cell Controversy in an Age of Press /Politics." *International Journal of Press/Politics* 8 (36): 36–70.

Norrander, Barbara, and Clyde Wilcox. 1999. "Public Opinion and Policymaking in the States: The Case of Post-Roe Abortion Policy." *Policy Studies Journal* 27 (4): 707–722.

———. 2001. "Public Opinion and Policymaking in the States: The Case of Post-Roe Abortion Policy." In *The Public Clash of Private Values: The Politics of Morality Policy,* edited by C. Z. Mooney, 143–159. New York: Chatham House.

Ollove, Michael. 2015. "States Not Eager to Regulate the Fertility Industry." *Stateline Blog,* March 18. Pew Charitable Trusts. www

.pewtrusts.org/en/research-and-analysis/blogs/stateline/2015/3/18/states-not-eager-to-regulate-fertility-industry.

Ortiz, Deborah. 2005. *Joint Informational Hearing of the Senate Health Committee, Senate Subcommittee on Stem Cell Research Oversight, Assembly Health Committee, Assembly Judiciary Committee: Implementation of Proposition 71: Options for Handling Intellectual Property Associated with Stem Cell Research Grants.* Transcript. October 31, 2005. http://shea.senate.ca.gov/sites/shea.senate.ca.gov/files/PROP_71_IP_TRANSCRIPT.doc.

————. 2016. "Bill to Expand Market in Women's Egg Donation Would Undermine Safeguards." *The Sacramento Bee,* August 4. www.sacbee.com/opinion/op-ed/soapbox/article93650762.html.

Osborn, Tracy. 2012. *How Women Represent Women: Political Parties, Gender, and Representation in the State Legislatures.* New York: Oxford University Press.

Ouellette, Alicia, Arthur Caplan, Kelly Carroll, James Fossett, Dyrleif Bjarnadottir, Darren Shickle, and Glenn McGeeg. 2005. "Lessons from across the Pond: Assisted Reproductive Technology in the United Kingdom and the United States." *American Journal of Law and Medicine* 31 (4): 419–446.

Papadimos, Thomas, and Alexa Papadimos. 2004. "The Student and the Ovum: The Lack of Autonomy and Informed Consent in Trading Genes for Tuition." *Reproductive Biology Endocrinology* 2 (56).

Petchesky, Rosalind. (1984) 1990. *Abortion and Woman's Choice: The State, Sexuality, and Reproductive Freedom.* New York: Longman.

Petersen, Anne Helen. 2017. *Too Fat, Too Slutty, Too Loud: The Rise and Reign of the Unruly Woman.* New York: Plume.

Pfeifer, Samantha, Samantha Butts, Saneil Dumesic, Gregory Fossum, Clarisa Gracia, Andrew La Barbera, Jennifer Mersereau, Randall Odem, Richard Paulson, Alan Penzias, Margareta Pisarka, Robert Rebar, Richard Reindollar, Mitchell Rosen, Jay Sandlow, Michael Vernon, and Eric Widra. 2016. "Prevention and Treatment of Moderate and Severe Ovarian Hyperstimulation Syndrome: A Guideline." *Fertility and Sterility* 106:1634–47.

Pfeifer, Samantha, Jeffrey Goldberg, Roger Lobo, Margareta Pisarka, Michael Thomas, Eric Widra, Jay Sandlow, Mark Licht, Mitchell

Rosen, Michael Vernon, William Catherino, Owen Davis, Daniel Dumesic, Clarisa Gracia, Randall Odem, Kim Thornton, Richard Reindollar, Robert Rebar, and Andrew La Barbera. 2014. "Ovarian Tissue Cryopreservation: A Committee Opinion." *Fertility and Sterility* 101 (5): 1237–1243.

Pierce, Patrick A., and Donald E. Miller. 2004. *Gambling Politics: State Government and the Business of Betting.* Boulder, CO: Lynne Rienner.

Piven, Frances Fox, and Richard Cloward. 1978. *Poor People's Movements: Why They Succeed, How They Fail.* New York: Vintage.

Price, Kimala. 2011. "The Quest for Purity: The Role of Policy Narratives in Determining Teen Girls' Access to Emergency Contraception in the USA." *Sexuality Research and Social Policy* 8 (4): 282–293.

Project Vote Smart. 2012. www.votesmart.org.

PBS (Public Broadcasting Service). 1999. "*Frontline,* Making Babies: Interview: George Annas." www.pbs.org/wgbh/pages/frontline/shows/fertility/interviews/annas.html.

Rapp, Rayna. 1999. *Testing the Woman, Testing the Fetus: The Social Impact of Amniocentesis in America.* New York: Routledge.

Rasmussen, Amy Cabrera. 2011. "Contraception as Health? The Framing of Issue Categories in Contemporary Policy Making." *Administration and Society* 43 (8): 930–953.

Reingold, Beth. 2000. *Representing Women: Sex, Gender, and Legislative Behavior in Arizona and California.* Chapel Hill: University of North Carolina Press.

———. 2008. *Legislative Women: Getting Elected, Getting Ahead.* Boulder, CO: Lynne Rienner.

Reingold, Beth, Rebecca Kreitzer, Tracy Osborn, and Michelle Swers. 2015. "Antifeminism and Women's Representation in the States." Presented at the annual meetings of the American Political Science Association, San Francisco.

Reingold, Beth, and Michele Swers. 2011. "An Endogenous Approach to Women's Interests: When Interests are Interesting in and of Themselves." *Politics and Gender* 7:429–435.

Resolve. 2016. "Insurance Coverage." www.resolve.org/family-building-options/insurance_coverage/insurance-coverage-facts.html.

Richardson, Sarah S. 2012. "Sexing the X: How the X Became the 'Female Chromosome.'" *Signs* 37 (4): 909–933.

Roberts, Dorothy. 1998. *Killing the Black Body.* New York: Vintage.

———. 2009. "Race, Gender and Genetic Technologies." *Signs* 34 (4): 783–804.

———. 2012. *Fatal Invention.* New York: New Press.

Robertson, John. 1994. *Children of Choice: Freedom and the New Reproductive Technologies.* Princeton, NJ: Princeton University Press.

———. 2008. "Assisting Reproduction, Choosing Genes, and the Scope of Reproductive Freedom." *George Washington Law Review* 76:1490.

Robinton, D., and G. Daley. 2012. The Promise of Induced Pluripotent Stem Cells in Research and Therapy. *Nature* 481:295–305.

Romney, Lee. 2006. "New Battle Lines Are Drawn over Egg Donation." *Los Angeles Times.* September 13. http://articles.latimes.com/2006/sep/13/science/sci-eggs13.

Romney, Mitt. 2005. *A Message from His Excellency the Governor Returning with Recommendation of Amendment, Pursuant to Article LVI of the Constitution of the Commonwealth, as Amended by Article XC, Section 3 of the Amendments to the Constitution, "An Act Enhancing Regenerative Medicine in the Commonwealth."* Senate, No. 2039.

Rorvik, David. 1974. "The Embryo Sweepstakes." *New York Times.* September 15.

Rose, Melody. 2006. *Safe, Legal and Unavailable? Abortion Politics in the United States.* Washington, DC: CQ Press.

Rosenthal, Cindy Simon. 1997. "A View of Their Own: Women's Committee Leadership Styles and State Legislatures." *Policy Studies Journal* 24 (4): 585–600.

Roxland, Beth. 2012. *Egg Donation for Stem Cell Research: How New York State Developed Its Oversight and Compensation Policies.* World Stem Cell Summit Report 2010. www.worldstemcellsummit.com/2010-report-egg-donation-stem-cell-research-how-new-york-state-developed-its-oversight-and-compensat.

Ryan, Timothy. 2014. "Reconsidering Moral Issues in Politics." *Journal of Politics* 76 (2): 380–397.

Saad, Nadine. 2013. "Sofia Vergara Talks Thyroid Condition, Freezing Her Eggs." *Los Angeles Times.* April 17. http://articles.latimes.com/2013/apr/17/entertainment/la-et-mg-sofia-vergara-thyroid-cancer-freezing-her-eggs-20130417.

Saint-Germain, Michelle. 1989. "Does Their Difference Make a Difference? The Impact of Women on Public Policy in the Arizona Legislature." *Social Science Quarterly* 70 (4): 956–968.

Sang-Hun, Choe. 2005. "Korean Lab Roiled by Egg Donor Disclosures." *New York Times.* November 23. www.nytimes.com/2005/11/23/world/asia/korean-lab-roiled-by-egg-donor-disclosures.html?_r=0.

SART (Society for Assisted Reproductive Technology). 2016. "Clinic Summary Report: 2013." www.sartcorsonline.com/Report/ClinicSummaryReportPublic?ClinicPKID=0.

Satz, Debra. 2010. "Markets in Women's Reproductive Labor." In *Legal and Ethical Issues in Human Reproduction,* edited by Bonnie Steinbock. Burlington, VT: Ashgate/Dartmouth.

Sauer, Mark. 2001. "Egg Donor Solicitation: Problems Exist, But Do Abuses?" *American Journal of Bioethics* 1 (4): 1–2.

Saul, Stephanie. 2009. "Building a Baby with Few Ground Rules." *New York Times.* December 12. www.nytimes.com/2009/12/13/us/13surrogacy.html?scp=1&sq=building%20a%20baby%20with%20few%20ground%20rules&st=cse.

Schmidt, Lucie. 2007. "Effects of Infertility Insurance Mandates on Fertility." *Journal of Health Economics* 26 (3): 431–446.

Schneider, Anne, and Helen Ingram. 1993. "Social Constructions of Target Populations: Implications for Politics and Policy." *American Political Science Review* 87 (2): 334–347.

Schön, D. A., and M. Rein. 1994. *Frame Reflection: Toward the Resolution of Intractable Policy Controversies.* New York: Basic Books.

Schreiber, Ronnee. 2008. *Righting Feminism.* New York: Oxford University Press.

Schroedel, Jean. 2000. *Is the Fetus a Person? A Comparison of Policies across the Fifty States.* Ithaca, NY: Cornell University Press.

Senate Bill 253. 2002. www.leginfo.ca.gov/pub/01–02/bill/sen/sb_0251–0300/sb_253_bill_20010215_introduced.html.

Senate Bill 322. 2003. www.leginfo.ca.gov/pub/03–04/bill/sen/sb_0301–0350/sb_322_bill_20030219_introduced.html.

Senate Bill 429. 2006. Louisiana State Legislature. Original Version. www.legis.la.gov/Legis/ViewDocument.aspx?d=374985.

Senate Bill 433B. 2006. http://assembly.state.ny.us/leg/?default_fld=&leg_video=&bn=S00433&term=2005&Summary=Y&Text=Y.

Senate Bill 452. 2006. Louisiana State Legislature. www.legis.la.gov/Legis/ViewDocument.aspx?d=375031.

Senate Bill 771. 2003. www.leginfo.ca.gov/pub/03–04/bill/sen/sb_0751–0800/sb_771_bill_20030221_introduced.html.

Senate Bill 1260. 2006a. Introduced version. www.leginfo.ca.gov/pub/05–06/bill/sen/sb_1251–1300/sb_1260_bill_20060209_introduced.html.

Senate Bill 1260. 2006b. Senate Health Committee Amendments. April. www.leginfo.ca.gov/pub/05–06/bill/sen/sb_1251–1300/sb_1260_bill_20060406_amended_sen.html.

Senate Bill 1260. 2006c. Assembly Health Committee Amendments. May. www.leginfo.ca.gov/pub/05–06/bill/sen/sb_1251–1300/sb_1260_bill_20060526_amended_sen.html.

Senate Bill 1272. 2002. www.leginfo.ca.gov/pub/01–02/bill/sen/sb_1251–1300/sb_1272_bill_20020115_introduced.html.

Sharp, Elaine. 2005. *Morality Politics in American Cities*. Lawrence: University of Kansas.

Shelley, Mary. [1818] 1999. *Frankenstein; or, the Modern Prometheus: 1818 Edition*. New York: Ballantine.

Shipan, Charles, and Craig Volden. 2012. "Policy Diffusion: Seven Lessons for Scholars and Practitioners." *Public Administration Review* 72 (6): 788–796.

Shotwell, Alexis. 2012. "Open Normativities: Gender, Disability, and Collective Political Change." *Signs* 37 (4): 989–1016.

Skocpol, Theda. 1992. *Protecting Soldiers and Mothers: The Political Origins of Social Policy*. Cambridge, MA: Belknap.

Smith, Anna Marie. 2007. *Welfare Reform and Sexual Regulation*. New York: Cambridge University Press.

———. 2009. "Reproductive Technology, Family Law, and the Postwelfare State: The California Same-Sex Parents' Rights 'Victories' of 2005." *Signs: Journal of Women and Culture* 34 (4).

Smooth, Wendy. 2011. "Standing for Women? Which Women? The Substantive Representation of Women's Interests and the Research Imperative of Intersectionality." *Politics and Gender* 7 (3): 436–441.

Solinger, Rickie. 2005. *Pregnancy and Power: A Short History of Reproductive Politics in America.* New York: NYU Press.

Sonfield, Adam, and Harold Pollack. 2013. "The Affordable Care Act and Reproductive Health: Potential Gains and Serious Challenges." *Journal of Health Politics, Policy and Law* 38 (2): 373–391.

Spar, Debora. 2006. *The Baby Business: How Money, Science, and Politics Drive the Commerce of Conception.* Boston: Harvard Business School Press.

———. 2011. "Room for Debate: Fertility Industry Is a Wild West." *New York Times.* September 13. www.nytimes.com/roomfordebate /2011/09/13/making-laws-about-making-babies/fertility-industry-is-a-wild-west.

Squire, Peverill. 2007. "Measuring State Legislative Professionalism: The Squire Index Revisited." *State Politics and Policy Quarterly* 7 (2): 211–227.

Stapleton, Patricia, and Daniel Skinner. 2015. "The Affordable Care Act and Assisted Reproductive Technology Use." *Politics and the Life Sciences* 34 (2): 71–90.

Stein, Rob. 2009. "New York to Pay Women Who Give Eggs for Stem Cell Research." *Washington Post,* June 26. www.washingtonpost .com/wp-dyn/content/article/2009/06/25/AR2009062501931.html.

Stone, Deborah A. (1998) 2002. *Policy Paradox: The Art of Political Decision Making.* New York: Norton.

Stump Legislative Website. 2012. www.azcc.gov/commissioners /bstump/.

Swers, Michele L. 2002. *The Difference Women Make: The Policy Impact of Women in Congress.* Chicago: University of Chicago Press.

———. 2013. *Women in the Club: Gender and Policy Making in the Senate.* Chicago: University of Chicago Press.

———. 2016. "Pursuing Women's Interests in Partisan Times: Explaining Gender Differences in Legislative Activity on Health, Education, and Women's Health Issues." *Journal of Women, Politics and Policy* 37 (3): 249–273.

Takahashi, T., and S. Yamanaka. 2006. "Induction of Pluripotent Stem Cells from Mouse Embryonic and Adult Fibroblast Cultures by Defined Factors." *Cell* 126 (4): 663–673.

Tatalovich, Raymond. 2017. "The Life Cycle of Moral Conflicts: Why Some Die, but Others Persist." *Journal of Policy History* 29 (4): 676–701.

Tatalovich, Raymond, and Byron Daynes. 1998. *Moral Controversies in American Politics: Cases in Social Regulatory Policy.* Armonk, NY: ME Sharpe.

Thomas, Sue, and Susan Welch. 1991. "Women Legislators: Legislative Styles and Policy Priorities." *Western Political Quarterly* 44 (2): 445–456.

Thompson, Charis. 2005. *Making Parents: The Ontological Choreography of Reproductive Technologies.* Cambridge, MA: MIT Press.

———. 2007. "Why We Should, in Fact, Pay for Egg Donation." *Regenerative Medicine* 2:203–209.

———. 2013. *Good Science: The Ethical Choreography of Stem Cell Research.* Cambridge, MA: MIT Press.

Thomson, J., J. Itskovita-Eldor, S. Shapiro, M. Waknitz, J. Swiergiel, V. Marshall, and J. Jones. 1998. "Embryonic Stem Cell Lines Derived from Human Blastocysts." *Science* 282:1145–1147.

Titmuss, R. 1997. *The Gift Relationship: From Human Blood to Social Policy.* New York: New Press.

Tolbert, Caroline, and Gertrude A. Steuernagel. 2001. "Women Lawmakers, State Mandates and Women's Health" *Women and Politics* 22 (2): 1–39.

Traister, Rebecca. 2016. *All the Single Ladies.* New York: Simon and Schuster.

US Census Bureau. 2010. *Statistical Abstract of the United States: 2010.* Statistical Abstracts Series. www.census.gov/library/publications /time-series/statistical_abstracts.html.

Von Hagel, Alisa. 2014. "Federalism and Bioethics: Women's Health and the Regulation of Oocyte Donation." *Politics and the Life Sciences* 33 (1): 79–91.

Waldby, Catherine. 2009. "Citizenship, Labor, and the Biopolitics of the Bioeconomy: Recruiting Female Tissue Donors for Stem-Cell

Research." In "Critical Conceptions: Technology, Justice, and the Global Reproductive Market," edited by Rebecca Jordan-Young. Special issue, *Scholar and Feminist Online.* http://sfonline.barnard .edu/reprotech/waldby_01.htm.

Waldby, Catherine, and Melinda Cooper. 2008. "The Biopolitics of Reproduction: Post-Fordist Biotechnology and Women's Clinical Labor." *Australian Feminist Studies* 23 (55): 57–73.

————. 2010. "From Reproductive Work to Regenerative Labor: The Female Body and the Stem Cell Industries." *Feminist Theory* 11 (1): 3–22.

————. 2014. *Clinical Labor.* Durham, NC: Duke University Press.

Waldby, C., and R. Mitchell. 2006. *Tissue Economies: Blood, Organs, and Cell Lines in Late Capitalism.* Durham, NC: Duke University Press.

Walker, Jack. 1969. "The Diffusions of Innovations among American States." *American Political Science Review* 63 (2): 880–899.

Washington Journal. 2006. "Regulation of Female Egg Donors." C-SPAN. March 25. www.c-spanvideo.org/program/EggD.

Waylen, Georgina, Karen Celis, Johanna Kantola, and S. Laurel Weldon, eds. 2013. "Introduction: Body Politics." In *The Oxford Handbook of Gender and Politics.* New York: Oxford University Press.

Weldon, S. Laurel. 2011. "Perspectives against Interests: Sketch of a Feminist Political Theory of 'Women.'" *Politics and Gender* 7 (3): 441–446.

WHO. 2016. "Sexual and Reproductive Health: Infertility Is a Global Health Issue." May 1. www.who.int/reproductivehealth/topics /infertility/perspective/en/.

Wilcox, Clyde, and Barbara Norrander. 2002. "Of Mood and Morals: The Dynamics of Opinion on and Gay Rights." In *Understanding Public Opinion,* 3rd ed., edited by Barbara Norrander and Clyde Wilcox. Washington, DC: CQ Press.

Wolbrecht, Christina. 2000. *The Politics of Women's Rights: Parties, Positions, and Change.* Princeton, NJ: Princeton University Press.

Young, Iris Marion. 1994. "Gender as Seriality: Thinking about Women as a Social Collective." *Signs* 19 (3): 713–738.

————. 2002. *Inclusion and Democracy.* New York: Oxford University Press.

Zaller, John. 1992. *The Nature and Origins of Mass Opinion.* Cambridge: Cambridge University Press.

Zegers-Hochschild, F., G.D. Adamson, J. de Mouzon, O. Ishihara, R. Mansour, K. Nygren, E. Sullivan, and S. Vanderpoel. 2009. "International Committee for Monitoring Assisted Reproductive Technology (ICMART) and the World Health Organization (WHO) Revised Glossary of ART Terminology." *Fertility and Sterility* 92 (5).

Zelizer, Viviana. 2010. "Risky Exchanges." In *Baby Markets: Money and the New Politics of Creating Families,* edited by Michele Goodwin. Cambridge: Cambridge University Press.

INDEX